Brought up in England, Jason Webster has lived for several years in Valencia, the setting of his Cámara novels. The first of these, *Or the Bull Kills You*, was longlisted for the CWA Specsavers Crime Thriller Awards New Blood Dagger 2011. He has appeared in several British TV documentaries, including *The Islamic History of Europe* presented by Rageh Omaar on BBC Television, and the critically acclaimed *Andalusia: The Legacy of the Moors* for Five.

THE SPY WITH 29 NAMES

To MI5 he was known as Garbo, though his aliases were many. But who, exactly, was Juan Pujol? Jason Webster tells of Pujol's early life in Spain and how, after the Civil War, a determination to fight totalitarianism took him on his strange journey from Nazi spy to MI5 star. Working for the British, he created a bizarre fictional network of spies that misled the entire German High Command just before the allied invasion of Normandy. Historians are agreed that without Garbo, D-Day would almost certainly have failed — and our world would be a very different place indeed. Meticulously researched, yet told with the verve of a thriller, *The Spy With 29 Names* uncovers the truth about the man behind one of recent history's most important and dramatic events.

Books by Jason Webster
Published by Ulverscroft:

OR THE BULLS KILL YOU
A DEATH IN VALENCIA
THE ANARCHIST DETECTIVE
BLOOD MED

JASON WEBSTER

◆

THE SPY WITH 29 NAMES

The story of the Second World War's
most audacious double agent

Complete and Unabridged

CHARNWOOD
Leicester

First published in Great Britain in 2014 by
Chatto & Windus
London

First Charnwood Edition
published 2015
by arrangement with
Chatto & Windus
The Random House Group Limited
London

A catalogue record for this book is available
from the British Library.

ISBN 978–1–4448–2497–1

Published by
F. A. Thorpe (Publishing)
Anstey, Leicestershire

Set by Words & Graphics Ltd.
Anstey, Leicestershire
Printed and bound in Great Britain by
T. J. International Ltd., Padstow, Cornwall

For Gijs and Alex van Hensbergen,
with thanks

'Reality is not always probable, or likely.'
Jorge Luis Borges

'Facts are the enemy of truth.'
Miguel de Cervantes

Contents

List of Illustrations

23. Harris in Spain, after the war
24. Pujol's grave in Choroní, Venezuela

Sources: 1, 5, 12, 13, 14, 16 German Federal Archives; 2 misaventurasfavoritas. com; 3 Italian airforce; 4 laopinondezamora.es; 6 Matt Whitby; 7, 20 HMSO; 8, 11, 15, 18 National Archives, Kew; 9, 10, author; 17 US Federal Archive (WM); 19 Imperial War Museum; 21 lapaseata.files.wordpress.com; 22, 23 Private collection; 24 webspace.webring.com.

Prologue

Morning off the Normandy coast. Finally: they have been waiting years for this.

An ashen dawn is trickling into the sky as the flotilla of British warships moves in closer. On deck, peering out over the grey-green sea, Private Jack Poolton of the Royal Regiment of Canada is waiting his turn to go ashore. The Channel is calm, the crossing has been easy.

Jack's letter home, to be sent if he does not return, is written and stored away. He tells his mother what is about to take place — a major attack against the northern coastline of Nazi-occupied France. Jack hopes that his generation will fight as bravely as their fathers did in the Great War. Much depends on what will happen that morning. To the east, the Russians are clamouring for this, a 'second front', to be opened in the west.

He remembers the past months' training in England: the manoeuvres and marches, and the children killed when a German Focke-Wulf bombed a cinema in Littlehampton before they embarked. To be here this morning Jack has lied about being able to swim, and has hidden the fact that he has trench mouth, caught from washing his mess tin in dirty water. But he is keen to see action. Perhaps, when he gets back, he will talk about today's events with Irene, the WAAF girl from Lancashire he met while sheltering from an air raid in the cellars of Birmingham railway station. She gave him a hat badge to remember her by; her mother ran a pub — the beer would be on the house whenever he could make it.

None of the men are interested in the tea and sandwiches laid on. Nor are there any rum rations or prayers: no one feels the need. The signal comes and they climb down into the landing craft. Jack is a mortar man, and sits near the back.

The first sign that things are going wrong comes when a German convoy intercepts British commandos on the Canadians' left. The gunfire alerts the defence forces on the coast, who fire star shells and chandelier flares to light up the sky. The attackers become visible, the element of surprise gone. Attempting to avoid detection, the Canadians turn in circles, slowing down their progress to the shore. Now, instead of a landing at dawn, it will be full daylight by the time their boots touch the beach.

A giant firework display begins, 'like a thousand guns firing': they are entering hell itself, Jack thinks. He is part of the second wave. Five hundred yards from the shore, his vessel is hit by heavy fire. A bullet passes through his tunic, near his shoulder, but mercifully draws no blood.

The landing craft is already reversing before all the men manage to get out. Jack jumps into 8 feet of water carrying the mortar, twelve high-explosive bombs, his grenades, and 250 rounds for a .303 rifle. Wading ashore, he realises that they are in the direct line of fire of a machine gun, bullets kicking up stones around his feet. Many of his comrades are already dead. The beach is littered with the shattered remains of the first wave.

Jack seeks cover behind a shallow abutment as the Germans accurately drop shells on their positions. It is, he thinks, as if the whole thing has been rehearsed. He sees Canadian soldiers trying to throw grenades at the enemy, only to be shot as they pull the pin, the weapon then exploding among their own men.

High explosives are useless in these conditions. Jack dumps his equipment and stretches out for the nearest rifle as men around him are cut down by enemy fire. He tries to join a group scaling cliffs nearby, but the man ahead of him is killed as he reaches the top, falling back on to Jack and dragging him to the bottom again.

The tide is coming in and wounded men on the beach are drowning. A landing craft comes ashore to take them away, only for the Germans to place a mortar shell in the middle of it. More men are shot dead as they cling to the sinking wreckage.

A white flag appears — someone has stuck an undershirt to a bayonet. Most in his regiment are surrendering. Jack and his company commander, Captain Houssar, decide to fight on. Alone, they charge down the beach armed only with rifles, but are pushed back by machine-gun fire.

There is no hope: they are trapped. Jack and Captain Houssar are the last Royals to put down their weapons. They are alive, but with surrender comes a deep feeling of humiliation. You can train a soldier to fight and accept death, Jack realises, but there is no way you can prepare him for being taken prisoner.

The attack has failed in only a few hours. Thousands have been killed. Thoughts of opening up a 'second front' are now almost as dead as the men on the shore, staining the seawater red. Pieces of body lie everywhere — feet with boots still on them; men stuck to barbed wire, burning where the bombs in their packs have exploded. The Germans are giving the seriously wounded *coups de grâce* to the back of the head.

As Jack climbs a ladder away from the beach and into captivity, an English-speaking German officer smirks and asks, 'What took you so long? We have been waiting for you for ten days.'

They knew they were coming all the time.

The Royals walk away from the battle, their hands held above their heads, while German photographers take snaps of the defeated enemy. This is great propaganda. The Germans can relax in the west now. Europe is theirs; they can concentrate on fighting the Russians.

Shattered yet defiant, the Allied soldiers start singing *La Marseillaise* as they march along. Their captors are furious. French civilians at the roadside start to weep and show the V for Victory sign.

For Jack there is nothing now except life in a prisoner-of-war camp. His role in the war — his Normandy — has come to an end. It will be years before he is free again.

Today, on 19 August 1942, almost 4,000 Canadian and British soldiers out of a total force of 6,000 have been killed, wounded or captured. The Dieppe Raid, as it is called, is a military disaster, an attack which the Germans themselves, with just over 300 dead, consider mediocre at best. Yet the lessons for the Allies are invaluable. Jack does not know this, but already the seeds have been sown for a second Normandy, two years later in 1944. Not here, not in and around the port of Dieppe, but over 80 miles to the south-west, towards the Cherbourg peninsula — an assault which will draw heavily on what has happened to him and his comrades this morning, attempting to avoid the same mistakes.

Firstly, never attack a port — they are heavily defended, and the cost in human lives is too high.

Secondly, any assault must be carried out on a much more massive scale and with greater cooperation between air, land and sea forces.

And thirdly, unlike at Dieppe, the enemy must not know where or when you are going to attack. Surprise, that most crucial of weapons, must be protected and used.

Even then, there remains the doubt: would surprise alone be enough?

One last scene catches Jack's attention as the defeated Allied soldiers are leaving the town. On the outskirts a woman approaches the column, walking alongside them for a few yards.

'Insult me in French!' she whispers to one of the men.

The soldier looks baffled, but something in the woman's expression makes him wonder. At her bidding, he starts to cuss and swear aggressively, shaking his fist and shouting obscenities.

On cue, the French woman responds and starts pelting him and the other soldiers with tomatoes, launching them with a look of rage on her face.

It seems odd: the tomatoes are not hitting the soldiers hard; despite her shouting and harsh words, the woman is actually tossing them rather gently. The defeated men are at their lowest ebb, their spirits crushed, yet are quick to catch on. Scooping up the tomatoes, they hide them in their tunics for eating later, grateful for this act of camouflaged charity. It will be a long time before the Germans offer them anything to eat or drink.

The Germans, however, think the woman is genuinely upset, and find the scene immensely funny. They even pat her on the back, praising her for her spontaneous act against the *Englische Schweine*.

They never realise they have been deceived.

PART ONE

picaresque, adj. of or relating to an episodic style of fiction dealing with the adventures of a rough and dishonest but appealing hero. ORIGIN from Sp. *picaresco*, from *pícaro*

'rogue'.**pícaro** *adj.*(a) crafty, cunning, sly, wily (b) mischievous, naughty, crooked.

1

England, 1941–2

Allied disasters in the Second World War were not limited to the Dieppe Raid. After the collapse at Dunkirk in 1940 and defeat in the Balkans in 1941, many doubted whether the British Army could prevail in a straight fight against the Wehrmacht. Even with the help of the United States, with its greater industrial strength and manpower committed from late 1941, it would be difficult to defeat a highly trained and fearsome opponent.

Other means — 'special means' — had to be developed to overcome the enemy. The Germans could pluck a seemingly endless supply of fighting men from a culture that valued discipline and glorified war. But the British applauded characteristics that would become effective weapons against them: wit and eccentricity. Intelligence, counterintelligence and deception were to become vital for the Allied war effort. There was a need for thinking in extraordinary and different ways, for talented men and women to set their minds on how to surprise and fool the enemy. Something like Dieppe could never be allowed to happen again.

In this atmosphere, the craziest schemes could tip the balance in the Allies' favour. And often such a scheme was the brainchild of a tiny group of people or an odd individual.

This is the story of one of those men and the decisive part that he played in the success of D-Day and the Normandy campaign. The tale has been told before, even by the man himself, but only partially: gaps were left unfilled, veils drawn over uncomfortable facts. The character at the centre remained an enigma, his true personality rarely emerging.

He was a Spaniard, from Barcelona — a dreamer, a cheat and a liar, and yet the noblest and kindest of men; a compulsive storyteller who could barely tell a story, so purple was his prose. If he were not real, he might appear like a character from a picaresque novel — a saintly rogue and compelling fantasist with unorthodox ideas about truth, someone who defies simple labels of 'good' and 'bad': at once innocent, like Don Quixote, and wily, like Sancho Panza.

He became the greatest double agent in history, creating a new truth by telling untruths. This is the story of who he was and what he did, and of some of the many lives that were changed by his achievements. The details and quoted conversations are taken from records, letters and memoirs of those who knew him.

At home, in Spain, he was known as Juan.

In the secret worlds in which he moved, he went under many different names . . .

Bletchley Park, December 1941

The 'Cottages' were a line of three small adjacent buildings near the main house. They

10

had served as the head coachman's quarters before the war, but now housed Dillwyn Knox's team of code-breakers — mostly pretty young women like Mavis Lever. People called them 'Dilly's Girls'.

Knox was one of Bletchley's 'characters', eccentric intellectuals working at the Government Code and Cypher School (GC&CS), trying to crack encrypted German wireless messages. They were the lifeblood of the place.

A classicist from Cambridge, Knox was often likened to a character from a Lewis Carroll novel, long and lean and, as one friend put it, with a 'face like a pang of hunger'. Now in his late fifties, he would sometimes wander around Bletchley in his dressing gown, not realising that he had not put his clothes on that morning, frequently losing his glasses or his tobacco tin under piles of decrypted messages. In one absent-minded moment he mistakenly stuffed bread from a sandwich into his pipe.

Mavis, still only nineteen at the time, felt a strong connection to Knox, seeing in him echoes of Alice's White Knight: 'endearingly eccentric and concerned about my welfare'.

'We're breaking machines,' he had said to her the day she first arrived in the Cottages, in 1940. 'Have you got a pencil?'

The respect and affection were mutual and the young recruit soon became the elder code-breaker's protégée. Mavis had broken off her German studies at London University to get the job, and if Knox started quoting Milton's *Lycidas* to her she would respond with something appropriate, perhaps from Heinrich Heine's poetry. There was an affinity between them; years later she would write his biography.

Bletchley Park was like a small town by this point in the war, with thousands of people working intensely on the enemy's codes, many of them in the huts that had been quickly assembled in the grounds. It got cold in winter. The Cottages were sturdier structures, better for keeping the heat in. Mavis was lucky.

The work was hard and there were rolling shifts throughout the day and night. A canteen was provided in the main house, but sometimes there was little more to eat at three in the morning than a handful of overcooked Brussels sprouts. There was a community spirit, however: when not code-breaking, Mavis enjoyed the concerts, the amateur dramatics group, and the Scottish country dancing.

Knox spent little time with them in the Cottage that December, he was seriously ill and was busy fighting a battle with Bletchley's operational head Alistair Denniston over how their decoded material was handled within the intelligence services. Mavis's work was built around Knox's methods, however, and the thinking required for solving the puzzles created by the enemy's Enigma machines.

'Which way do the hands on a clock go round?' he would ask.

'Clockwise.'

'That depends on whether you're the clock or the observer.'

They had already enjoyed one great success

together, breaking the Italian naval codes earlier in the year. This had played a vital role in the Battle of Matapan in the spring, when the Italian Navy suffered a major defeat at the hands of the British. Churchill described it as the greatest sea triumph since Trafalgar.

'Tell Dilly we have had a great victory in the Mediterranean,' Admiral Godfrey rang through to Bletchley. 'And it's entirely due to him and his girls.'

As a reward, Knox had taken Mavis out to dinner, driving in his Baby Austin to the Fountain Inn at nearby Stony Stratford, and arranged for her to get a raise on the 35 shillings a week she was then earning.

That was in April 1941. Now it was December, yet as Mavis and her colleague Margaret Rock worked to piece together a new puzzle, it was clear that something just as important — more so, even — was happening.

After months of effort, carrying on from Knox's first hammer blow against the cipher in October, on 8 December Mavis and Margaret finally cracked the code used by German intelligence and were able to look at their first deciphered Abwehr message. If the Allies could listen in on what Germany's spies were saying to each other, then the enemy would have few secrets left indeed.

Knox was delighted.

'Give me a Lever and Rock,' he said, 'and I can move the universe'.

It was a great achievement, one which vindicated his unusual methods — using

13

linguists and even a speech therapist to help him break 'mathematical' codes. Yet despite insisting that the credit be given to his 'girls', the 'rodding' system that they were using to break the German encryption was his making, and henceforth the decrypted messages would bear his name — even after, just over a year on, he died of lymph cancer.

Around them, the war carried on. The morning after her breakthrough, Mavis heard of the Japanese attack on Pearl Harbor. It seemed clear that the Americans would be joining them soon. Meanwhile, to the east, the Red Army was finally starting to push the Germans back from the outskirts of Moscow. It was not obvious at the time, but these events, taken in conjunction with her own success of the day before, meant that those few days in early December would prove to be a pivotal moment in the conflict.

After reading the first coded message, they had much more work to do. Mavis and Margaret were 'in', but it would take weeks before a proper stream of Abwehr messages could be produced. Out of a team of seventeen 'girls' they were the only ones with any German: more linguists would be needed. It was Christmas Day 1941 before this new, important source of information could be passed on to the rest of British intelligence, a service which, at the beginning at least, involved decoding anything between fifty and a hundred Abwehr telegrams a day. Later that figure would be multiplied several times over and a total number of 140,000 messages were read by the end of the war.

Mavis was on her own that day — Knox was ill and had to stay at home, where Margaret was taking him material to carry on their work. There were no celebrations. All the same, it was a significant moment. 'On Christmas Day 1941 the geniuses at Bletchley broke the Abwehr Enigma . . . ' Hugh Trevor-Roper wrote. 'When that was done we really were in a new age.'

British intelligence officers could now read what their German opponents were saying to each other almost as easily as they read the morning newspapers. It was not Mavis's job to analyse the messages that she and her colleagues cracked, however. That was the work of the intelligence officers at MI6 — of which GC&CS was a part — busy absorbing the material with which Mavis and Knox were now providing them.

In the German texts that they were reading, however, one curious name appeared, mentioned in the disturbing traffic between Abwehr headquarters at 76/78 Tirpitzufer in Berlin and its Madrid spy station. These were references to the 'Arabal[1] undertaking', a mysterious Nazi spy ring operating from inside Britain itself, headed by an agent called 'Alaric'.

The thought caused a shudder. A phobia about enemy spies was gripping the country. There were rumours of jackbooted nuns parachuting into Warwickshire, signals ploughed into remote fields for German spotter planes, and chalk symbols on telegraph poles. One elderly lady had even concluded that her neighbour was sending

---

[1] Also sometimes spelled 'Arabel'.

15

messages to the enemy through a form of Morse code based on the long and short garments on her washing line. It was hard to know who to trust.

They were less excitable at Bletchley. Nonetheless, over the following weeks and months Mavis and her colleagues were to come across many more references to the sinister 'Alaric'. The question was, who was he?

St Albans, January 1942

Desmond Bristow spent most of his day checking hotel registers sent over by agents in Madrid and Lisbon. His job was to look for anyone suspicious — a name that did not tally, or that had cropped up somewhere before. Still, he told himself, it beat being an infantryman. Back in May 1940, while waiting for a train at Oxford station, he had caught sight of badly wounded soldiers returning from Dunkirk: that had rid him of any ideas about fighting on the front line.

He had not imagined that being a spy would be quite so dull, though. Betty was pregnant, and he missed her. Worcester was a long way from St Albans. At least he had his beloved Matchless motorbike and could use spare petrol coupons to drive over to see her occasionally. But apart from the odd pint at the King Harry pub with his boss, there was little to break the tedium.

After two and a half years of war there were plenty of reasons to be spying abroad, which was what MI6 — the Secret Intelligence Service — concentrated on. But there were no foreign postings for Bristow. Not even in Spain, where he had been brought up. Yes, they valued his knowledge of the language and the culture and that was why he had been taken on. But he had been placed in Section V of MI6, the branch that dealt with counter-espionage, and Section V had moved out of London to Glenalmond, an Edwardian red-brick town house in the sleepy town of St Albans.

He was still only twenty-six, too young to enjoy drinking pink gins with the others after work in the conservatory. The 'snakepit', they called it.

At least there was Philby.

His boss had a bit of a stutter, but knew and loved Spain as Desmond did, having been *The Times's* correspondent there during the Civil War. Older than Bristow by about five years, he was easy to talk to. Before long they became friends and Bristow would take him around St Albans on the back of the motorbike, heading out to the pub after work. Kim Philby made life in Glenalmond that bit more bearable.

Colonel Felix Cowgill was part of the problem. Formerly of the Indian Police, the head of Section V treated Glenalmond like a medieval castle. He was a suspicious man and had fallen out with most of the other chiefs in the intelligence services. His department's role was to work through counter-intelligence reports from foreign countries — information about attempts to spy on Britain — and, where

17

necessary, pass them on, not least to the other major counter-intelligence organisation, MI5, the Security Service. Where Section V of MI6 dealt with 'abroad', MI5 handled Britain and the Empire, with a large degree of overlap between the two. This should, in many people's minds, have led to high levels of cooperation. But Cowgill thought otherwise: he suspected MI5 wanted to take over his territory. Citing a need to protect MI6 sources, he only allowed a portion of his material to be passed on.

Philby hated him.

'Lack of imagination, inattention to detail and sheer ignorance of the world we were fighting in . . . ' he wrote. 'Glenalmond . . . felt like a hedgehog position; Cowgill revelled in his isolation.' What was the point of receiving so much intelligence if they were not going to share it? Now that the Abwehr codes had been properly cracked, Cowgill was becoming more difficult than ever. Philby had to resort to passing information on to friends in MI5 verbally, informally, 'to avoid needless trouble'.

Decrypted German messages were referred to as ISOS, standing for 'Illicit Services Oliver Strachey', after the GC&CS man in charge of breaking Abwehr messages that had been enciphered by hand. ISOS had been online since April 1940, before Bristow had joined. More importantly, though, the new German messages coming through had been enciphered not by hand, but using Enigma machines. These messages were far more complex and useful than previous ones, and had only recently been

18

broken by the GC&CS team headed by Dilly Knox. They had started arriving properly on Christmas Day 1941, and were officially referred to as ISK — 'Illicit Services Knox'. Like many people, however, Bristow did not differentiate between the two, and ended up referring to all the deciphered Abwehr material as ISOS.

The messages were biked over by special courier to Glenalmond in the morning, arriving at 10.30. It was foggy and icy the day that they first heard of 'Arabal'. Bristow had just lit the fire and Philby was sitting by the bay window wearing a scarred leather jacket he had picked up during the Civil War in Spain. Tim Milne, one of their colleagues, read through the intercepts dealing with the Iberian Peninsula.

'This sounds very odd,' he said, staring at one of them.

Bristow looked up from his hotel registers. From the window, Philby glanced over.

'What does it say?'

Milne handed it to him. Bristow walked across and looked over his shoulder. He saw a typed message written in capital letters, and there, in front of them, was the text from the Abwehr's station in Madrid to headquarters, telling their Berlin masters about a new *Vertrauungsmann* — a 'trusted man', or spy — reporting from London. This agent, this *V-mann* code-named 'Alaric' by the Germans, was being run by the Abwehr station in Madrid. What was worse, as Bristow and Philby read on it appeared that this new enemy spy was not alone. Alaric claimed to have recruited three sub-agents to work with

19

him: 'Senhor Carvalho', a Portuguese travelling salesman based in Newport, south Wales, where he spied on shipping movements in the Channel; 'Herr Gerbers', a German-Swiss businessman based in Bootle, near Liverpool, spying on the Mersey; and a wealthy Venezuelan student based in Glasgow.

The Germans were referring to this spy network as 'the Arabal undertaking'.

'Alaric'? 'Arabal'? None of them had seen the names before. Yet here, on the decrypted Abwehr message in front of them, this new Nazi spy was reporting the formation of a shipping convoy in the bay of Caernarfon, clearly with a view to alerting German U-boats for an attack. What should Section V do?

Philby wasted no time. He picked up the green scrambler phone to warn their colleagues at MI5: the spy was on home turf and the Security Service needed to be informed.

Bristow, like everyone else in the office, stopped what he was doing and listened in on the conversation. This was by far the most interesting thing that had happened since his arrival at Glenalmond. Philby got through to Herbert Hart, the head of MI5's research department. Bristow noticed how Philby clicked his fingers while he spoke, trying to control his stammering.

'Have you seen his message from M-M-Madrid on the Caernarfon convoy, Hart?'

It appeared that MI5 had also seen the Arabal message, and were equally worried and per-plexed.

20

'Get Scotland Yard on to it,' Philby said.

The spies had a lead, but the police were the best people to start a physical search for any German agents. Meanwhile, MI5 would talk to their liaison officer at the Admiralty about the Caernarfon convoy.

'We'll go on watching and see what comes of it. Bye for now.'

Philby put down the phone, and the office became a buzz of conjecture.

Who was this new enemy agent?

'Surely he must be a Spanish sailor off one of those merchant ships tied up in Liverpool?' Jack Ivens, another member of the team said.

'Why should he or she be a Spaniard?' Bristow replied, playing with a cigarette. 'He could be a Dutchman or woman, Swedish national or whatever.'

They all looked at each other. None of them had any idea.

'I wonder what means of communication our mysterious Arabal used?' Bristow asked.

Philby shook his head.

'We must not get c-c-carried away on a guessing game,' he said. 'It wastes time, and if this character is important there will be another reference from ISOS soon enough.'

Bristow and the others took the hint: they went back to their work, wondering in silence.

The following communications only deepened the mystery.

First was a written report sent through from Commander Ewen Montagu, MI5's liaison officer with the Admiralty, who had been asked about the reported Caernarfon convoy. To their surprise, Montagu told them categorically that no such convoy existed.

A few days later, Scotland Yard's Special Branch also reported back. After a thorough search, no trace of an enemy agent had been found.

There was, it seemed, no German spy, and no Caernarfon convoy, yet the following week Alaric and the Arabal network were mentioned once again by the Abwehr in the Bletchley intercepts, the Madrid station telling Berlin that according to their man, 'CONVOY SAILED FOUR DAYS AGO IN SOUTHERLY DIRECTION.'

Philby became exasperated when he saw it.

'What's going on? We know there is no bloody convoy.'

He looked at Bristow.

'Who is Arabal? Why is he so obviously lying?'

London, 22 February 1942

Major Thomas Argyll Robertson, head of MI5's B1A section, was a busy man. For ten days Luis Calvo, Spanish journalist and member of a pro-Nazi spy ring operating under orders from Madrid, had been locked up in MI5's interrogation centre, Camp 020 on Ham Common. Within twenty-four hours the Spaniard had confessed. Stripped naked, he only had to catch sight of camp commander 'Tin-eye' Stephens cracking his swagger stick against his riding boots to break down.

There was cleaning up to do, however, after the public exposure of a Spanish reporter with close ties to the embassy. Staff there were anxious to avoid an escalation of the crisis. After this, other countries would take a second look at the Spanish diplomats on their territory.

Nonetheless, it had been a success for MI5: simple counter-espionage, stopping the enemy's intelligence operations in their tracks. Not that Spain was officially an enemy, but she was certainly no friend.

The case might not have involved Robertson (he was always called Tommy, or 'Tar', after his initials) had it not been for the fact that one of his double agents had played a part in exposing Calvo. Gwilym Williams was known by his initials, G.W., the only one in the double-cross pack not to have a proper code name of his own. 'Snow', 'Tricycle', 'Tate' — the others were all part of Robertson's special club; once they had been taken into the fold, either willingly or not, all were re-baptised. But not G.W.

MI5 had got G.W. in to keep a watch on Arthur Owens — double agent 'Snow' — the shifty Welsh nationalist who thought he could play one side off against the other. That was not how double-cross worked, however. To be on Robertson's team, agents worked exclusively for him, only ever pretending to be working for the Germans. It was a simple and necessary rule. The whole structure, all the double agents they had painfully built up since the beginning of the war, would collapse if the enemy got an inkling that one of 'their' agents had been turned and

23

was working for the British.

Hence the use of G.W. to keep a track on 'Snow'. They could trust Williams, a former policeman. He was also a Welsh nationalist, which helped with the cover story of a man happy to work for the Nazis in the hope of one day liberating his homeland.

Now he had claimed his biggest scalp. G.W. posed as a link man between Calvo and the Abwehr. His efforts had been invaluable in incriminating the Spaniard. But it meant that his MI5 work was finished. His connections to the Abwehr were broken the moment that Calvo was arrested. He could no longer work as an 'enemy spy'. To maintain the pretence he would have to cease operations for fear of being discovered by the British. Any other behaviour would be out of character. So Robertson would have to close him down as a double agent.

That was a problem with double-cross: the patterns of lies were so complex that success — as with the Calvo case — could also bring loss. Using the system against the enemy often meant that double agents — sometimes carefully nurtured over years — had to be discarded like empty bullet casings. You got one shot, that was it.

The other problem with double agents was that most of them only worked under duress. Captured German spies — pathetic creatures, many of them, trying to move around the country with a few quid in their pocket and heavily accented English — were given a choice: the noose or turn against their former masters.

Some chose death but plenty opted for the alternative. Robertson had been the one who suggested the option be given them in the first place. A dead German spy was no use to anybody. But one who continued communicating with the Abwehr yet was actually being controlled by the British? That was different. Using all these agents in tandem, getting them to tell the same story to the Germans, could be very useful indeed. Double agents were as old as warfare itself, but no one had tried to do anything on this scale before.

It needed coordination, funds, organisation, cooperation and a lot of man-hours. Then they had to get the right Whitehall people on board — without telling them too much.

That side of things was John Masterman's job. As head of MI5's B1A section, Robertson ran the double agents, each with their minders and housekeepers and wireless operators and whole teams around them, making sure they did what they were told, and told the Germans what they were meant to tell them. John Masterman, meanwhile, a tall, reedy fifty-year-old bachelor don from Christ Church, detective novelist and future Vice-Chancellor of Oxford, was better suited to dealing with the process of deciding how and when the agents were to be used, working with representatives from the various government authorities. A 'back-room boy', Masterman later described himself, the head of the Twenty Committee that oversaw the double-cross system as a whole — 'Twenty' because in the playful minds of those who worked on it, the Roman numerals XX formed a 'double-cross'.

Masterman had been in Germany at the start of the First World War and spent the entire four years of the conflict as a civilian internee, so he knew both the language and the people well. And as a former MCC player he liked drawing parallels between running the Twenty Committee and captaining a cricket XI. His intellect and scholarly manner were perfect for the job.

Robertson was no intellectual, as Masterman and others commented. But he did have nous. The others might be cleverer, but they did not always see things clearly. They needed Robertson for his ability to read people and situations. He got things right, almost always, and sometimes when 'logic' suggested otherwise. And he was a natural leader. Masterman and the others respected him for that.

Working for MI5 was a far cry from Robertson's earlier, hellraising life, when the nickname 'Passion Pants' had stuck — a reference to both his womanising and the colourful tartan trousers he had worn as a Seaforth Highlander. The debts he had accrued back then with all the parties and nightclubs meant he had to resign his commission. First he had gone into the City, before a change of tack had taken him to the Birmingham police force as a rank-and-file copper. At some point during this period he came to the notice of MI5, when the organisation's founder, Vernon Kell, recommended Robertson because he had been at Charterhouse with his son, John.

Charming, courteous and easy to be with, Robertson was likened by one of his colleagues to the actor Ronald Colman, a Rudolph Valentino type who, with Hungarian star Vilma Bánky, had formed a silent-movie duo that had rivalled that of John Gilbert and Greta Garbo. Robertson was most at ease doing business in bars and restaurants: the banter over a few drinks often showed a man's true character, brought in the best results.

Now he was the head of B1A section, and although it was a Sunday, he was off to have a chat with Ralph Jarvis, MI6's man in Lisbon, who was over in London for a few days. It would be useful to meet, to see how things were over there.

Luis Calvo had not been the only Spanish spy on Robertson's mind. For the past month or so they had been chasing the mystery man the Germans referred to as 'Alaric' or 'Arabal', with his phantom shipping convoys. They still had not found him. Herbert Hart, the head of MI5's research unit, had come to the conclusion that 'Arabel' — as he preferred it — was Spanish, as some had suspected from the start. (By now most were referring to him as 'Arabel', choosing the more English-sounding spelling of his German code name so that he sounded more like an imp or a fairy than a spy: someone you were not sure even existed.)[1] Arabel was reporting to the Abwehr spymaster in Madrid, so Hart's theory made

---

[1] From here onwards I generally use the spelling 'Arabel' unless in direct quotation from, or reference to, the German.

sense. Yet despite his claims to the Germans, it was clear that Arabel was not in London. No one actually present in the country could come up, as he did, with such comical material about life in Britain.

Liverpool's amusement centres, according to his reports, were hives of 'drunken orgies and slack morals'. Perhaps that was not entirely mistaken, yet clearly he had never travelled to Glasgow, where he claimed that owing to so much wartime hardship the local men could be persuaded to carry out acts of sabotage and terrorism for the novelty of 'a litre of wine'. 'This product does not exist on the island,' Arabel insisted. Although Robertson had been born in Sumatra, his parents were Scottish; few understood better than he the beer-drinking preferences of his fellow countrymen. Just as surprisingly, Arabel had informed the Germans that during the summer months London effectively shut down due to the heat, with diplomatic missions taking refuge on the cooler shores of Brighton. He appeared to have little idea of British ways, or the country itself. Judging by an expenses sheet he sent to the Germans, he clearly had no grip on £ s d (a train journey between Glasgow and London cost him '£0 s87 d10'). By now it was obvious to the British that he was only pretending to be in London.

The question was whether the Germans also guessed that. Some of his mistakes were amusing, but others were more worrying. He had told his spymasters that minesweepers were being used as escorts for shipping convoys over the Atlantic.

That was bad enough, but one that he named as still being in operation, HMS *Chestnut*, had been sunk in November 1940 — 'a fact that', a Navy representative reading his material concluded, 'the Germans can hardly have failed to notice'.

Even if he was making his reports up, the double-cross system was so delicate that MI5 could not allow people to freelance like this. If the Germans found out that Arabel was duping them — and it could only be a matter of time before they did — they might start to suspect all their agents. And even if they did not, Arabel's reports might contradict information sent by genuine double agents. The risk was too great. Arabel had to be found, and stopped.

Unless, of course, MI5 could get him and persuade him to join the Twenty Committee's special team. It was a long shot. Even if such a feat could be pulled off, the chances were that he would be compromised in some way. There were plenty in the intelligence community who thought he could not be trusted, that he might be a German plant meant to infiltrate British intelligence. Others preferred to wait and see.

First he had to be located, though.

The search was split between two sections of MI5. Robertson in B1A checked his double agents' communications with the Germans for possible clues to his identity. Meanwhile, B1G, which dealt with counter-espionage in the Iberian Peninsula, searched through their sources. Tomás (Tommy) Harris was in charge of that section. Half-Spanish on his mother's side, he was a wealthy artist who helped his father run the Spanish Art Gallery in Mayfair selling El Grecos and Goyas. Harris spoke Spanish like a native, yet neither he nor Robertson had had any success in locating Arabel.

It was not just that Arabel was a German agent supposedly operating from London. The fact was, the counter-intelligence chiefs were confident that they had picked up most of the Nazi spies that had been sent to Britain by this point. Not only that, thanks to double-cross, Robertson was only months away from concluding that MI5 was running *all* German intelligence operations inside the country. Arabel was an anomaly, one that had apparently slipped through the net. It had been over a month now since they had first become aware of him, his name appearing on the Bletchley intercepts. His material might be bogus, but it was imperative that they find him.

Sunday, 22 February wore on, and the time came for Robertson's meeting with Jarvis: an informal chat, an MI5 man and an MI6 man smoothing over the fault lines where the two organisations joined and sometimes clashed. There were plenty of matters to talk about — Lisbon had become an espionage centre when the war began. But over the course of their conversation, Jarvis threw out an unexpected question.

'Do any of your double agents', he asked, 'write messages to their German case officers with addresses in Madrid?'

Robertson nodded.

'The address *Apartado 1099* mean anything to you?'

It was a PO box number.

Robertson told him it was genuine, that one of his double agents sent letters to the same address.

Jarvis excused himself and got up to make a phone call to his section head in St Albans, Felix Cowgill. Once he got the necessary clearance, he returned to Robertson.

There was something important that MI5 needed to know, Jarvis said, something about a Spaniard in Lisbon who had been pestering MI6 for months . . .

2

Spain, Autumn 1941

For a time he had feared for his life, but the immediate threat had passed and now Karl-Erich Kühlenthal had reason to believe that he was on the cusp of a major triumph.

Outside the embassy, skeletal horses pulled delivery carts up and down the Avenida del Generalísimo. Madrid was a poor city, its people suffering after the destruction and pain of the Civil War. All over the country mothers scavenged for food for their children, surviving off scraps and stealing whatever they could to stay alive, while in prisons, tens of thousands awaited retribution for having fought on the losing side. The firing squads and garrotters were kept busy cleansing Spain of Reds.

German diplomats had an upmarket address in the centre of the capital, not far from the Real Madrid stadium. This was the centre of the new Spanish Establishment, where the victorious made their homes and came to watch the State-favoured football team. For the embassy staff, Madrid was an important posting in a friendly, if austere, country. Franco had defeated his Republican enemies in April 1939, just five months before the new world war began, and he had done so thanks in large part to help from Mussolini and Hitler.

Since then, and against the Germans' best efforts, he had resisted calls for Spain to join the Axis. Franco was a Galician, from the northwest, where caution and inscrutability were applauded. Exhausted after so much fighting, Spain could not, he told his ally, become a full player in a new conflict. It would remain officially neutral, but it would still be Hitler's friend.

Big and important as it was, the German Embassy was more than a symbol of this amicable arrangement. As with many foreign legations, it was also an espionage hub, with an active Abwehr station at the heart of it, the biggest in any neutral country. And Kühlenthal was becoming one of the most important officers of the hundreds on the payroll.

His connection with Spain went back years. In the 1930s his father, General Erich Kühlenthal, had been military attaché to both France and Spain, and had made friends with members of the Spanish armed forces. As a result, when Franco had joined the military uprising against the Spanish Republic in 1936, he turned to General Kühlenthal to seek German support for his campaign — which quickly turned into the Spanish Civil War.

The upshot of Hitler's subsequent decision to help Franco was the creation of the Condor Legion, a unit of several thousand military volunteers from the German armed forces sent to fight alongside Franco's army. Spain became a testing ground for new military ideas, concepts that would later turn into the 'blitzkrieg' tactics that won the Germans such rapid victories across Europe. Despite efforts to cover it up, most blamed the Condor Legion for the massacre at Guernica.

The Legion had also had an intelligence corps, headed by Joachim Rohleder. In 1938, Kühlenthal, then in his late twenties, became Rohleder's secretary.

Kühlenthal was tall and slim, with light brown hair smoothed back with a parting on the left side. His nose was thin and 'hawk-like' according to those who met him, while his eyes, a typically German blue-grey, were described as 'piercing' and 'searching'. He dressed well, usually wearing double-breasted suits, and had the appearance of a German of 'the better class'. As a young man, Kühlenthal had wanted to follow his father into the army, with dreams of reaching high rank. But there was a problem, one which, after Hitler came to power in 1933, made his entry into the German armed forces impossible: his grandmother on his mother's side was Jewish. Under the Nuremberg Laws passed in 1935, in which the Nazi state gave legal definition to its anti-Semitism, a quarter-Jew was regarded as a 'second-degree mongrel' (*Mischling zweiten Grades*), and while not persecuted quite as heavily as those considered 'more Jewish', was still denied certain basic rights.

Kühlenthal had initially come to Spain to escape the pressure of his racial 'impurity', and for a while he ran a business in Madrid selling radios imported from the United States — 'Elcar' he called it, the name coming from a combination of his wife's first name, Ellen, and the Spanish version of his own name, Carlos. Then the

Spanish Civil War broke out and he was forced to return to Germany. But shortly afterwards he was back in Madrid, this time in German intelligence through his father's military connections.

During the First World War, his father had become friends with a diminutive naval officer. Admiral Wilhelm Canaris was now the head of the Abwehr, and had become the young Kühlenthal's mentor. A former U-boat captain, Canaris had been made head of the German secret service after Hitler came to power. He was a conservative, a right-winger, but there was much about the Nazis and their ideology that Canaris did not agree with, including their ideas about race. Kühlenthal was one of many Jews whom he assisted; until Himmler ousted him in February 1944, the Abwehr chief helped save the lives of hundreds, sometimes naming them as his agents, sending them abroad as he did with Kühlenthal, getting them out of sight.

Ironically the threat of persecution only seemed to make Kühlenthal work harder, running spy networks from Madrid. In 1941 he was thirty-three years old. He was industrious and his passion for his job had, with time, made him one of the most important figures in the Abwehr station, to the annoyance of some of his colleagues who resented the fact that, despite his lack of military training, he had been made 'specialist-captain' and put in charge of the section running secret agents.

People regarded him as stand-offish and serious. And while many in the Abwehr were drawn by the excitement and adventure of espionage — the money and sex — Kühlenthal, married with two children, was noted only for his passions for tennis and for cars, of which he owned two: a brown French coupé with changeable number plates for daytime driving, and a black German car for cruising the streets at night.

And yet, despite his invaluable work for the Reich, he could not be entirely at ease. Since the previous summer Germany had been at war with its former ally, the Soviet Union. The killing of Jews was now a large-scale enterprise with special murder squads — *Einsatzgruppen* — sent in behind the front-line troops to execute Jewish populations in newly conquered territories. Kühlenthal could busy himself with work, show that he was a useful intelligence officer, but how much longer could he survive, even in Madrid? When would it be his turn, the knock on the door in the middle of the night?

For the Abwehr was not the only covert German organisation operating from the embassy in Madrid. Himmler's secret police, the Gestapo, and his Nazi-controlled intelligence body, the Sicherheitsdienst or SD, also had agents on the ground there. Himmler had made an official visit to Spain in October 1940, meeting Franco to pave the way for his men to enjoy full cooperation from the Generalísimo's police. This effectively gave them a free hand.

Kühlenthal could not feel safe. Perhaps Spain was not the haven that he had imagined. Franco was sitting out the world war, yet had quickly set up a special military force for Spanish young men wishing to help the Führer. Once the invasion of the Soviet Union had begun in June 1941, the Spanish Blue Division recruited tens of thousands of eager volunteers to be sent to the Eastern Front.

The truth was that Spain was becoming even friendlier with Germany, which was fine for ordinary embassy employees, sharing in the glory of the Reich's victories against the Reds; they went down well in Franco's Madrid. But Kühlenthal needed something to make his position more secure.

And salvation had come — not once, but twice.

Himmler's Nazi spies — the SD — had been on the prowl. Their Madrid office had found out about Kühlenthal's grandmother. But then help had arrived. Canaris, his mentor, had almost certainly had a hand in it. A piece of paper that could save Kühlenthal's career — perhaps even his life — landed on his desk: he had been officially created an Aryan. At the stroke of a pen, like the waving of a magician's wand, his Jewishness had been made to vanish.

The SD had queried the measure. They were furious. There was 'no legal authority for such an act', they insisted.

Drop it, came the reply from Berlin.

The fact was, Kühlenthal's hard work was paying off. He was becoming too important a person to lose. For the network of spies he had patiently been building up was beginning to show real promise. Not all of them, certainly.

The British were skilful adversaries when it came to espionage. Yet Kühlenthal had high hopes for a new network at the heart of enemy territory. Since the summer of 1941, one of his men had been reporting directly from London, writing letters in secret ink sent via courier to Lisbon. He had a keen eye, this one, even if he did get muddled about English ways sometimes. No matter, he would learn. The information he had sent about troop movements and shipping convoys would raise Kühlenthal's stock in Berlin.

He had first met his new spy a short walk from the embassy, at the Café Correos. At first the little Catalan had not impressed him — Señor López, he had called himself. A false name, of course, just as Kühlenthal had introduced himself as 'Felipe' — later he would also use his preferred pseudonym 'Carlos'. The new agent was inventive, a problem solver: through some clandestine means he had managed to get himself a passport and exit visa for travel abroad, no easy task for an ordinary Spaniard then. And his political leanings were in the right direction. Plenty of Spaniards wanted to help defeat communism. They had, after all, done so themselves at home. Now their anti-Red fervour needed new battlefields.

Gradually, Kühlenthal had been won over. All right, he said, show us what you can do. You're of no use to us here in Madrid. What we really need is for you to get yourself to London. Then we might be interested.

He and his subordinate gave the man training in secret inks, some money, and a code name:

'Alaric', after the Gothic chief who had sacked Rome. Could his new agent help bring down the British Empire from within?

He had had his doubts. Would Alaric even get to England? Then the first letter arrived. His man was in London, passing on his correspondence to a KLM steward flying the civilian route from Portugal to Britain in order to bypass the enemy censors. It was a clever move, if expensive — the courier was demanding a dollar a letter. But it was worth it to have a new agent on the ground.

In their replies, Kühlenthal's office had to remind Alaric to number his future letters, and his new agent's baroque prose style made his messages wordier than necessary. But it was a good start. Better even than Kühlenthal might have imagined, for already his *V-mann* had taken his advice and recruited three other sub-agents to work under him. Abwehr headquarters would be pleased.

Kühlenthal was calling this network, with Alaric at its head, 'Arabal', the name of a gushing waterfall in British-held Kashmir.

First the certificate of Aryanisation, and now a new intelligence operation in London itself.

It was just the beginning.

3

Lisbon, December 1941

Araceli was worried. The train journey from their home in Estoril to central Lisbon took a little over half an hour. Before long her husband would be in the city library again consulting reference books and the day's newspapers. Just a few more reports for the Germans, he insisted, and he would shut everything down.

The emigration paperwork from the Brazilian Consulate was almost complete. Soon they could book their passage and get away. But they were in danger, and time was running out.

She had reason to be frightened. What if it went wrong, if someone found out? Little Juan was barely four months old.

They had not meant for things to turn out like this. Neither of them really wanted to go to Brazil. Or to be in Lisbon, for that matter. Back in Madrid, just after the Civil War, when they had managed the Majestic Hotel together, the dream had been to get to London, or perhaps America, to a better life, away from the misery and austerity of Franco's Spain. Once the world war had broken out, they eschewed the official reports from the Spanish media, which were careful never to say anything that might offend their German friends. Instead they listened to the news in Spanish broadcast by the BBC. Few

40

people did that: it was risky.

London appeared like a beacon of a better world, a place of higher values, even opportunity. German bombs may have been falling on it, but it was preferable to the grey limitations of Franco's National-Catholicism, the poverty of a deeply wounded country. Salazar's Portugal was just as bad.

With curly black hair and fine features, Araceli had a dark, seductive beauty not uncommon to her native Galicia in north-west Spain. She had certain airs — which would later cause frictions — and was convinced that she was descended from aristocracy. But like her husband she was intelligent and had a taste for adventure: she had made the first exploratory approach to the British on her husband's behalf in January 1941 with an offer to help in the struggle against Hitler. It had been a failure, however: the staff had barely given her the time of day. Later, her husband himself had tried to talk to the British on numerous occasions, all to no avail.

Now it was late 1941. In Madrid a couple of weeks earlier she had been hopeful: a passport official at the embassy had finally agreed to meet her husband. But yet again the people they were trying to help turned them away, uninterested in what he had to offer. There was no choice, her husband said, but to return to Lisbon and prepare to leave Europe altogether. If the Germans discovered the truth their lives would be in danger. And every approach to the British only exposed them even more.

Perhaps her husband was right about moving

to Brazil. They would be safe there, and could start a new life. But he would always bear the weight of failure. He had set so much on this, his pride, his self-esteem. He was more than just a dreamer. His imagination was even more powerful than her own, but he could work things to make those dreams come alive through his scheming, his sleight of hand, his ability to lie with a straight face. Neither of them had thought things would go this far, or get quite so bad, but the rejections from the British authorities — it was easy to lose count of them by now: five? six? seven, even? — had driven them here, to the far edge of Europe. Brazil, far across the ocean, seemed the only escape route left.

There was one last thing she must try, however. Everything had to be prepared before she took her next move — the right papers and proof to take with her, someone to look after the baby for a few hours. Her husband must never find out that she was making her own plans.

German money was paying for all this — the grand house, their Lisbon life. German money paying for the false reports her husband was now working on at the library, pretending to be based in London but actually gathering information from a *Blue Guide to Great Britain*, French newspapers, a Portuguese book on the British fleet, a French-English dictionary of military terminology, and a map of Britain that he had been given in Madrid. Not having any English made it more difficult.

At home, he would write a cover letter,

42

ostensibly to her, Araceli, detailing his experiences as a novelist in England, wishing her well and hoping that he might see her and their baby son again soon. Other letters might be addressed to a supposed Catalan nationalist friend or a mistress he had invented in Madrid. In between the lines he would write the intelligence reports in secret ink, basing his stories on material in his reference books. Two works of fiction on the same page, running in parallel. One visible, the other hidden. With no word of truth in either.

The Germans had no idea that he was really in Lisbon, and not in London: the letters were forwarded to them from a Portuguese poste restante address. But the money could not last for ever. Their situation was all too precarious: the Germans would not be understanding if they learned about her husband's ruses. A new solution was needed.

She checked her bag to make sure she had everything. The nice American had said he could get a British man to come along as well today.

It had taken a while for Theodore Rousseau Jr, assistant naval attaché at the US Embassy, to consider her proposals seriously. She had first approached him the month before with stories of a Spanish spy working for the Germans against the Americans. The US was not in the war, not yet at least, but she had thought it better to make out that there was a direct threat to them.

And she had been bold, asking for 200,000 dollars for her precious information. Her husband would have been proud. That made Rousseau start taking her seriously. In the end she had given him proof for no payment at all: a message written in secret ink, stating that 'Agent 172' in Chicago was ready to start his sabotage plans.

It was written in French. Araceli did not speak French. She thought that producing a message in a language she could not write would help her story. All it took was to ask a French friend to jot down a short note for her, then she changed some of the key words. So 'Paris' became 'Chicago', and the 'publication' of 'journals' in the original became the 'sabotage' of 'factories'. She had learned a lot over the past months.

After that Rousseau had become very interested. But in November 1941 the US was not a combatant in the war: that would come a few weeks later, once the Japanese attacked Pearl Harbor. At this stage, he decided she should talk to a representative of the British government about her German spy.

And so now here she was, about to meet Rousseau for a third time, with his counterpart from the British Embassy in Lisbon, Captain Arthur Benson, who was, Rousseau told her, a member of the British intelligence services.

She started her story, repeating what she had told Rousseau before: she had information about a Spanish spy working for the Germans. To prove it she opened her bag and pulled out a piece of microfilm, a flask of secret ink, and a letter from the spy's German controller. She thought for a moment of her husband's reaction: he would be annoyed if he found out what she was doing. Not angry, or furious. He never spoke harshly, that was not his way. But she had no other choice.

Benson glanced briefly at the 'proof' she had brought with her, but his expression and manner suggested that he was not impressed. What did he think? That these were fakes? She was risking her life, and her family's, by coming here.

But yes, that was precisely what Benson thought. There was nothing, he told her, of any interest in what she had to say or show him.

A whole year of having doors shut in their faces by the British, both in Lisbon and in Madrid. She had put everything on this one last chance, hoping that by coming through the Americans she might have a greater possibility of being heard. But in Benson's eyes she was a mere adventuress, trying to grab some quick money or excitement.

She had had enough. This last-ditch attempt had come to nothing. Her mind should turn to other things: to little Juan, and the emigration papers. They would have to move quickly. If the Germans ever found out . . .

She made to leave. Seeing her stand up, Benson himself got to his feet, and with a cruel grin, leaned over to place a 20-escudo coin on the table in front of her.

'Here you are. Take this for your trouble and your fare.'

A final insult.

Rousseau could only apologise. He was concerned. There was no need for a scene. Yet there was a question in the air: what was really going on here?

Araceli realised that she had no choice: she

45

would have to tell them everything, to explain to Rousseau — and to Benson — the real reason why she was there, the reason why she had got in touch in the first place.

This man, she started saying. This German spy . . .

Rousseau and Benson listened.

This spy is my husband.

★　★　★

Later, Benson passed the information on — to the Admiralty in London, and to the Section V man in Lisbon, Ralph Jarvis.

The Spanish woman had brought along German secret inks to 'prove' her story, and the Americans seemed to be going along with what she had to say, but the British had more experience dealing with the Abwehr — appearances were, more often than not, misleading. And Lisbon was a den of spies, or people trying to become spies.

A Spaniard working for the Germans, pretending that he was in London spying for them. When all the time he was in Lisbon. And, according to his wife, the people he really wanted to work for were the British. So she said. Who could tell? The chances were that he was a plant by the Germans, trying to get one of their men inside British intelligence.

She had given them her husband's name: Juan Pujol García. It sounded plausible enough. Benson would pass it on.

But making up a name was easy.

4

Southern England, April 1942

A painter and a circus impresario were chosen for the pick-up.

Tomás Harris sat in the back of the car. They had a long drive ahead and he made himself a cigarette, flattening the paper smooth before adding black tobacco and rolling it into a cylinder. Slim and elegant, with pushed-back black hair and a penetrating gaze, there was a rare power about Harris, an enthusiasm and love of life that few failed to notice.

'He was ebullient and vibrant,' recalled a close friend. 'Everything fascinated him. He was magnetic, unpretentious, and passionate about everything that he did.'

A multi-talented artist, Harris had won the Trevelyan-Goodall scholarship to the Slade School of Fine Art when he was only fifteen. He went on to study sculpture at the British Academy in Rome before returning to London. There he set up his own art business on Bruton Street, but later joined his father to run the Spanish Art Gallery, which sold works by the Spanish masters. Lionel Harris was a Jewish businessman who had worked in Spain. He married a woman from Seville — Enriqueta Rodríguez León. Of their seven children, Tomás was the fourth and last son.

When the Second World War started, 'Tommy' — as he was usually called by colleagues — took a job with his wife Hilda at the SOE training facility at Brickendonbury Hall after a recommendation from his friend Guy Burgess. In 1940 he moved to MI5.

His self-portraits show a dark, intense side, but outwardly he was a warm, sociable character.

'He was a wonderful raconteur and was never happier than when telling anecdotes and stories.'

Others were struck by his strength of character.

'Tommy was a very, very strong personality,' one colleague said. 'He was a very persuasive person. If you looked at a picture with him you found at the end of twenty minutes you were thinking the same as him.'

Anthony Blunt, also working at MI5 at the time, was a friend — Blunt had reviewed an exhibition at the Harris gallery — and he, too, held Harris in high esteem.

'Tomás was one of the most complete human beings I have ever known.'

Harris's Spanish background gave him a touch of exoticism (his maternal grandfather had been a distinguished bullfighter) and labelled him as something of an outsider — despite his connections he never felt completely at home in British upper-class society. Yet apart from his painting and art dealing, he was also a piano and saxophone player as well as being a talented MI5 intelligence officer: there was a whiff of genius about him.

Cyril Mills, from MI5's B1A section, was next

to him as they set off, heading out of London along the A4. Mills was forty and older than Harris by about six years. Before the war he had been a famous circus manager and used to fly a de Havilland Hornet Moth around Europe looking for new acts. Then one day, soaring over Germany in 1936, he had caught sight of a train line disappearing into a mountainside. Mills had studied engineering at Cambridge, and to his technical eye this looked suspicious, not unlike a secret military factory. He told MI5, who asked him to keep snooping for them. When the war started, it was obvious there would not be many more circuses for a while, so Mills swapped his impresario life for a full-time MI5 position.

The two men sat back in the car. It would be late afternoon before they reached Plymouth. Jock Horsfall was reliable, a former racer and the best driver in the service. They could think and talk for a while.

At long last they had found their mystery Spaniard. 'Arabal', 'Alaric', 'V-Mann 316', 'V-Mann 319': the Germans gave this new man and his supposed sub-agents many names. MI5 had been chasing him for months. Now he had been located in Lisbon and was being flown over to Britain for interrogation. Some of their questions would be answered on his arrival, but new queries would inevitably arise. Would they be able to trust him? Was he really as good as he appeared?

MI6 had first heard of him way back in December: a Spaniard asking to become a British spy, claiming that he had already fooled the Germans into thinking he was working for them. And it looked as though the same man had made various approaches, not only in Lisbon, but in Madrid as well. On each occasion he had been shown the door, while all the time he was sending false reports to the Madrid Abwehr claiming that he was actually in London.

Now it was late April. Four months had gone by trying to find the new enemy 'spy', wondering how he had escaped detection, while all the time he was in Portugal trying to work for the British. Harris repeated the phrase that kept running through his mind: it was a minor miracle he had survived this long. Which only made the sceptics suspect even more. The man must be a plant, otherwise the Germans would have liquidated him by now.

Yet Dilly Knox's decoded Bletchley transcripts of Abwehr traffic clearly showed the trust the enemy had in Arabel as their man in London. There was no hint there of a set-up.

For MI5 this was a great opportunity. The double-cross system was working well — a nest of German spies now safely working on behalf of His Majesty's Government, feeding lies to the other side. Could they take this new man on board as well?

MI6 were calling him 'Bovril' because, they said, like the drink, he helped 'avoid that sinking feeling'. All those messages to Madrid about non-existent convoys had something to do with it, perhaps. It was not clear who had come up with the code name. It was said that MI9's man in Gibraltar, Donald Darling, who helped Allied soldiers escape from behind enemy lines, had given it to the Spaniard when he arrived from Lisbon a couple of weeks before. But 'Bovril' had been used to describe him earlier than that — at least a month before. Were MI6 trying to wash their hands of him, knowing full well they were about to lose him to MI5?

Perhaps Philby, Harris's close friend in Section V, had something to do with it. Philby was one of the regulars at Harris's grand Mayfair home, using number 6 Chesterfield Gardens as a kind of private club, as did Victor Rothschild, Anthony Blunt and Guy Burgess — a small set enjoying one of the best wine cellars in London.

Arabel might never have been brought to Britain had it not been for Philby, often acting behind Cowgill's back. It was now becoming clear quite how much Bletchley material on him Cowgill had been keeping from MI5. The head of Section V saw a threat, knowing perfectly well that the Spaniard might be perfect double agent material. Which is why he had tried to hide him from MI5 for so long.

'I do not see why I should get agents and then have them pinched by you,' he told Guy Liddell, Harris's boss and the head of MI5's B section. As far as Cowgill was concerned, 'the Yanks' had brought Arabel to him. If he was to belong to anyone it was to MI6 — he would be *their* man working from Lisbon.

But double-cross was not about winning battles, it was about winning the war itself. And from operating as a means of controlling and curtailing German espionage work inside Britain (why send any new agents over when the ones they had were working so well . . . ?), it would eventually move into a new, more significant phase, that of actually deceiving the enemy.

The car had driven far from London now, with fewer reminders around them of the war, except the military vehicles and lack of road signs. The flying boat from Gibraltar was scheduled to arrive just before sunset. The flight lasted twice as long as in peacetime as they had to fly so far out into the Atlantic to avoid German fighters.

If they could just make things with this new man work . . .

The double-cross system was not without its problems. Many captured spies who were 'turned' to work for the British had to be threatened to assure their cooperation. Few were willing double agents, and the business of building them up in the Germans' eyes, making them increasingly credible so that eventually false and misleading information could be fed through them, was fraught with difficulties.

With Arabel, however, if he was who he said he was, some of the teething problems might be avoided. If he was already trusted by the Germans, MI5 had a chance to use a fully fledged double agent who had been willing to work for the British in the first place.

They would have to proceed cautiously. In the past double agents had shown promise and then had to be dropped over fears that they might be compromised. Security was paramount, and as with the Bletchley material, double-cross could only work if the enemy suspected nothing.

But still, Arabel, or Bovril, or whatever name they gave him in the end, had promise. He had made it this far on his own. And after the Malta convoy message, what might he be capable of once they finally got him under their wing?

It still was not clear if Arabel had been behind the report on the convoy to the besieged island. The Abwehr report had not said, putting it down to Kühlenthal's 'V-Mann 372'. It was one of the many points that would be covered over the coming days of questioning and interrogation. Bletchley had picked it up on 2 April, over three weeks previously. By then the decision had already been taken to bring Arabel over to Britain. In the meantime, however, while the would-be British agent waited in Lisbon for the territorial battles between MI5 and MI6 to be sorted, he was still sending messages to his Abwehr controller.

That last one had created ripples — in more ways than one. There was, it said, a convoy of fifteen ships, including nine freighters, heading from Liverpool with relief supplies for Malta. Not only food, but war materiel including anti-aircraft ammunition and RAF personnel, were also on board.

Previous aid convoys to Malta had sailed from Mediterranean ports with the loss of many ships, sunk by the Germans and Italians. This was the first such convoy reported to be sailing from Britain itself. The enemy responded to the intelligence handsomely. German U-boats were sent to ambush the convoy as it passed close to Gibraltar on its way into the Mediterranean, while Italian planes armed with torpedoes were amassed in Sardinia for later strikes.

All to no avail. The convoy to Malta never appeared. The Germans were angry — they blamed the Italians. A great deal of war effort — man hours, fuel, supplies — had gone into the operation, with no result.

For there had never been a Malta convoy. It was made up.

Amazingly, no one on the German side blamed the intelligence or the agent who had supplied it. As far as the enemy were concerned, the convoy had existed; they had simply failed to find it. So whoever had sent that report — and there were still doubts about whether Arabel was behind it — had not only proved his credentials with the Germans, but had single-handedly had an important, if relatively minor, effect on the war itself.

It had been enough to tip the balance in favour of those wanting to get Arabel to London. Even Cowgill gave in eventually. He could still claim it was his idea to bring him over, but no one from MI6 would be there for the reception.

They finally reached Plymouth and Jock Horsfall pulled the car in behind the Mount Batten flying-boat terminal. Rooms had been booked at a nearby hotel where they could have dinner and spend the night before driving back to London the next morning.

It was sunset when the launch finally brought the passengers over from the flying boat. Harris watched as a short Spanish man stepped on to British soil. He looked older than his thirty years

— prematurely balding on top — although his small yellow-brown eyes had a keenness about them, mischievous almost. It was extraordinary that someone so unassuming and humble in appearance could have caused so much trouble, for both the Germans and the British.

Harris stepped forward and held out his hand in greeting. Then spoke in perfect Spanish:

'*Bienvenido a Inglaterra, señor Pujol.* Welcome to England. My name is Tomás Harris, and my colleague here — ' he used the false name they had agreed for Mills — 'is Mr Grey. We will both be taking you to London.'

Juan Pujol smiled politely at them. He had finally made it — in Britain at last, with the people he had been trying to work with for a year and a half. He shivered, and made a comment about the cold. Harris and Mills grinned. No, Harris said, this was not southern Europe. He would have a lot to get used to.

Pujol chuckled with his characteristic laughter, like a 'sly rabbit'.

★   ★   ★

Days later, in London, when they had heard and been amazed by Juan Pujol's story, Mills spoke to Harris.

The code name Bovril did not fit. Besides, Pujol was their man now, he belonged to MI5. Mills proposed a new code name, one which suited him better. Pujol, he said, must be the 'greatest actor in the world' to have fooled so many people and survived. They should name him after that other great actor: Greta Garbo. A film of hers was showing, *Two-Faced Woman*, about a character living a double life. What could be better?

Yes, it was ideal. Not only because of Pujol's acting skills, but, Harris also knew, because of an intelligence and liveliness about the man. The Spanish word *garbo* had no direct translation into English, but it could mean 'graceful', or 'panache', with connotations of perfectionism and generosity.

Mills had no Spanish, but he had found the perfect code name.

PART TWO

'One's real life is often the life that
one does not lead.'
Oscar Wilde

5

Spain, 1912–39

The original building at 70 Carrer Muntaner was pulled down in the early 1980s and replaced by a modern block of flats, but most of the neighbouring structures from the end of the nineteenth century still stand, and the character of the street, in the heart of Barcelona's modernist Eixample, remains virtually unchanged from when it was first conceived. It was and remains a residential and shopping district for the wealthy middle classes, Catalan merchants and traders. The Pujol family, owners of the Juan Pujol y Compañía textile-dyeing firm, celebrated for the quality of its black silk dyes, had made their home here.

And it was here, on Valentine's Day 1912, that Juan Pujol García was born.

Or at least that was what he always said, and 14 February was the day that he celebrated his birthday. His birth certificate in the Barcelona civil record, however, tells a different story. There, his mother Mercedes registered his birth on 1 March 1912, stating that he had been born two days earlier, on 28 February (it was a leap year). The surnames that she gave her baby boy were García Guijarro — her own. Only four years later did Juan's father legally adopt him, and his surname changed: Pujol from his father's side; García from his mother's, as is Spanish custom.

For the first few years of his life, Juan's parents were not married, and all four of their children were born out of wedlock. It was a curious, even scandalous, situation for a religious, middle-class family, particularly in such conservative times.

The problem was that although he was in a relationship with Mercedes, Juan's father was already married — to a woman called Teresa Llombart Puig. Teresa's story with Pujol Sr did not end happily.

It is not known what separated the couple. They had no children — perhaps that was a reason. Teresa was born around 1870. Before she turned forty her husband had started his relationship with Mercedes, a younger woman who worked for them as a cleaning lady. Mercedes gave birth to her first child by Pujol Sr — Joaquín, Juan's elder brother — in 1908.

At that point Juan Pujol Sr and Mercedes became, to all intents and purposes, 'married', living together and raising a family: Juan was their third child. There was no divorce at the time. Perhaps they erased Teresa from the story, pretending to their bourgeois neighbours that they had taken their vows.

Teresa was still around, however. While Pujol Sr and his new family lived comfortably in one of the city's better quarters, her lot was considerably worse. She was living in the Poblenou district, to the north-east of the port, not far from her husband's factory. The area had been the centre of Barcelona's industrial expansion from the end of the nineteenth century and had even been dubbed 'the Manchester of Catalonia'. Yet as in Britain's industrial north, living conditions were appalling. Teresa lived on the ground floor of a small building at Carrer Sant Pere IV 58 — today an abandoned former truck depot.

It was here, at 2.00 in the afternoon on 10 August 1915, that Teresa died. Her death certificate gave cause of death as 'mucomembraneous enteritis', an acute inflammation of the gut producing colic and diarrhoea. There is no indication of how she became ill, but sanitation in the area at the time was minimal, resulting in numerous cases of typhoid and cholera — both illnesses that can cause acute enteritis. Thousands were dying from drinking dirty, bacteria-infected water — an epidemic in the second half of 1914 had infected over 9,000 people, killing around 2,000. Teresa may have been a victim of a similar outbreak. It is perhaps no coincidence that she died in August, when the summer heat made such cases more common. Her death was brought to the attention of the authorities by a man called Agustín Cádiz, described as a married carpenter who lived nearby on Carrer Mariano Aguiló.

For Juan Pujol Sr, his estranged wife's death removed a problem: he was now free, and less than three months later, on 3 November 1915, he and Mercedes wed at the Church of Los Angeles, a five-minute walk from their upmarket home. Now the process of legitimising their children could begin. Juan Pujol was three and a half years old.

It seems apt for someone who would later play such an important role in history as a storyteller, moulding, turning and shaping the truth for great effect, that there should be uncertainty and subterfuge concerning his entry into the world. In spite of the religious and social mores of the time, his mother and father raised a family — for the first few years at least — without the official blessing of either Church or State. It showed bloody-mindedness and an ability to shape the world rather than be shaped by it — both attributes that characterised Pujol in later life.

Pujol himself never mentioned the complications in his parents' marital affairs. His autobiography portrays his father as an upstanding character: 'the most honest, noble and disinterested man that I have ever known'. He was a role model, someone who taught Pujol the values of tolerance and non-aggression that he followed throughout his life. 'He despised war, and bloody revolutions, scorning the despot, the authoritarian . . . So strong was his personality and so powerful his hold over me and my brother that neither of us ever belonged to a political party.'

Later, during the most intense period of his adult life, Pujol would do much to live up to the ideals of liberalism instilled in him by his father.

Despite their secret, the family was otherwise respectable and well-off: they never suffered the kinds of privations of the city's poorer inhabitants. Politically and socially, however, it was a difficult time in Barcelona, with growing workers' movements, social unrest and assassinations. The recently formed CNT anarchist trade union was engaged in frequent battles with gangs organised by company directors. During the worst period, between 1916 and 1923, 27 bosses, 27 managers and 229 workers were killed in the violence. One of Pujol's earliest memories was of his father leaving for work in the mornings during these troubles, saying goodbye to his wife and each one of his children as though he might never come back.

Mercedes, the mother, was more of a disciplinarian than Pujol Sr, instilling in her children the strict Catholic ideas that she had inherited from her own Andalusian family — Los Beatos as they had been known in Motril for their rigid adherence to Church doctrine. Yet despite this the young Juan was a difficult child, unruly, headstrong, whimsical, and he would frequently break all his own toys, as well as those of his brothers and sisters. His father may have tried to teach him the values of pacifism and tolerance, but by nature he was rebellious and combative.

For a time he was sent with his elder brother to a Catholic boarding school in the town of Mataró, to the north of Barcelona, in an attempt to discipline him. It worked, to a degree, but his adolescence was marked by frequent radical changes of direction. He left school aged fifteen to become a blacksmith's apprentice. After a matter of weeks he decided that he wanted to get a place at university studying philosophy and literature instead. There followed a period in which he read almost every book in his father's ample library, fascinated by history and etymology. At this time the family moved house as their fortunes rose, first to Carrer de Septimania 21, then to a magnificent home in the same neighbourhood on Carrer de Homero. All the children received private French lessons three times a week with a tutor from Marseilles.

In 1931, when he was nineteen, Pujol's intense self-education was cut short by an acute case of appendicitis. The wound became infected after the operation and he came close to death, passing in and out of consciousness and suffering a high fever. His father held his hand through the night, weeping at the thought that he might lose his son.

When Pujol eventually recovered some weeks later, he emerged into a changed country: during his illness the Spanish monarchy had fallen and a republic — the Second Republic — had been proclaimed in its place. Whether this was the cause of his next change of direction is unclear, but from philosophy he now decided that chicken farming was where his future lay. On finishing his studies in *avicultura*, he carried out his military service, being drafted in 1933 into a light artillery regiment where he learned to ride a horse, although only after several beatings from his commanding officer.

His father's death from flu in January 1934 came as a severe blow, and seemed to presage a new phase in which the comforts of his middle-class life were exchanged for intense hardship and suffering. At first, the shift was gentle: his mother sold the family share in his father's company to the other business partners; a transport company that Pujol set up with his brother soon folded, as did a chicken farm they established together. In later life almost every business that he set up — from cinemas to farms and hotels — ended in failure. Yet he was an impresario by nature, never happier than when engaged in a new project.

More serious problems arose a couple of years later.

The Civil War began in July 1936. Like many Spaniards, Pujol heard the news of a military coup over the radio, apparently starting in the Spanish territories in northern Morocco. He had plans for a trip with friends to the nearby Montseny mountains that hot day, but as the news seemed to get worse with each bulletin, and there was talk of barricades being erected in the streets and people being shot, he headed over to his fiancée Margarita's house, also in the Eixample area, on Carrer Girona. Margarita's parents were old family friends. Around them, neighbours were hanging white sheets from their balconies to show that they were peaceful and wanted no trouble, but soon events were to change everyone's lives dramatically.

At the start of the coup Barcelona, like most of the major cities except Seville, failed to fall into the hands of the rebel generals and remained under government control. Barcelona, however, quickly became a centre of a radical counter-coup movement. Anarchists and different left-wing groups took over: checkpoints were established in the streets, curfews imposed; people were shot for suspected sympathy with the military rebels. Overnight the city became a dangerous place.

Pujol's family was caught up in the chaos. His sister and mother were arrested as 'counter-revolutionaries' because their names were on a parish list for a visit to the monastery at nearby Montserrat. Anti-clerical fever was at its height, and they were only saved by a friend in the anarchist trade union, who managed to get them released. Their jailers never found out that during those first few days of the conflict, Mercedes had been hiding other Catholics in her home, including a priest called Celedonio. He would later play an important role in Pujol's story.

Meanwhile, Pujol's brother Joaquín was press-ganged into the army to defend the Republic against the rebels. He managed to escape from the front, crossing a great distance almost naked through the snow before finding refuge with family members in the Pyrenees. The experience took a heavy toll, and years later Pujol would blame it for his brother's death at the age of sixty-two.

Elena, Pujol's younger sister, was even less fortunate. Her boyfriend was arrested by the city's revolutionaries as a suspected Franco sympathiser, taken to the hills nearby and shot.

During these difficult first few days and weeks, Pujol remained in his fiancée's house, not daring to walk out into the street, too frightened to try to get out of the city, where the danger was greatest. Patrols and checkpoints were everywhere on the lookout for 'fifth columnists' — a phrase recently coined by one of the rebel generals — and he lacked any forged paperwork that might aid his escape.

The weeks turned into months. He could not appear at the window, or speak in a loud voice for fear of being heard by the neighbours. Whenever anyone knocked at the door he had to hide in a back room.

Shortly before Christmas armed men burst into the flat. Pujol was in the kitchen breaking nuts with a hammer, but he heard the noise as the militiamen began their search. As things turned out, they were not looking for him, but for valuables left in safekeeping with his host family by others who had fled the city. Someone — they did not know who — had tipped the authorities off. It did not take long for the search party to find what it was looking for — gold and jewels stuffed inside a door frame. But as the men passed through each room in the flat, they also discovered Pujol with the hammer in his hand. Along with Margarita's father and brother, he was whisked away.

Pujol was relatively fortunate that his destination that night was the Police headquarters on the Via Laietana. It offered some minor guarantee: had he been taken to one of the less formal 'police' stations — *chekas*, they were referred to, after the kangaroo courts of the Russian Revolution — he might well have been killed out of hand. As it was, he was placed on his own in a dark cell, unsure if these moments were to be his last.

He remained there for a week. Then one night, in the early hours, his cell door was opened and he was asked to step out. A mysterious man took

67

him through a labyrinth of empty offices to a small side door which opened out into the street, thrust a piece of paper in his hand with an address on it, and sent him on his way.

Confused and frightened, Pujol set off. It was cold, but thankfully he only had a short distance to go: the address scribbled on the piece of paper was in the Barri Gòtic, the medieval part of the city between the Cathedral and the port. Arriving at a little street just behind the Town Hall, not sure what he was letting himself in for, he walked up the stairs in the dark and knocked softly. A woman opened and silently let him in.

Pujol discovered later that he had been helped by an organisation called Socorro Blanco, a secret Catholic group operating in Republican territory which rescued people who had fallen foul of the authorities. Fearful for his safety in prison as a draft-dodger, Margarita had got in touch with them and they had made efforts to get Pujol freed, using one of their operatives — a woman posing as a 'revolutionary' who was having an affair with an officer at the police station.

All this would become clear later. For now he was in hiding again, living in the home of a taxi driver who had been forced to drive soldiers to the Aragón front. His wife and nine-year-old boy offered Pujol what security they could. Again Pujol was reduced to silence, to living inside, never showing his face at a window. Conversations, for example when the taxi driver returned with news from the front, could only take place with the radio on, drowning out any sound of his voice that might be picked up by neighbours.

Months passed. In the mornings the wife went out in search of food, leaving Pujol with her little boy.

One day, while she was gone, the police raided the flat. In the seconds before they managed to get inside, Pujol indicated to the boy that he was going to hide under his bed.

The boy showed the police around with unusual *sangfroid*, telling them that his mother was out and that his father was at the front fighting the rebels. The policemen looked carefully in each room, finding nothing. When they were about to enter the room where Pujol was hiding, the boy himself opened the door for them, switched on the light and declared it was his own room. At which point the policemen turned and left. Pujol had been saved once again.

He was so grateful that for the next few months he did his best to teach the little boy whatever he could: the schools had closed and his education had suffered. It was a new form of stimulus for Pujol as well, helping to pass the time. But life in the city was getting worse: it was being bombed by the Francoists and the queues for food were getting longer. By the middle of 1937 the taxi driver's family could stand no more, and decided to leave the flat to stay with relatives out of town.

Pujol was on his own. Socorro Blanco organised thrice-weekly visits to bring him food, but now, with no company at all, Pujol was forced to live in a blackened silence, unable to turn on the lights or make a sound of any kind. He became depressed and withdrawn and his health started to deteriorate. The visits became less frequent, the food rations smaller and smaller. He lost a lot of his hair and over 20 kilos in weight, looking more like a man in his late forties than his mid-twenties.

He knew that he could not remain like this indefinitely. By now it was early 1938 and he had been in the flat for over a year. Fearing for his physical and mental health, he decided that he had to get out. Again, Socorro Blanco helped, providing false identity papers which made him out to be a man too old for military service.

When he stepped out into the street, not only had the city changed thanks to the bombs and revolutions, but so had he. He had been in self-imposed captivity for a year and a half. Through a contact in the Socialist trade union, the UGT, he got a job running a chicken farm in San Juan de las Abadesas, in northern Catalonia, near the border with France. It seemed a perfect place from which to complete his escape.

Slowly he got his strength back, taking long walks once his daily work was done, calculating how far he would have to go to get across the border. Once his preparations were finished, however, and he was about to leave, another group of would-be escapees were involved in a shoot-out near the border with police, and several were killed. As a result, patrols in the area were intensified: just as it had opened, the door to freedom had been closed again.

With the route to France now cut off, Pujol

had to think of other ways to get out of Republican Spain. The farm was not a success and made no money, owing to a lack of investment from the union. After a number of arguments over the running of the place, Pujol handed in his resignation and weeks later was back in Barcelona. This time it seemed there was only one way out: to join the Republican army and try to cross over to the Francoist side at the front line.

He decided to chance it and presented himself at a recruitment centre. It was ironic that after so long he should volunteer to join up in the very army he had been trying to stay out of. Yet with his false identity and older appearance, he was greeted with open arms. It was the spring of 1938 and the Republican side was clearly losing the Civil War. Pujol was given basic, two-week infantry training and sent to the front, near the town of Flix on the River Ebro.

Life in the infantry did not appeal to him, and he was determined not to become 'cannon fodder', so he lied to his officers, telling them that he knew about telegraphy and Morse code. He was duly sent to a signals unit attached to the International Brigades, but his ignorance about the job was all too evident and eventually he was ordered to lay cables between the trenches and the command post. Finally, his unit was sent to the front line, relieving a force that had lost 50 per cent of its men, largely through desertions to the other side. Morale on the Republican side was low, not helped by the fact that all they had to eat, for every meal of every day, was lentil stew. At night, Francoist troops would call out mouth-watering details of the food that they enjoyed on their side, encouraging the Republican soldiers to try to cross the lines.

Pujol did not need any persuading — that was precisely why he was there. Soon he discovered that others were thinking of attempting the same thing. It was risky. If they failed and were caught they would be shot. On one occasion the company's barber was executed in front of the entire battalion for an unsuccessful escape attempt. This was the only dead man that Pujol saw in the entire Civil War.

The Francoist lines lay 200 metres away across a valley with a stream running at the bottom. One clear evening, Pujol, 'starving and disenchanted with life', decided to make a run for it. Later he would claim it was the craziest thing that he ever did.

Just as he was leaving his trench to head out across no-man's-land, armed with a couple of hand grenades, two of his colleagues jumped out of their position to escape as well, causing a small landslide of stones. The sentries were alerted by the noise. Pujol hesitated for a moment, but this was, he told himself, his only chance, and he set off with the patrol hot on his heels. At the bottom of the valley he hid in a patch of pine trees, but quickly became disoriented. Once the patrol had gone, he started heading up a hill, thinking he was inching towards the Francoist side, only to discover that he was going the wrong way — back to the Republican positions.

'Halt!' came a cry.

'Don't shoot,' Pujol replied coolly. 'I'm a Republican passing over to the other side.'

Shots rang out. Realising his mistake, Pujol raced once again into the valley, while the patrol rushed down to try to root him out.

Sneaking through the pine groves, he reached a stream, where he lay down in a reed bed, covering himself as best he could with leaves. The patrol came very close, pushing at the undergrowth with their rifle butts. At one point they stopped for a smoke. The full moon appeared from behind a cloud and Pujol could see their silhouettes, only metres away from him.

He started a silent prayer, calling out to the Virgen del Pilar, the Madonna of the Pillar, to save him. He would, he said, pay homage to her in the cathedral of Zaragoza if she saved him then. He clung to the two grenades he had brought with him, wondering if he would have to use them. Just at that moment, the moon was clouded over again, the night became darker, and the patrol moved away.

Pujol stayed where he was for a while, and shortly afterwards the Francoists began their usual banter, calling out to the Republicans on the other side. Pujol decided to use their voices to orient himself, and he got up out of the river bed, took his boots off so that the sound of his footsteps would not give him away, and started the long climb up the slope to the other side. Eventually he made it and, exhausted and suffering from his shredded feet, he was hauled over into their trenches, almost passing out with fright. 'Don't worry now,' he heard them say as he made a final effort to reach them.

Bleeding and hungry, he had crossed the lines successfully. He spent the next couple of days in the Francoist trenches eating as much as he could.

Yet if he thought that his life was about to improve having finally made it out of Republican territory, two years since the Civil War had begun, he was sorely mistaken. Long, tiring interrogations soon began, before he was finally sent off in a goods train to Zaragoza along with other ex-Republican soldiers. From there they were taken to a Francoist concentration camp in Deusto, in the Basque Country. Once again, Pujol, as a former Republican soldier, found himself a prisoner.

The camp had been the university building, yet conditions were harsh. Lice had infested the place, while the men had to sleep on the bare floorboards of the lecture halls. During the day, they congregated around a fountain in the campus, which was the only place they could wash. To pass the time, some of the men would conduct lice races, betting their rations on the result. Pujol had not eaten properly for a long time, and he found that he could not hold down his food. For a while he was put in the infirmary, where he was given a diet of milk and broth to help his digestive tract recover.

By now he had gained some experience in survival: he sold a Parker fountain pen that he had managed to keep hold of, and with the money bought himself a cheaper pen, some paper and stamps. With these he wrote to every family member and friend that he could think of, asking for help. Some answered, others even with small amounts of money, but the response was not enough to get him out.

But help did finally come. Celedonio, the priest whom his mother had sheltered in Barcelona at the start of the war, had managed to get across to Francoist territory and was now the head of a hospital in Palencia, near Salamanca. He travelled to see Pujol in Deusto, insisting to his captors that Pujol was honest, apolitical and Catholic. He then went one step further and called in at the Francoist capital, Burgos, on his way back to Palencia, where he personally vouched for his family friend and made such a noise that within three days he was released from the concentration camp.

At first Pujol was sent to Celedonio's hospital to recover for a week. By now he was suffering from acute bronchitis, yet he was still obliged to join the Francoist army. In Burgos he enlisted, this time under his own name and giving his true age.

It seemed as though his problems might finally be over. Living the life of a junior officer in the conservative, traditional city of Burgos, he made friends and found a new girlfriend, despite struggling to get by on only one-third-pay. Then one day in December, at a victory celebration after the Francoists had won the Battle of the Ebro, Pujol was caught by his commanding officer exchanging his soldier's cap with a Carlist militiaman's red beret. The officer was infuriated

— such an act was strictly forbidden. Summoning Pujol to his office the next morning, he struck him hard across the face, ripped the braid off his uniform and sent him down to the cells.

Pujol was incarcerated once again, and soon he found himself being sent with other soldiers to the front lines in Aragón. The Civil War was about to end, yet Pujol was in danger of becoming one of its last casualties.

When he got a chance, he called his girlfriend in Burgos, asking her to pull strings: she worked in the Ministry of War and was friends with an influential general. The plan worked. Three weeks later Pujol was called back from the front and reinstated as a junior officer, working with telegrams and communiqués inside the Francoist General Headquarters. It seemed that finally, after so many years of hardship, he could relax. Pujol lived out the last weeks of the Civil War in Burgos, staying at the Condestable Hotel. There, two days before it ended, he met another young woman, a beautiful and seductive black-haired Galician who had a nursing job. Araceli González would later become his wife.

Curiously, at that time Kim Philby was also in Burgos. Accredited to the Francoist side, he was *The Times*'s correspondent in the Civil War, and had already been secretly recruited by the Soviets. By now it was early 1939; the Civil War ended on 1 April. Three years later, Philby would be leading attempts from within MI6's Section V to find a man who had also been a regular face at Franco's GHQ. Did he and Pujol ever meet in Spain? There is no evidence to the fact, yet the

76

coincidence is curious enough for one Spanish writer, Rafael Fraguas, to conclude that Philby and Pujol did get to know each other during this time.

Did Philby even recruit Pujol as a Soviet agent, as Fraguas suggests? This is a conspiracy too far, one that turns Pujol, history's greatest double agent, into a *triple* agent, who was secretly working for Moscow all along.

Fraguas's theory is based on conjecture and nothing has emerged from the Russian archives or anywhere else to support the idea.

But the temptation to speculate about Pujol and his motives is understandable, because little in his story is either simple or straightforward.

6

Spain and Portugal, 1939–41

The Civil War was over and Pujol had survived, proud of the fact that despite serving in both armies, he had not fired a single shot in battle. Yet Spain was in a desperate situation. To this day, the post-war years — La Posguerra — hold a place in popular Spanish consciousness as an emblematic time of want and suffering.

Pujol was still a Catholic, but if he had had any idealised notions about what life would be like on the Francoist side, these were quickly undermined. Now the war was over, he suffered much less than many of his fellow countrymen thanks to his position as a demobbed junior officer from the winning side. Yet attempts by friends and colleagues to get him to join the Falange, the Spanish fascist party, were met with firm refusals. He reacted to the ideology of Franco's Spain as he had to that of 'Red' Barcelona: he wanted nothing to do with it: it clashed with the ideas of liberalism and tolerance handed down by his father.

More important than the matter of party membership, however, was that of making a living. Answering an advert in a newspaper, he got the job of manager of the Majestic Hotel, in the upmarket Castellana district of Madrid. The best days of the hotel were behind it by this point, however. Owned by a Gypsy woman called Señora Melero, it had enjoyed something of a reputation during the 1920s and 1930s, but had been used as lodgings for the International Brigades during the Civil War, and had become almost a ruin, a far cry from the 'majesty' of its name. There was little that Pujol could do to help it recover its former glory: rationing and austerity severely curtailed his efforts.

Pujol was never a man to give up — something that he demonstrated time and again in the face of setbacks and disasters — and around this time the idea began to form in his mind of a better life, of getting out of post-war, Francoist Spain and moving to a country more suited to his ideas: Britain and the United States both appealed.

He started listening to the Spanish-language broadcasts from the BBC, to hear what the British had to say about Hitler and the Germans. Through the BBC he heard about the beginning of the new world war. That in itself was unusual. Spain is not, in general, a country of Anglophiles — the exploits of 'the pirate Drake' and humiliation over Gibraltar can still rankle even today. In the early 1940s, when Nazi Germany and Fascist Italy were the country's closest friends, to have a pro-British attitude was even stranger. Yet a desire for freedom and democracy were such a part of Pujol's character, having been passed down from an early age by his father, that an image of Britain became a beacon for the political ideas that he valued.

In April 1940 he married Araceli, the

ambitious Galician beauty he had met in Burgos. By now Pujol was making some progress in his plans to leave the country. It was very difficult to get a passport — the Francoist authorities demanded good reasons, or good contacts, before handing over such documents to ordinary citizens. An opportunity for Pujol arose, however, from an unlikely quarter: a young guest at the hotel called Enrique who styled himself the Duke of La Torre de Santo Domingo, was friendly with a couple of aristocratic ladies in the city who were known as 'the Princesses of Borbón'. These grandes dames had been complaining about the difficulty of getting any Scotch in Spain, and how important it was for them, in their position, to have a few bottles at home for entertaining. The 'Duke' turned to Pujol, who saw his chance and came up with a plan: if they could get him a passport, he could take them all to Portugal to pick up some whisky. Within days the passport was in his hands. With Pujol at the wheel, the 'Duke' and his friends drove to Évora, just over the border from Badajoz, loaded the car up, and headed back. Impressed by the ladies' titles, the border guards did not even search the car as they passed back into Spain.

And now Pujol had a passport. It was a first and important step, using guile and imagination — his key strengths — to get past a seemingly impassable bureaucratic hurdle. He was soon to use them many times over in the face of similar obstacles.

Away from Spain, the world war had moved

into a more active phase: over the previous months France, Holland, Belgium, Denmark and Norway had fallen to Hitler. Pujol began to link his ideas about leaving Spain with a desire to help Britain, then standing alone against the Nazis, in whatever way he could. He was approaching a Rubicon, the crossing of which would determine the course of the rest of his life. How great a role was played in his decision by the shadow of his father, urging him to act from beyond the grave?

Pujol was no hesitating Hamlet, however. In January 1941 he made his first move: an approach to the British in Madrid offering to work for them.

The details of this first contact are hazy: Pujol later claimed that he had gone to the British himself. The MI5 account of his story, however, written just after the war and based on the interrogations Pujol underwent on his arrival in London, states clearly that his wife went to the British Embassy on his behalf. Pujol's domestic situation when he wrote his autobiography, in the mid-1980s, after more than thirty years of estrangement from Araceli, can account for the discrepancy. What Araceli told the British on her husband's behalf, however, remains unclear. Was he actually offering to spy for them, as the MI5 version has it? Or was he thinking more in terms of a job with the BBC, as Pujol later claimed?

'I wasn't thinking about spying at the beginning. Not at all.'

Whatever Araceli's exact message was, the response from the British was a resounding 'no'.

Questions over Pujol's motives and reasoning, particularly at this crucial first stage of his career, have never quite gone away. In his autobiography he would later say that his ideals, his father's moral values, drove him to help Britain in her time of greatest need. Fascism appeared all-conquering in Europe, and Pujol, who had suffered under both communism and fascism during the Spanish Civil War, was determined to do what he could to stop it.

Is that believable? There are inconsistencies in Pujol's story, as well as details that differ between his own account and the MI5 version. In his memoirs, Desmond Bristow said that Pujol justified his desire to work against the Nazis because once, while in France, his brother had witnessed atrocities being carried out by the Gestapo. Years later, Bristow learned that Pujol's brother had never crossed into France, and could never have seen such an event. Much of this, however, can be seen merely as an attempt to give believable explanations to the British — not to dupe them, but to convince them of his loyalties. Pujol had a subtler understanding of lies, where an untruth, on occasion, may be told to get closer to the real truth.

But what was driving Pujol? What of his motives? He himself later wrote that his plans at this stage were 'fairly confused'.

He thought about becoming a spy because he was a dreamer. But unlike many dreamers, he was also practical, a problem-solver and someone who could play the system — attributes that had helped him survive the Civil War. His imagination conjured up the ideas, the visions, but his guile meant that he could navigate his way through the world in order to make those dreams manifest. In time he would make an excellent double agent, the most important in history. For the time being, his mind filled with stories from films and novels, espionage seemed a perfect way to combine an urge to get out of Spain with a general desire to do some good — however vague that idea might be.

Later he said that the possibility of espionage emerged in his mind as a result of his initial rejection. The British might not want him, he thought, but what about the Germans? If they took him on in some capacity, then perhaps it would be easier to return to the British and persuade them that he was serious: he could spy for them from inside German diplomatic circles. He was stubborn, and his *amour propre* had been stung by the rejection. It seemed an obvious step to take.

This time he made the approach himself. After putting through a number of calls to the German Embassy, insisting that they listen to him, after several weeks he was eventually told to visit the Café Lyon on Calle Alcalá at 4.30 the following afternoon, where a man wearing a light-coloured suit and with a raincoat over his arm would be waiting for him.

It was February 1941. Pujol gave his name as Señor López.

Pujol had been exposed to enough fascist rhetoric while serving on the Francoist side in the Civil War. Now he studied the Nazi version of it, learning the set phrases and formulae, before heading off for his café rendezvous. The German who greeted him wore a double-breasted grey suit and spoke perfect, unaccented Spanish. Blond-haired and with blue eyes — a 'classic Aryan' in Pujol's mind — he gave his name as 'Federico'. In fact he was Friedrich Knappe-Ratey, a member of the German Abwehr working under Karl-Erich Kühlenthal.

Pujol later remembered the first meeting between himself and Knappe as being a little strained. Getting into character, he started ranting in the manner that he had perfected, talking of a 'New Europe' under the glory of the Führer and the Third Reich. Knappe was happy to hear of his enthusiasm, but kept trying to bring Pujol round to what he was actually offering them. Finally, Pujol said he wanted to work for them, inventing off the cuff some 'contacts' in diplomatic circles with access to 'information'. Knappe said he would talk it over with his superiors, and get back to him.

Knappe was friendlier at their next meeting, two days later at the Café Correos. Pujol took it as a good sign: he knew that everything depended on him being able to convince the Germans that he was genuine. Knappe told him, however, that they were not interested in extending their network of collaborators inside Spain. If Pujol really wanted to be of use to them, he would have to get himself to Britain.

Pujol did not bat an eyelid and accepted the challenge. Britain had, after all, been in his mind as a possible destination in his attempts to leave

Francoist Spain. But he knew that such a move was highly complicated — not only because of the war, but because of the paperwork that he would need from both the Spanish and British authorities: he had a passport, but the Spanish would have to provide an exit visa with permission to travel to Britain, while the British would have to issue a visa allowing him entry. Knappe made it clear that Pujol was on his own, that he would have to sort these matters out for himself.

Over the next few weeks they met several times in the cafés of Madrid — the Aquarium, the Maison Dorée and others — as Pujol's imagination produced another story. He had a contact in the section of the police that dealt with currency scams, he said. This policeman wanted him to go to Lisbon, and then to London on his behalf, chasing a supposed lead. That way, Pujol told Knappe, he would be able to get the right paperwork. But the Germans did not like the sound of this complicated story. He should try to get an accreditation with a newspaper and get sent to London as a journalist, they said.

Meanwhile, behind the Germans' backs, Pujol attempted to get a visa through legitimate means from the British Consulate. He was told that none was likely to be forthcoming.

There were further meetings with Knappe, each man sticking to his position, Pujol with his story of working for the police, the German insisting on journalism being the better route. Eventually they came to a compromise: Pujol should leave for Portugal, where he was to continue his attempts to get the right paperwork for travelling to London.

Again, there are differences between Pujol's account and MI5's. According to the official report Knappe handed over 1,000 pesetas for expenses; Pujol claimed that he travelled to Lisbon with a gold chain smuggled on his person, selling it and using the money to keep himself alive. What is clear is that on 26 April 1941, he left Madrid for the Portuguese capital.

Once there he registered at the Spanish Consulate as a resident, his occupation given as writer. This was not entirely false: within a short time he had met another Spanish ex-patriot, a poet by the name of Luances, and between them they wrote a number of pamphlets in support of the Allied cause which were distributed for propaganda purposes at various embassies. Pujol did not sign them, however, not wanting his name to be spread around.

He also went to the British Consulate to try to secure a visa. He was not surprised by the subsequent refusal, but he felt it important to keep up pretences, in case the Germans were watching him. He was stuck, however. He had sold a lie to the Germans, and now he was in Lisbon with no way of backing up his story, let alone of getting to London.

Then luck played a hand. A fellow guest at the Hotel Suisso-Atlántico was a Spaniard called Jaime Souza. Pujol fell in with him, and one evening, Souza happened to show him his diplomatic passport, which he was intending to use to carry out an official mission in Argentina.

He was in Lisbon waiting for a seat on the flying boat to become available.

Pujol was very interested in this special passport — with something like that he could not only travel much more easily, but also impress the Germans. A new plan quickly formed in his mind. One night, as he and Souza were gambling at the Estoril casino, just outside the city, Pujol faked stomach cramps and went back to their shared room, where he took photographs of the passport.

Soon after, Souza was gone, bound for South America, but Pujol used enlargements of the photos to produce his own fake version of his valuable travel document, posing as a member of the Spanish Embassy and asking a Lisbon printer to produce 200 copies for him. Such a large order meant that the printer suspected nothing, and by May, Pujol was back in Madrid, having smuggled several copies in with him and discarded the rest.

On his arrival, he called the German Embassy to ask for a meeting. At the subsequent rendezvous Knappe was angry — Pujol should never call the embassy, he said. Pujol excused himself, saying the matter was urgent, as he had managed to obtain the necessary paperwork to travel to London.

By this time Pujol had left the Hotel Majestic, establishing himself in a small *pensión* on the Gran Vía. Araceli was also heavily pregnant with their first son.

Several more meetings followed with Knappe. Pujol insisted on his story about working for a

Spanish policeman in Lisbon, called Varela, who was trying to bust international currency scams. Slowly, Knappe began to believe the tale. Then Pujol offered him some 'proof'. Telling a friend in Lisbon that he wanted to return to Portugal to visit a mistress there, but without arousing his wife's suspicions, he asked him to send a telegram with the following message: 'You must come here urgently. The affair has been arranged. Signed: VARELA.'

Pujol duly showed the telegram to Knappe at their next meeting. Knappe kept the note and when they saw each other the next day, he told Pujol that he should go immediately to Lisbon as 'Varela' asked, handing him 500 pesetas and telling him to contact the Abwehr in Portugal when he arrived. This Pujol did, getting more funds from Knappe's Lisbon-based counterparts, before returning once again to Madrid.

He now told Knappe that 'Varela' had made all the arrangements, and that soon he would have his final paperwork for travelling to London, all issued through the police. They agreed to meet again the following afternoon. Early the next morning, however, Pujol telephoned Knappe in an excited state, saying that he had to meet him immediately. Annoyed, Knappe agreed. At the café Pujol told him that he had finally been given his new passport and that he had to go immediately to the Foreign Ministry for it to be stamped. The fact was, Pujol's fake diplomatic passport lacked the necessary stamps to be taken as genuine, and it was a ruse to let Knappe see his travel documents without giving him the time to inspect them properly. It worked. On seeing the passport Knappe's mood quickly changed and he slapped Pujol on the back to congratulate him. Pujol then hurriedly bid him goodbye and dashed off in a taxi, asking in a loud voice to be taken to the Foreign Ministry.

The Germans were now convinced by Pujol and his story. They asked for instructions from Berlin, and over the next few days gave him a crash course in how to become a spy, teaching him about secret inks and handing over questionnaires for him to study, giving him an idea of the kind of intelligence from Britain that they were expecting him to provide.

At the last meeting, Knappe's Abwehr superior appeared — Karl-Erich Kühlenthal. He gave Pujol his final instructions: he was to try to pick up as much information as possible, Kühlenthal said, and to recruit sub-agents to build up an espionage network. In addition, Kühlenthal handed over some more money and cover addresses for Pujol's letters, within which his messages were to be written using the secret inks.

Knappe told Pujol that he envied him, that he would like to be in his position, travelling on a dangerous mission into enemy territory.

Kühlenthal was more circumspect. Pujol should not, he said, underestimate the British. They were a formidable enemy.

Four years would pass before Pujol would see either Knappe or Kühlenthal again. By then the war would be over and their circumstances

89

would be very different. But for now, armed with the Germans' inks and funded by their money, he picked up Araceli from her parents' home in Galicia before travelling on to Lisbon.

Scheming, rejected and alone, Juan Pujol was now a fully fledged Nazi spy.

7

Lisbon, 1941

It was July. Pujol was in Lisbon, pretending to the Germans that he was in London.

Living in the city centre was risky — people knew him there and might threaten his cover story, so he took a small fisherman's cottage along the coast in Cascais, where Araceli gave birth to their first son, Juan, shortly after. A few weeks later they moved into another, larger villa in nearby Estoril, at Rua do Porto 14, close to the casino.

Knappe and Kühlenthal had given Pujol 3,000 dollars, which he had smuggled over the border hidden inside two condoms — one stuffed inside a tube of toothpaste, the other in a tube of shaving cream, both opened at the bottom and resealed.

His first move, once established back in Portugal, was to approach the British again. His hopes were not high, and indeed he failed even to get a hearing. He would have to collect more proof that the Germans considered him one of their spies before he could make another attempt.

He therefore sat down and wrote his 'first letter from London' to his German controllers. Dated 15 July, he sent it from Lisbon on the 19th. To get around the fact that it clearly did not have a British postmark on the envelope, he came up with an elaborate tale. He had, he said, made contact with an official in the airline company flying from Lisbon to Portugal, which he had used on the 12th to fly out from the country. This was BOAC, but the staff on the flights were Dutch as four of the planes used were KLM DC3s. The official, Pujol told the Germans, thought that he was a Catalan exile sending urgent letters home, and agreed to take them on the flights, charging a dollar each time, posting them from Lisbon and so bypassing the British censors. The Germans were to send their return letters to an address in Lisbon, where the airline official would pick them up and take them back to Pujol 'in London'. This courier, code-named J(1), was the first member of a large network of collaborators and sub-agents that Pujol would eventually invent, becoming in time what the Germans would refer to as the 'Arabal undertaking'. Some appeared as willing helpers, aware of Pujol's work for the Nazis, others aided him unwittingly. All of them, however, were mere figments, the fruits of his powerful imagination.

Sending and picking up letters from the poste restante office in Lisbon, by the end of July he received his first reply from the Germans, confirming receipt of his letters and stating that they were eager to hear further news from him.

Pujol now thought that he had all the proof he needed, and he made yet another approach to the British in Lisbon. After some difficulty he was interviewed by someone in the Military Attaché's office. Pujol explained that he could provide secret inks and questionnaires from the Germans to back up his claims. He pointed out, however, that it was extremely dangerous for him to keep coming to the British Embassy, and that should he hand over the material he mentioned, he would never be allowed back into Spain, and would probably have to leave Portugal as well. So he insisted that the British could only have the material which would expose the German spy network in Madrid in exchange for helping him leave and get to the United States.

The British official said he would discuss the matter with his superiors and agreed to meet Pujol the following day at the English Bar in Estoril at 7.00 in the evening. Pujol duly showed up, but after a long wait it was clear that the British were not coming. Furious, he returned to the British Embassy, where the official told him that he had not been able to locate the superior whom he had intended to bring along for the meeting. Eventually Pujol left in disgust. There was no one, he concluded, among the British delegation in Lisbon who was at all interested in what he had to offer. If he was to make any progress at all, it could only be through the British Embassy back in Madrid.

Pujol was in a difficult situation: the Germans thought he was in England and were demanding intelligence reports. Yet the British, the people he was trying to help, wanted nothing to do with him. If the Germans found out that he was lying, and worse, that he was trying to make contact with the British, his life would be forfeit. He was twenty-nine years old, living in a foreign country, and his wife had just given birth to their first child. Resourceful and imaginative as he was, the danger involved was all too clear.

He had to do something, so he fell back on Kühlenthal's orders — to build up a network of sub-agents. He had already started with his KLM courier. Now he would begin creating new characters. In his second letter back to Madrid, he introduced the first two. Agent 1 was a Portuguese citizen living in Newport, South Wales, called Carvalho, who had agreed to watch the shipping convoys coming in and out of the Bristol Channel. Agent 2 was a German-Swiss named Gerbers, based in Bootle, keeping an eye on the Mersey. In a later letter, he created a third sub-agent, a Venezuelan student based in Glasgow who eventually became known as Pedro. These were the characters appearing on Bletchley intercepts read by Philby and Bristow at Section V, who would cause British Intelligence so much concern.

The invention of the sub-agents had a double benefit: firstly, by passing on information to the Germans as having come from them, Pujol put in a safeguard should 'their' intelligence prove to be wrong: any mistakes and he could easily liquidate them. Secondly, these agents demanded money for their reports: Gerbers wanted 2 dollars a day, plus 25 dollars for any important information that he passed on. The more 'sub-agents' he had, the more money Pujol could ask of the Germans.

Kühlenthal was delighted. But still the demand came for real information that the Germans could use. From making up characters, Pujol had to start inventing 'intelligence'.

By now it was September 1941. Pujol did not have any English, but he could check newspapers written in French. He travelled into Lisbon city centre, visiting libraries to pick up whatever information he could from reference works about shipping and military matters. From British newspapers he gleaned information about certain firms — their names and addresses — with which he could pepper his reports to add to their realism.

His letters to the Germans were verbose — a ruse that he later claimed to have adopted deliberately in order to say as little as possible with a maximum number of words. The truth was that it was his natural prose style.

I had an agent near Avonmouth. Unloading was mostly of foodstuffs. This I gathered from a dock worker who said: 'Fortunately a hungry winter is finished for us.' From the information from North America it is judged that this convoy is that indicated by Churchill when he referred in his speech to the largest convoy which has ever crossed the Atlantic . . .

Number Three agent reports the following: The latest recruits called up a few days ago in the Glasgow area go out every morning in formation to effect military exercises on the Rangers football ground. This ground is on the left bank of the Clyde near Broomstown Street [sic] . . .

In his third letter he talked about convoys arriving in the Clyde. The last thing he wanted was to unintentionally endanger any real convoys, so he said that before docking, the convoy broke up and dispersed all around the coast, thus making themselves more difficult targets for German U-boats. It was a good plan, so good that a couple of years later the Admiralty in London adopted it in all reports about convoys fed back to the Germans through double agents.

For the time being, however, Pujol was on his own and living by his wits. He made a further attempt to approach the British, this time through a passport official in Madrid. Araceli went with him, but again it came to nothing: Mr Thompson, he was told, was away.

It was even more dangerous for him to be in Madrid than in Lisbon; he would have to return as soon as possible. In the meantime, he wanted to confirm that the Germans believed in him as their spy in London. What if they were deceiving him just as he was them?

He concocted another plan: Araceli was to deliver a letter by hand to Knappe in Madrid. This she then did, and at the meeting she started quizzing the German, wondering about her husband's unusual behaviour. What was this letter about? What was going on? Why was she passing it on to him, a man she had never met before? Eventually she confided that she thought her husband was having an affair. Knappe, anxious to get his hands on Pujol's letter, told her everything. He was actually working for them, he said, spying for the Germans from inside Britain. Feigning doubt at first, Araceli finally accepted the story, handing a photo of her little son to Knappe to pass on to her husband.

Araceli was as good an actor as Pujol, and had secured the proof that the Germans did indeed think that her husband was genuine. Their minds could be put at rest on that point, at least. Yet still Pujol was getting nowhere with the British, and still he had to produce intelligence for his controllers.

In Lisbon he bought a *Blue Guide to Great Britain* and a Portuguese book on the British fleet. The reports began to flow — often concentrating on shipping, but also talking about troop movements that he observed as he pretended to travel about the country:

Along the Windermere — Barness [sic, presumably Bowness] road, and along the road which follows the shores of the lake to where it crosses the Windermere — Ambleside road (at a point called the Wood where there is a small chapel of Santa Catalina) there are camps full of troops. These forces are excellently equipped and have modern weapons.

The Germans swallowed it all, even the pieces about non-existent minesweepers and the summer heat in London.

Months passed, and Pujol's situation became more desperate. He would not be able to sustain the pretence indefinitely, yet already, in one of their replies, his controllers had told him that his mission in Britain would be a long one, and that on no account should he try to return to Spain. There was no option but to carry on. Eventually the British would have to listen.

In October he made a last attempt to make contact. Again in Madrid, he got through to the passport official named Thompson, producing German questionnaires and promising to provide evidence of German secret inks and other methods. But Thompson, like so many other British officials, refused to believe him. He failed to even take note of the questions asked of Pujol by the Germans. They included many on the situation in the Pacific, including: 'How does England expect to resist Japanese aggression? What help is expected from the USA in case of war with Japan?'

A little over a month later, on 7 December 1941, the Japanese attacked Pearl Harbor and the world war extended into the Far East.

Meanwhile, in Lisbon, Araceli was worried. There had been so many rejections. Her husband was at a low ebb. He started talking about emigrating to Brazil. They had to get out: there was no way they could carry on as they were.

He was close to giving up. He would, she knew, make the most of a new life in Latin America, but this failure would hang over him for the rest of his life.

It was at this point that she decided she would have to act alone, without his knowledge: a last-ditch attempt to make this work before either the Germans discovered the truth, or circumstances forced them to leave Europe for good. In November she went to the US Embassy in Lisbon, asking for an interview with the assistant naval attaché, a man called Rousseau. She had information, she told him, about a man spying for the Germans from within the United States itself. She had a telegram from him talking about sabotage plans in Chicago.

Would Rousseau listen . . . ?

PART THREE

'And, after all, what is a lie? '
Tis but the truth in masquerade.'
Lord Byron

8

The Eastern Front, Southern Sector, 25 December 1941

It was Christmas Day. At Bletchley Park Mavis Lever and Dilly Knox were starting to stream the first decoded Abwehr messages to Bristow, Philby and others in British intelligence. At that moment, far from London and the Home Counties, the heaviest fighting in the war was taking place in the Soviet Union, where, on the shores of the frozen Azov Sea, at the southern tip of the Eastern Front, the temperature was dropping to minus 40 degrees.

There the SS troops whose fighting lives would in time be profoundly affected by Pujol's stories were expecting a special visitor for lunch, flying in from Berlin to celebrate with this elite unit. To insiders like Jochen Peiper, their guest was known as King Heinrich — 'K.H.' — the reincarnation of Germany's first king. Others referred to him by his official title: Reichsführer-SS Heinrich Himmler.

The advances of the summer and autumn had now ended, yet vast areas of the Soviet Union had been conquered. To the north, Moscow itself had been within reach only weeks before, while in the south, Rostov-on-Don had briefly been theirs. The Soviets had fought back and pushed them out of the city, westwards to Taganrog,

Chekhov's birthplace. Yet the thaw of spring would see another German offensive. In a short time they would push towards the Caucasus again, with its mineral and oil wealth so important for the Reich.

Conditions at the front line had deteriorated over the past weeks: rations had been reduced to 150 grams of food a day. At the winter headquarters, however, no effort would be spared to make the best Christmas lunch possible for their guest.

There were many sections of the SS, acting as front-line troops, concentration-camp officers and death squads. Yet within the Nazi Praetorian Guard, one unit was held higher than any other, a privileged inner corps: the men of the Leibstandarte Adolf Hitler — the LAH[1] — were proud to bear on their uniforms the name of the Führer himself, whose life it was their mission to protect. No other body was closer to the top ranks of the Nazi Party.

Despite the brutalising experiences that he had already lived through, Jochen Peiper still had a boyish face, with pushed-back dark-blond hair, pink cheeks, heavy eyebrows, pale eyes, a long straight nose and cleft chin. He had turned eighteen on the day that Hitler had come to power, 30 January 1933. Weeks later he joined the SS. The officer training programme was infamous: people claimed that a recruit had to stand still while a grenade was let off on top of

---

[1] Later renamed the Leibstandarte SS Adolf Hitler, LSSAH. For the sake of simplicity I refer to it as the LAH throughout.

his helmet. The story was untrue, but contained a truth nonetheless — about the commitment required, the importance given to following orders, and a cavalier attitude to physical injury and death. Officers of the Wehrmacht — the traditional German armed forces — might frown at the methods and high casualty rates of SS soldiers, the Waffen-SS, but for Peiper and his comrades theirs was a war of *Weltanschauung*, of ideology, of building the dream of the Reich. They were a new Order of Teutonic Knights, men who one day, in the hall of Valhalla, would reminisce about the battles they had fought and the sacrifices they had made for Germany.

Peiper was no ordinary member of the LAH. From before the war, and during the first years of the conflict, he had been adjutant to Himmler himself, and the Reichsführer had come to value the young man who was bright, ideologically passionate and obedient. 'My dear Jochen', he called him in his letters. Peiper had married Sigurd Hinrichsen, one of Himmler's secretaries, who was best friends with Hedwig Potthast, Himmler's mistress, and with Reinhard Heydrich, his deputy.

Working so close to Himmler was second only to being adjutant to Hitler himself. But Peiper had craved the life of a soldier from a boy, inspired by his father's experiences as an officer in the Imperial Army. Himmler had allowed his adjutant a brief stint away to fight with the LAH during the conquest of France. Now, however, Peiper had been on the Eastern Front for months, proving that he was more than a mere desk officer, that he could also fight and lead men. And his superiors were pleased with him. Hauptsturmführer Joachim Peiper — Jochen to those who knew him — was still only twenty-six, yet was already a captain, decorated with an Iron Cross, First Class.

Now it was Christmas. His wife Sigi was pregnant with their second child and a new year was about to begin, one that would put the failures of 1941 behind them. They had not taken Moscow, but once the Russian winter came to an end they would strike again.

And they had something important to tell Himmler.

Heinz Seetzen was commander of Einsatzkommando 10a, a sub-unit of the SS death squads sent in behind the front-line troops. He was wintering near the LAH, and while the fighting continued he and his men were kept busy. The LAH had helped where it could: tank-trap ditches were useful for disposing of corpses. Seetzen was even using a new machine to carry out his work — a *Gaswagen*, a truck on which the exhaust was piped back into the body of the van. The screaming could still be heard from outside, and the truck had to drive a few kilometres around the city before everyone inside was dead, but by the time it returned to Taganrog the job was done, and it prevented some of the stress that the task could cause Seetzen's men. Thousands had already been killed using this method: Communist Party members, the mentally ill, and particularly Jews. The fact was — and this was the news they could

106

tell Himmler on his arrival — with the work of the *Gaswagen*, Taganrog was now *Judenfrei* — free of Jews entirely.

Peiper had not seen Himmler since the late summer. It was possible, he knew, that the Reichsführer would ask him to return as his assistant. The two men got on, and he had heard that his replacement was not doing well. He enjoyed soldiering, yet being next to Himmler allowed him to witness the inner workings of state. There was little he did not know about the Reichsführer's plans for their struggle against international Jewry and communism. And it had allowed this Berlin boy from a middle-class family to see more of the world than he otherwise might have: there had already been official visits to France, Greece, Norway, Italy and Spain. Franco had treated them to a bullfight in Madrid, before Himmler's entourage had moved on to Barcelona. They had visited a monastery in the mountains — Montserrat. Obsessed with his search for ancient sacred relics, Himmler thought he might find clues there to the location of the Holy Grail.

Now there was talk of a new move, a new chapter. Not just *Gaswagen*, but other, bigger machines that could do the work of thousands of men. Heydrich would be put in charge; it would only be a matter of time before their final objectives were met.

Peiper took his place, ready to welcome his chief and mentor.

A salute: *Heil Hitler*. Arms outstretched.

And Himmler in front of him, thin mouth, weak chin, eyes black and still behind circular glasses.

A smile.

'My dear Jochen.'

9

London, Spring 1942

The change from sifting through hotel registers was more than welcome. Bristow spoke fluent Spanish, and although MI5 was taking over the case, MI6 still needed a man there before handing over 'Bovril'. Besides, there was plenty of legwork to be done, translating messages to the Abwehr into English from the original Spanish — copies that Pujol had brought with him from Lisbon. Then there would be many days of hearing the man's story over and over again, cross-referencing, looking for possible inconsistencies.

Bristow, posing as 'Captain Richards', caught the train down from St Albans early in the morning on 28 April 1942, before taking the Tube to Hendon, and 35 Crespigny Road.

The MI5 safe house was an unremarkable late-Victorian place, painted white and with brick-red roof tiles, on a street of houses all quietly distinct yet essentially the same. Inside, behind the lace curtains, it was sparingly decorated: chairs and tables had been set in a back room where the interviews took place. The window looked out on to a small garden. Mrs Titoff, an elderly Russian émigré and MI5 employee, was the housekeeper.

Cyril Mills, from MI5, had been named the

new man's case officer, and made the introductions. Bristow's impression of Pujol was favourable from the start. The small Catalan appeared relaxed. His brown eyes had a warmth about them, with something of a mischievous glint.

After the first day at Hendon, Bristow rushed back to Glenalmond from the train station, wanting to tell Philby and the others about the mysterious Nazi agent who had kept them guessing for so many months.

'Well, Desmond, h-how is our friend?' Philby asked.

It was getting late, and his colleagues were already in the snakepit, sipping after-work cocktails.

'Very well,' Bristow said. 'Surprisingly relaxed. Seems to enjoy answering any questions I put to him. Without any doubt it is he who sent the notes to our opponents in Berlin. He is Arabel.'

'No doubt in your mind at all, Desmond?' Philby asked.

No, there was none.

'He knows the dates and the contents of the messages,' Bristow said. Pujol could recite almost word for word the reports he had written in secret ink in the letters forwarded to the Abwehr spymaster in Madrid.

'And I don't think he is a German agent,' he added. 'It seems as though he has invented himself out of some romantic notion about spying, or else just for the money. Apparently the Germans were paying him quite well.'

Everything pointed to Pujol being who he said

he was: a Spaniard, pretending to work for the Germans, who really wanted to work for the British.

For the following few days, Bristow continued his new routine of heading down to Hendon in the mornings. Cyril Mills was always there, but he did not speak a word of Spanish and could not make anything of the man. Too pompous by half, Bristow thought; it was not the best of arrangements.

And then, on 1 May, as he turned up for another day's interviewing and debriefing, a different, happier face opened the Hendon door to him.

There was someone else in MI5 much better suited to the job of running this potential new agent, a Spanish speaker, a good friend of Philby and the man who had been with Mills to pick Pujol up at Plymouth: Tomás Harris.

Bristow had met Harris a couple of times before, the first a few months previously when Philby had invited him down to London for dinner. Driving in the dark after the headlights on Philby's Vauxhall car fused, they had arrived at Harris's Mayfair home. Tommy and his wife Hilda — an attractive and impulsive woman who became renowned among their friends for her cooking skills — were wealthy, and the food and wine they served were of a quality that was becoming increasingly rare in wartime. Philby had spoken openly about service matters in front of them, which had perplexed Bristow until it was explained that Harris was in MI5. His mother was from Seville, and he had spent a good deal of time in Spain collecting works of art. Much of the collection was in the Mayfair house. Bristow ended up staying the night, sleeping in a room with a seventeenth-century Spanish wardrobe, brass-studded latticework decorating the doors. Much of the furniture on the landings seemed to have come straight from a museum.

He liked Harris; he was a talented and charming man. Like Philby, Harris shared a love of Spain, which felt so far away as the snow began to fall on London and Philby drove Bristow back to St Albans.

Now, though, a little part of Spain — a curious Spaniard — had come to them. Bristow was delighted that Mills had stepped aside. Harris would be the perfect case officer.

At Hendon, the two men greeted each other warmly. Bristow had heard most of it already, but Harris needed to listen to Pujol's story in full.

Pujol was in the back room, waiting. After drinking some of Mrs Titoff's coffee, Harris and Bristow went through, and the interview began. Pujol was cold, unused to the British climate, and Mrs Titoff made sure the fire was lit. He was enjoying her English breakfasts: he had not eaten bacon for years.

It took several days. Bristow and Harris were in and out of Crespigny Road for over a week, going over the story time and again. Harris was soon convinced that Pujol was indeed who he said he was, that he was, at least in the Germans' eyes, a genuine agent.

'Desmond,' he told Bristow after his first day with Pujol, 'he is obviously Arabel, but I do find it hard to believe such an outwardly simple man still has the Germans fooled and had us worried for so long. He is such a dreamer, and so willing, he is going to be a marvellous double agent to operate with as long as the Germans continue to swallow his communications.'

The MI5 man and his Section V colleague were convinced. The job now was to persuade those above them that Pujol was worth adding to the double-cross team. Bristow was asked to report first, joining the Thursday afternoon meetings of the Twenty Committee at MI5 headquarters on St James's Street. Later, on his recommendation, Harris came along as well, soon becoming a regular member. Bristow would leave shortly after to become MI6's man in Gibraltar.

The room where the meetings were held was 'square, bare and cold'. The chair was held by John Masterman, with John Marriot, a former solicitor, as secretary. Tar Robertson was present, as head of MI5's B1A section, as were various representatives of MI5 and MI6, directors of intelligence for the Army, Navy and Air Force, and delegates from the Home Forces and Home Defence.

Harris and Bristow had heard Pujol's long and involved tale: they also studied the copies of the letters that he had brought with him from Lisbon, replicas of the messages he had been sending over the previous months to the Germans. Thanks to the Bletchley intercepts, they were able to cross-check what Pujol showed them with what the Abwehr in Madrid were reporting back to Berlin about Arabel. The texts matched.

There was a letter missing from Pujol's collection, however, the one about the Malta convoy. When it was mentioned to him, Pujol wrote out the letter again, matching the original almost word for word. This was proof, as far as Harris was concerned, that he really was who he claimed to be. Later, the original letter emerged — it had been mislaid by MI6 when they transferred Pujol and his materials from Portugal.

The question was whether Harris and Bristow could convince the members of the Twenty Committee of Pujol's usefulness. They would be the ones to decide to take him on or not for double-cross work. The problem was that not everyone on the committee had access to the Bletchley decoded transcripts, or were even aware of their existence. The Twenty Committee may have been one of the secret services' most secret organisations — the 'club', as Masterman called it — but secrets were being kept from at least some of its members; not least the fact that the British had cracked a good number of the German Enigma codes, including that used by the Abwehr.

Not having access to this material meant that, on hearing Pujol's story, many committee members refused to believe it. It was, quite simply, preposterous. How on earth could they take such a man seriously? Surely he was a fantasist, or a German plant. It would be impossible to use him as a double agent.

Only a handful of members — those from the Admiralty and MI6 — knew, thanks to Dilly Knox and Mavis Lever's decoding work at Bletchley, that almost everything that Pujol said could be confirmed by what German intelligence was reporting about him in its internal communiqués.

The situation became untenable. The Twenty Committee was close to rejecting a man who had the potential to become an invaluable double agent. Members from MI5 had some knowledge, at least, of Bletchley, but representatives from the Services were in the dark, and if they could not believe in Pujol it would be impossible to come up with false or misleading material for him to pass on to the Germans. Finally, in desperation, Masterman wrote to MI6 chief Sir Stewart Menzies explaining the situation. A few days later Menzies wrote back, reluctantly clearing all members of the committee to receive Bletchley material relevant to the work of double-cross. The doubters could finally see the proof: Pujol was genuine.

Now word quickly came back from the Twenty Committee: yes, they would take the Spaniard on as a double agent.

At long last, under Harris's guidance, Pujol's work as Garbo could begin.

10

London, Spring–Summer 1942

Garbo is commonly thought of as one man — Juan Pujol. 'Garbo' was the code name MI5 gave Pujol and that was how he was referred to in official documents — always in the singular. Yet in reality the double agent was a double act: the character of Garbo was forged by two men. Putting Pujol and Harris together might have appeared the obvious thing to do, given the Spanish connection, but it was an inspired decision by 'Tar' Robinson.

'Harris and Pujol worked very well together,' said Sarah Bishop, who later acted as their assistant.

The little Catalan and the brilliant, half-Spanish half-Jewish artist were an ideal, Quixotic match, with echoes of Cervantes's duo in both of them. Hands-on and highly creative, Harris had the flair to mould the raw material of Pujol into what Garbo would eventually become. And both of them were keen storytellers.

Yet their relationship was not built simply on the fact that they spoke Spanish. They also shared a common language of mischief. *Pícaro* is a common word in Spain, often used to describe someone who is both sharp-witted and a troublemaker. It is morally neutral — you may criticise the person one minute and admire them

116

the next. There tends to be something slippery about them, hard to nail down, almost as though they were obeying some other code of conduct or morality — one which is invisible or unknown to ordinary society. The *'bandidos'* of the Spanish sierras, colourfully depicted by writers such as Mérimée in *Carmen*, belong to a similar tradition.

In Spanish literature, 'picaresque' novels were stories published during the sixteenth and seventeenth centuries, inspired by the classic *Maqamat* tales of 'rogues' in medieval Arabic literature. The writer Gerald Brenan summed up the picaresque genre:

> *These novels depict as a rule a child growing up under sordid conditions and making his way through the world where everything is hostile and dangerous. He has no arms but his mother wit: by using it he becomes a criminal, but essentially he is innocent and well intentioned and it is the wickedness of the world that corrupts him.*

They are satirical and funny, commonly episodical and depicting a realistic view of the harshness of everyday life. Hypocrisy is a frequent target, while fate and chance act as a permanent backdrop. Most striking, though, is the insistence on the need for cunning, a sense that only a fool takes the world at face value, playing by its rules and following its logic. Be smart and be light, the stories seem to tell us — almost as though imparting a teaching — otherwise the world will lock you in its jaws.

'Garbo' may have worn a suit and spent most of his time in central London offices rather than begging on the streets of Toledo, but there is a parallel. Pujol and Harris could not have created their character had it not been for a shared world view born from *Lazarillo de Tormes* or *El Buscón* — classics of the picaresque genre.

Pujol was no mere 'front man' for Harris. In the official account of the Garbo operation that he later wrote for MI5, Harris was at pains to point out that Pujol was hard-working and imaginative, and was vital to the functioning of the Garbo operation. In no way did he act 'purely as a scribe', as many of the other double agents did. 'On the contrary, his entire existence remained wrapped up in the successful continuation of the work which he had so skilfully initiated.'

Nor did Pujol sit back or slow down once he arrived in London. His workload increased now that he was officially employed by the British. Over the course of the next three years he would write 315 letters, some of which were up to 8,000 words long. Each one of these letters not only contained writing in secret ink, but a plausible cover letter as well — two texts on the same page.

'There was a lot of work,' Sarah Bishop remembered. 'There were so many things to do — writing letters to the Germans. Garbo would change them and write them in his own style. Then they had to be written out again.'

Later, his communications with Madrid

118

included wireless messages, and he produced the final version of around 1,200 of these, dressing the dry communiqués in his own unique style. Were anything to be sent in his name with a different voice, questions might be raised at the other end and his cover blown.

'He jealously examined the development of the work lest we should choose to pass material to the enemy through his medium which should result in discrediting the channel with which he had supplied us,' Harris wrote.

In addition there were bureaucratic tasks to perform, such as sending his accounts every month to Kühlenthal, and keeping a diary of the movements of each of his imaginary agents.

Once Harris got the green light, he rented a tiny office for their joint use near the Piccadilly Arcade, on Jermyn Street. This was very close to the MI5 building at 58 St James's Street, and Harris could cross from one to the other in a short time: at a brisk pace it takes just over a minute door to door.

The office had little natural light and just enough space for a couple of tables and some chairs, and a lamp that was almost always switched on. Pujol would tend to sit next to the wall, sandwiched between a desk and a filing cabinet where copies of his messages were kept.

Harris was not there all the time, but Pujol was kept company by an MI5 employee who became an integral part of the Garbo team. Sarah Bishop had worked previously in the War Cabinet before moving to the French section of MI5. She spoke fluent Spanish, and bumping into her on the stairs one day, Harris asked her to join him on the Garbo team. Soon she became Pujol's translator, assistant and close friend.

It was clear that the best arrangement would be to have Pujol stay in London for the long term. Pujol willingly agreed, but on condition that his wife and son be brought over from Lisbon to join him. Araceli was now expecting their second child.

The couple had been communicating by letter over the previous weeks — always passing through the wartime censor first. Pujol was clearly anxious for news from his wife, and wrote in his usual style:

> *I am writing to you again today with the natural surprise caused by my not having yet received any letter from you in reply to mine, and my surprise is the greater since my letters asked you for particulars which I am particularly interested in receiving; I hope therefore that without further delay you will reply to this letter and will give me some more news about Juan Fernando and about yourself, I want to know how you are . . .*

He told Araceli the arrangements for her leaving Lisbon: she was to tell her mother that she was travelling with Pujol to America; and she was to leave summer clothes behind — they would not be needing them in London.

Pujol clearly missed his wife and son, but the letters show how happy and relieved he was to have finally reached England:

I am feeling quite well and getting better acclimatised than I thought I would to the country in general, which to me is charming and smiling, and above all one breathes the real air of liberty, which I never thought or ever suspected would be possible. I promise you many pleasant surprises when you come and get to know the country.

For her part, Araceli wrote back telling him how their son's first teeth were coming through, how the doctor had told her that her new pregnancy was going well, and assuring him that they were both well, but missing him too.

You cannot know, my dearest Juanito, how I long to be at your side. I cannot imagine life without your affection and attention. I would tell you so many things right now if Mr. Censor weren't so curious . . . Just to say that before finishing the letter I will give the baby lots of kisses from you, and tell him that Daddy loves him and will see him soon, right?

And you be careful with the pretty girls over there. You know how much it would hurt your little wifey. I believe you to be a good man and you wouldn't do anything like that for anything in the world. You just remember how much I adore you and concentrate on working like a madman against that gentleman in Central Europe, that no matter how much is done against him can never be enough.

Araceli clearly thought it wiser not to refer to Hitler by name. By the early summer of 1942, after some complications, the British authorities finally brought her and her son over to London to be with Pujol. Jorge was born in September 1942.

To allow Pujol to move freely in wartime London, Harris arranged some identity papers in the name of Juan García — Pujol's second surname, that of his mother. He also arranged for him to have a nominal posting within the BBC as a translator, as well as a job in the Ministry of Information's Spanish section.

Pujol's mornings at this early stage were spent in the office, working on new letters and messages to be sent to his German controllers, then at lunchtime he and Harris would eat at a nearby restaurant — either Garibaldi's on Jermyn Street, or Martínez, just across Piccadilly on Swallow Street, where they served Spanish food. The intense German bombing of the Blitz was over a year in the past now and air raids were less frequent, but damaged buildings in the area were a visual reminder of the war. Just across the street from the office, the crooner Al Bowlly, the world's first 'pop star', had been killed when a German parachute mine blew up outside his flat. Some structures had been pulled down completely and vegetable patches — 'Victory Gardens' — planted in their place.

In the afternoons Pujol went to English classes at a nearby Berlitz school, before heading home to Hendon. The Crespigny Road address was soon swapped for another, very similar house a two-minute walk around the corner at 55 Elliot Road. Although a relatively safe part of London, the area had suffered some damage during the earlier part of the war, when high-explosive bombs had been dropped on nearby streets. It was a short stroll to Hendon Central Underground station, from where the Northern Line went straight down into central London. MI5 paid Pujol £100 a month for his services, which he considered more than enough — his rent cost £18 per month, while lunch in a restaurant cost around 6 shillings.

Harris and Pujol combined brilliantly, with Pujol's imagination and eagerness sculpted by Harris's intuitive brilliance and inside knowledge. Later, Pujol would commonly refer to Harris as 'always smiling' and his 'best friend'. Harris was held in high regard by his colleagues: Masterman wrote that he was 'the most remarkable' of all the people he collaborated with during his time on the Twenty Committee.

But while they could communicate in Spanish and quickly developed a personal rapport, security measures still had to be enforced. Pujol was never a member of MI5, as a result of which much of what Harris knew — for example the existence of the Bletchley intercepts — could never be passed on to him. Trust in Pujol strengthened over time, but for the first five months in London he was accompanied twenty-four hours a day by an official, his personal phone was tapped and his letters back to family members in Spain were censored. It was never properly explained to him who he was working for or how things were organised around him. Over the months and years he gained a sense of some of this, but the fact that he rarely asked any questions helped to deepen the trust in him, and in particular the esteem in which Harris held him.

One of the first tasks facing Garbo, once Pujol was established in London, was to account to his German controllers for the long gap in between his letters. The journey from Lisbon to Gibraltar and then to Britain had taken several weeks, during which time he had not communicated with them. It was vital that he resume his messages lest the Germans conclude that he had been caught. The Luis Calvo affair was still fresh: the Spanish spy formerly working for the Germans was now languishing in Camp 020. There was a danger that Kühlenthal might conclude that Pujol had suffered a similar fate.

Pujol had had the foresight to bring the same stationery with him that he had used for his messages written in Lisbon. Also, in the run-up to his leaving Portugal, he had mentioned that he was suffering from pneumonia — a ruse to give him the alibi of illness to explain away what he already imagined would be a lengthy period without corresponding.

Once in London, he made up for some of the time gap by predating his first letter, and sending it along with the second, claiming that he had gone to see his KLM courier only to discover that he had left for Lisbon the previous night. Thus two letters, the first and second, would be sent simultaneously on his return. In this way he was able to cover up almost a week of silence.

The first letter from London — the first 'Garbo' letter — was dated 12 April and sent on 27 April, only three days after his arrival. Pujol continued sending more, all in the same style, as though nothing had changed. The important difference was that now, rather than having to make up the information, he was being given genuine material by Harris. It was all 'chicken feed', but at least it was accurate. No more 'chapels of Santa Catalina' or nonsensical expenses accounts.

Given that Pujol was not sending the letters himself from Lisbon, MI5 had to come up with a new way of getting the letters there. It was decided to send them by diplomatic bag at first, with MI6's man in Lisbon forwarding them on and picking up the Germans' replies.

The new letter had been sent, and the system to move the Garbo operation forward was put in place. Yet, puzzlingly, no word came back from the Abwehr. The Germans' last letter was dated 2 March. Since then Pujol had had no word from them, despite continuing to send further letters himself — a total of seventeen in the end. What was going on?

Just when everything should have started operating smoothly there was nothing from the other end but silence.

11

Britain, Summer–Autumn 1942

The first letter from the Germans finally arrived in the second half of May, a month after Pujol had landed in Britain. In it, his Abwehr controllers explained that they had been disturbed by their agent's silence and had decided not to write for a while so as not to attract any attention to him; they feared that he had been caught or was being watched by the British. Now, however, they felt confident enough to carry on the correspondence, providing new cover addresses to send his letters to, along with promises of more money.

Harris and Pujol were delighted. The final step in setting Garbo up as a double agent had been completed and the channel between MI5 and the Germans was open. Kühlenthal himself was becoming more interested in the Garbo material, and from now on some of the letters were to be sent directly to a cover address of his in Madrid, to a Don Germán Domínguez. When signing his missives, Pujol was also to adopt certain pseudonyms: Germán Domínguez was to receive letters from 'Jaime Martínez' or 'Jorge Garrigan', while for his letters to 'Manuel Rodríguez' Pujol had to sign as 'Rodolfo'.

The German's choice of pseudonym is interesting. The writer Ben MacIntyre has described Kühlenthal as 'a one-man espionage disaster area' who, among other blunders, played an important part in the Germans' falling for the 'Man-who-never-was' hoax. Kühlenthal appeared fully convinced that his new spy in London was working for him and was sending over genuine intelligence. That the British should have fooled him might be understandable — it was more a testament to their skills of deception than to his credulity — yet his choice of pseudonym seems positively reckless. 'Germán', pronounced *kher-MAN*, is a bona-fide first name in Spanish. It also means 'German', plain and simple. Not the best cover name for an Abwehr intelligence officer, one would imagine.

Nonetheless, from now on Kühlenthal was to play a greater role as Pujol's Abwehr controller.

A line of communication through Garbo went directly to the Abwehr. In time the British would try to use that connection to its fullest capacity, stretching it almost to breaking point, but for the moment the emphasis was on making it stronger — building up German trust in their 'Arabel' to the point where not only the Abwehr might be fooled, but perhaps even the German High Command. This chain of possibility could, if it worked, lead from a cramped office off Piccadilly, through the German espionage centre in Madrid to the highest levels of the enemy's military structure.

In the summer of 1942, all this was some way off. For now Harris, Pujol and Sarah Bishop had to lay down the foundations for what would become, in Kim Philby's words, 'one of the most creative intelligence operations of all time'.

Much of that creativity came in the form of the various characters that were invented to populate Garbo's network: 'notional' agents, to use MI5's parlance, bona-fide sub-agents in the Germans' eyes. Although none of these people existed outside Pujol's imagination, real people would eventually play the parts of some of them as the network grew and became more complex.

Carvalho, Gerbers and Pedro had all been invented in Lisbon. In his first message to Madrid from London, Garbo mentioned a new contact — an RAF officer who told him about anti-aircraft batteries in Hyde Park. Up in Scotland, Pedro was also allowed to make friends with an NCO in the RAF.

The idea was to spread Garbo's contacts as far as possible, with potential sources of information in various key points of the country, as well as in the various wings of the armed services, and even within government itself. Some information might be handed over knowingly by 'traitors', other material might be passed over unwittingly by people unaware that Garbo was 'spying for the Germans', while yet more might be overheard in conversation.

To this last end, Fred was created — Agent 4. Fred was a Gibraltarian waiter, a man who loathed the British, not least because he had been forcibly evacuated from the Rock, and now found himself in Britain. Hating his new home, he was a convinced supporter of the German cause and, as a waiter, was ideally suited to picking up titbits of conversation, particularly at tables where officers were seated. Garbo claimed to have become friendly with him and made him a fully fledged member of his network. And given that there was a shortage of waiters thanks to the war, Fred could find work in any one of several areas: between Hull and Newcastle, around Maidstone, or in Colchester.

Garbo sent the Germans a message telling them about Fred and asked where they themselves preferred him to be based. In the Hull-to-Newcastle area, came the reply from Kühlenthal. So there Fred went, on the direct recommendation of his new German masters. Without realising, by 'sending' him there, the Germans had told the British which part of the coastline they were most interested in, and as a result defence systems in the area could be built up.

One of the most important unconscious sources of information for the Germans was created shortly after Fred. Working at his new job at the Ministry of Information, Garbo claimed to have become friendly with his boss, the head of the Spanish Department who thought that Garbo was a Republican Spanish refugee. With time, this man became more indiscreet, so that he even allowed Garbo to see Top Secret material. Garbo referred to him as Agent J(3) — the 'J' standing for 'Juan', in that he was one of Juan's (i.e. Pujol's) direct sources. No name was ever given for him, but the Germans were forwarded enough information to draw the conclusion that he was W.B. McCann — the real person in charge of the Spanish section at the Ministry of Information. McCann himself was later informed that a notional agent had been built up around him and he was obliged to 'play' his own alter ego on one occasion as part of the deception plan, a job that he was delighted to carry out.

The next new sub-agent to be created was Agent 5, the brother of Agent 3, Pedro. Agent 5 was never named, although the Germans gave him the code name 'Moonbeam'. He was recruited by Garbo in June 1942 and described as an ambitious young man of independent means who would take any risks for the Germans. At that time MI5 was trying to find out if the Abwehr had any agents operating in Northern Ireland, and if it was an area that they were interested in. To this end Garbo suggested that Agent 5 be sent there. Yes, came Kühlenthal's enthusiastic reply.

With that, MI5 had their answers: yes, the Germans were interested in Northern Ireland; and no, they almost certainly did not have anyone working there for them.

In truth the British did not want to send anyone over to Ulster — fictional or not — so Garbo had to backtrack, making the process of crossing the Irish Sea so complicated that it proved impossible to get Agent 5 over there. Thankfully, the Germans did not seem to mind too much. They were also interested, they said, in finding out about the Isle of Wight — then, in wartime, a virtual fortress. Getting anyone there, let alone a young Venezuelan, was practically impossible, but Garbo landed his man on the island nonetheless, inventing a story about his adventures that, as Harris described it, read like something out of 'any spy novel'. The Germans believed it, and Agent 5 rose greatly in their estimation.

Finally, in midsummer of 1942, Garbo recruited a South African into his network — Agent 6, known as Dick. Dick was a virulent anti-Communist who was more than happy to work for the Nazis. Garbo promised him an important role in the New World Order when the war was over. Clever, capable and a top-class linguist, he had a number of contacts in government ministries, and was the person who had originally put Garbo in touch with the man who became his boss in the Ministry of Information. Dick hated Britain and was determined to get out of the country. His chance would come some months later, when an opportunity arose to send him to Algiers. Eventually the Garbo network would stretch over half the globe, with spies based from Ceylon to Canada.

All these agents, and the many that came later, were Garbo's puppets, creations in a highly complex performance that was played out over the following years. Each one had to speak his or her own lines, in an authentic voice, never falling out of character as they slowly concocted a narrative causing the audience — the Germans — to reach conclusions that the Allies wanted them to. In the eyes of the Abwehr, the spectacle that Garbo put on for them was real — the living out of actual events. Any slip-up — an agent's

131

message striking a different, wrong note, for example; a contradiction between one character and another — and the Germans might start to suspect that what they took as real was anything but, and the whole fragile edifice would collapse.

It was imperative, therefore, that verisimilitude be the watchword for the entire operation. John Masterman later described how double agents were encouraged to live a life as close as possible to the one that they were putting across to the enemy. So, for example, if an agent was asked by the Germans to go and visit such-and-such a factory, MI5 would arrange for him — or at least a substitute — to travel there in person before replying. 'If an agent had notionally a sub-agent or cut-out in the country, he ought actually to have met such a man.' Otherwise the danger of getting facts wrong, of contradicting himself, was too great.

Another potential risk was the passing on of information that could be harmful to the Allied cause. Nothing of this kind would willingly be sent over by MI5. But what if an agent — even a fictitious agent — was ideally placed to report on something which the British did not want him to report? The characters had to perform as real people at all times. Failure to send information could be just as damaging to the credibility of a network as sending wrong or false intelligence.

In Garbo's case, it became clear over the summer of 1942 that Herr Gerbers — Agent 2 — the German-Swiss living in Bootle, would be ideally placed for reporting on the build-up in Merseyside for the eventual Allied invasion of

French North Africa — Operation Torch, scheduled for later that autumn. Clearly the Allies did not want such information to be passed on. Yet for Gerbers to remain silent about these shipping movements, or for that silence to go unexplained, was not an option. A solution had to be found.

As it turned out, Gerbers had failed to file any reports for some weeks. Garbo therefore travelled to Liverpool to check up on him. There he found that Herr Gerbers had fallen seriously ill and was about to undergo an operation, meaning that he would not be able to send any information for some time. Garbo reported this to Madrid and the Germans replied that he should continue to pay Gerbers through his illness; that he would be able to repay them with more shipping reports once he got better.

Sadly, however, Herr Gerbers never did get better. In fact he got steadily worse, his silence continued through the autumn and on 19 November, eleven days after the Allies had successfully landed in Morocco, Algeria and Tunisia, he died.

Garbo did not get to hear about this straight away. In early December, wondering what had happened to his sub-agent, and astonished that he had not even acknowledged receipt of his payment for the previous month, Garbo took the train back up to Liverpool. There a distraught Mrs Gerbers told him of her husband's demise, showing him the obituary that MI5 had had inserted in the the *Liverpool Daily Post* which read: 'GERBERS — November 19 at Bootle, after a long illness, aged 52, WILLIAM MAXIMILIAN. Private funeral. (No flowers, please.)'

Garbo sent the obituary notice to the Germans, who replied with condolences for his wife. Mrs Gerbers — 'the Widow' — would later reappear in the Garbo story, and become a fully paid-up member of the organisation.

Operation Torch was not only used to kill off the unfortunate Herr Gerbers: Garbo took advantage of it to build his reputation further in the Germans' eyes. On 1 November, a week before the invasions started, he wrote a letter which included information from Pedro in Glasgow that a convoy of battleships had left the Clyde painted in Mediterranean colours. In the same letter, Garbo claimed to have seen a secret file in the Ministry of Information containing certain directives in the event of an Allied invasion of French North Africa. There was clearly a connection, he said, between this and the rumours circulating of action soon to come in North Africa.

Despite being dated the 1st of the month, the letter was not sent on to Lisbon until 7 November — the day before the invasion. Thus it did not arrive in the Germans' hands until after the initial Allied assault had already taken place. It was too late for them to act on the intelligence that Garbo had provided them with, but the fact that he was trying to tell them about the landings before they actually happened was a major step in building him up as a source of valuable information.

Not only had Garbo shown that he had access to good intelligence, the time delay in getting his material to the Germans meant that, in their eyes, he should have a wireless transmitter. Garbo had suggested this to Kühlenthal back in August, after Fred, the Gibraltarian waiter, told him he knew a man in Soho who could provide him with the necessary kit. Kühlenthal had turned the offer down, but now, after the Operation Torch letter, he was coming round to the idea.

It would not only mean that he could receive his agent's intelligence faster. Garbo's wireless messages would have to be less wordy than his interminable letters and become considerably more concise.

Indeed, Kühlenthal's spy in London could show himself to be moody, even petulant, at times. In his first proper letter sent to his Abwehr controllers after arriving in London, Garbo had complained, not unlike a jilted lover, that he was not being valued enough, and told them so in no uncertain terms:

I have often wondered whether you are satisfied at your end with my class of work, as in spite of some comforting letter which you sent me once in a while, I begin to suspect that they are intended to pay me compliments. If this were so it would greatly disillusion me for my work as I am only here to fulfil a duty and not for pleasure. You do not know how homesick I sometimes feel for my own country. You cannot imagine how miserable

135

life here is for me since I arrived. Since I arrived I have made a point of avoiding all contact with Spanish society or individuals, this in the interest of our work. My Catalan character does not adapt itself to casual friendship more so when it concerns Spaniards who talk through their arse and compromise one for less than nothing.

The letter was pages long, hidden inside a tin of Andrews Liver Salts and sent via the KLM courier in the usual way. It was in keeping with the messages Pujol had sent from Lisbon, but now that he was in London, it was also part of the MI5 plan. In Harris's words, 'Kühlenthal was encouraged to regard Garbo as a quixotic, temperamental genius, whom he learned to be cautious not to offend. He came to regard Garbo as a fanatic, prepared to risk his life for the Fascist cause.'

Over time, Harris and Pujol noticed that the more insulted and spurned Garbo appeared, the deeper Kühlenthal fell into their trap.

In Madrid, Kühlenthal was becoming increasingly reliant on his agent as a source of intelligence. The Spaniard's eccentricities were, in his mind, a small price to pay for having a spy operating from the heart of enemy territory.

Yet it would be worth getting him a radio set, if only to force him to write shorter messages.

12

London, Glasgow and Madrid, March 1943

Winter was coming to an end. Weeks before, the Germans had suffered their first major military defeat on the Eastern Front, at Stalingrad. The course of the war, so long in the Germans' favour, was slowly and painfully beginning to turn.

In Glasgow, Pedro — Garbo's Agent 3 — had found something that would interest the Abwehr. During the spring of the previous year he had become friendly with an NCO in the RAF, a man of rather weak character who was often short of money. In conversation with Pedro one day, the NCO happened to show the Venezuelan a copy of an RAF aircraft recognition handbook. The airman did not know that Pedro was a Nazi spy, and allowed him to flick through the loose-leaf booklet with its illustrations and specifications on the planes then being used by the British Air Force.

How interesting, Pedro said, handing it back to the RAF man. Would he be prepared to sell it? It would be nice to have as a souvenir. The NCO agreed, but before negotiating a price, Pedro discussed the matter with his chief in London — Garbo.

Garbo — Alaric — put the matter through to

his master in Madrid, Kühlenthal. He would, Garbo told Kühlenthal, authorise Pedro to buy the booklet for a maximum of £100. Would Kühlenthal be prepared to pay that amount?

Yes, came the reply. The Abwehr thought it a fair price for an RAF recognition guide.

Garbo relayed this information back to Pedro. But wait, said the Venezuelan. If I offer this man as much as £100 he might become suspicious and start suspecting my motives. Far better, he said, to pay him a mere pound or two. Garbo agreed.

In the end, the RAF man was happy to sell his guidebook for £3. Pedro took possession of it and sent it down to London, to Garbo.

Garbo was very impressed — his agent had shown his integrity by refusing to take the large sum of money suggested by the Germans. He was a man who could be trusted. Garbo mentioned this in his messages to Madrid, and how Agent 3 had risen in his estimation. The Germans concurred. They too were impressed, not only with Agent 3, but also with Garbo, who had likewise demonstrated his own integrity.

Now that Garbo had the booklet in London, there was the small matter of getting it to Madrid to deal with. It was decided that the best option was to send it baked inside a cake. Mrs Gerbers — 'the Widow' — was now part of the network and working as an assistant at Garbo's home. The poor woman had been left penniless after her husband's death and had sent an urgent message to Garbo only a few weeks earlier pleading for help. Garbo's answer had been to head up to Liverpool and bring her back down to London with him, taking her on as a housekeeper — she was someone he could trust inside his home.

Now helping to look after the Garbo household, with Garbo's wife and two small boys to take care of, Mrs Gerbers baked the cake that the RAF booklet would be sent inside, sealed in greaseproof paper. Garbo himself wrote with chocolate icing on the top: 'With good wishes to Odette'. Inside the packaging he wrote a cover letter to a Miss Odette da Conceição, making out that it was a birthday gift from a seaman, sending a present to his girlfriend in Lisbon. Then in secret ink, in between the lines of text, he wrote a different message to the Germans:

Inside the cake you will find the book on aviation which was obtained by [Agent] Three [Pedro] . . . The cake itself was made for me by the Widow and I did the lettering myself. I had to use several rationed products which I have given in a good cause . . . if it does not arrive too hard it can be eaten. I hope you appreciate the culinary art of the Widow. Good appetite!

Some time later, having been sent via Lisbon, the cake arrived in Madrid. Kühlenthal was delighted with the contents. He was becoming increasingly happy with his London agent, whose occasionally odd behaviour merely added a certain charm to the excellent intelligence that he was starting to provide. It made Kühlenthal look good, and he was proud to be able to share stories about his spy with his superiors.

Admiral Canaris, the head of the Abwehr, even got to hear about the story of the cake. He made frequent visits to Spain during the war. On this occasion he was in Madrid, meeting his intelligence officers at the Abwehr station, and each one was able to regale the chief with stories about their agents. Kühlenthal stole the show, however, with tales of his man in London — Alaric, head of the Arabal network. Alaric, he told Canaris, was not only a spy, he was also a chef. But despite the fact that the cakes he sent them through the post were not great for eating, their contents were of the highest possible quality.

The story did the rounds within the Abwehr, and came back to the British more than once in decoded Bletchley transcripts.

In London, Harris read the Abwehr messages with great interest, watching as, through Garbo, he himself set something in motion, passed it on to the Germans, and then monitored the reaction in the Germans' comments. Kühlenthal was the closest he had to a personal adversary — Pujol's *other* spymaster, his German controller. Part-Jewish, like Harris, yet working for a regime that was starting to murder Jews in their hundreds of thousands. Doubts about him in Berlin persisted, not least because of his Jewish blood; some within the Abwehr counter-espionage section suspected that he might be working for British intelligence.

The RAF aviation guide was genuine enough,

but the most recent information had been removed to leave it several months out of date. Indeed, it was identical to a similar guide that the British believed had fallen into German hands some months before during the North Africa campaign.

The truth was that the British were merely feeding the enemy what they already knew. They had no need to buy off Kühlenthal. By his own efforts and blunders, and thanks to Garbo, he was becoming MI5's own mouthpiece within German intelligence.

13

London, 1943

The National Archive at Kew has a wealth of material on Garbo. Some of the files are several inches thick, their tattered, ageing pages delicate and fraying, often scribbled with pen and pencil marks from the various people through whose hands they passed before being filed: 'Tar' Robertson, 'Tommy' Harris, Guy Liddell.

The papers are now available to the public and shed a clear light on one of the most fascinating chapters of the Second World War. Details are given of the hundreds of messages that Garbo sent, how they were then reported by the Abwehr, and subsequently spread through the German military system. There are delightful titbits of information about certain individuals — for example, Kühlenthal's passion for tennis, and his attempts to have one of his agents send him a racket from London. He received a racket all right, but not of the tennis kind.

Much as I searched, however, there was one file that I could not find, the file that might give a window on to life inside the Garbo office, of how Harris, Pujol and Sarah Bishop worked together. In his account of the Garbo operation, Harris often compares Pujol's imagination to that of a novelist. 'It read', he said of a story that Pujol fed to the Germans about a sub-agent trying to blackmail him, 'like a scene from a commonplace detective story in which the hero outwits the less subtle, though cunning, crook.'

Indeed, Pujol's original cover story had been that he was 'a writer' based in Britain. His prose style may have been wordy and baroque, but time and again Pujol comes across as a story-teller, even a compulsive one: a fantasist who could change the world around him by the tales he told — often to deceive people or make them think what he wanted, or needed, them to think.

Not least was his ability to create rich, colourful characters. In the end, he dreamed up twenty-seven fictional sub-agents in his net-work:[1] they became vital elements of 'Garbo' itself, as Ewen Montagu, the Royal Navy representative on the XX Committee described.

'Tommy and Garbo 'lived the life' of all these imaginary sub-agents,' Montagu wrote, 'remembering all their characteristics and foibles. For example, if I suggested that [Agent] No. 1 at, for instance, Bristol, should report so and so, it might be that he was no use as he *never* reported 'I believe' or 'I've heard that'. *He* always reported something as a fact, but Tommy could get No. 3 to a suitable port in a couple of days and *he* could report a rumour. On the other hand No. 4 who knew about a subject I wanted reported, could not make the journey because

---

[1] The twenty-seven fictional members of the network, along with the German code name 'Alaric' and the British code name 'Garbo', make Pujol 'the spy with 29 names'.

143

his wife was ill. Every one of these notional sub-agents was like a close personal friend of Tommy and Garbo and lived in their minds.'

Anthony Blunt painted a similar picture.

'[Harris] 'lived' the deception, to the extent that, when he was talking in the small circle of people concerned, it was difficult to tell whether he was talking about real events or one of the fantastic stories which he had just put across to the Nazi Intelligence Service.'

But how did Harris and Pujol conjure up their fictitious sub-agents? What would it have been like to sit in that cramped, dark office on Jermyn Street, and watch them work together?

Let us imagine them in a real situation. It is the autumn of 1943. The Allied invasion of France, they know, will be coming at some point over the following year and the Garbo network will soon be needing new sub-agents to help fool the Germans.

* * *

Harris had concluded that an entire, ready-made organisation should be created, a small group of potential sub-agents whose loyalties could be relied on from the start, as there was little time to build up trust in them before a deception plan covering the invasion had to be implemented. Everyone at MI5 felt the pressure: they knew that the Germans were a formidable foe. 'The enemy is still proud and powerful,' Churchill had said a few months before. 'He still possesses enormous armies, vast resources and invaluable strategic territories.' Memories of Dunkirk and Dieppe were fresh. Schemes to hoodwink the German military would be vital if the Allied landings on the French coast were not to result in disaster.

Stepping into the office one morning, Harris outlined his ideas to Pujol and Sarah Bishop. He suggested a pro-Aryan organisation of some sort, people who felt an affinity with Nazi ideology and who could therefore be easily accepted by the Germans.

Sitting at his desk, his hands illuminated by the pool of light from the table lamp, Pujol listened and quickly put his mind to the task.

'Aren't there people in Wales who feel strongly anti-English?' he asked.

Harris grinned. Pujol already knew the answer. They had been working together closely for a year and a half, and he could already sense where this might be going. His friend was Catalan, and knew how regional resentments could simmer for many years, even centuries.

'Would that be a useful starting point?'

'Yes,' Harris said.

Pujol shuffled in his chair.

'The Welsh are Celts ¿verdad? And aren't the Celts also considered one of the Aryan peoples?'

'They were the last time I checked.'

'Perhaps we could ask Herr Hitler to confirm,' said Sarah Bishop.

Pujol smiled.

'A group of Welsh Aryan nationalists might provide a useful source of future sub-agents,' he said.

Harris placed his fingertips to his forehead and

closed his eyes. Pro-Nazi Welsh Aryan nationalists? Could they really get away with it? And yet he knew by now that the cheekier and more bizarre the idea was, the greater chance it had of success.

'It's perfect,' he said, looking up with a grin. His opponents in the Abwehr were unlikely to question the existence of such a maverick group. In fact he felt sure that they would happily accept 'intelligence' from anti-English Welshmen with dreams of aiding the Reich.

What was more, he knew that they already had a Garbo character who could help them build up these new recruits. Stanley, Agent 7, was Welsh, a former merchant seaman who was acting as a military reporter after being invalided out of the Merchant Navy.

Sarah Bishop was one step ahead of him. She went to the cabinet and pulled out the detailed information that they had built up on Agent 7.

Harris took the files and thanked her. Glancing through, he remembered that Stanley was interested mostly in money, and had pestered Garbo many times for payments. But he also had nationalist leanings and, as such, was anti-English.

He dropped the file on to Pujol's desk.

'I think we need Stanley to make some new friends.'

Pujol's fantastical imagination was already working on it. Harris knew that it was best now to hold back and watch.

'Welsh nationalists, like him,' Pujol said, his eyes fixed on Harris's, 'but even more revolutionary in their thinking. More radical. And they need a name.'

Harris waited. From the look on Pujol's face, he knew that his friend was on the brink of dreaming one up.

'I've got it,' Pujol said. Harris and Sarah Bishop leaned in. 'The Brothers in the Aryan World Order.'

They all laughed, but Pujol carried on speaking as the characters in the group began popping up in his mind.

'They're former members of the Welsh Nationalist Party,' he said, still giggling. 'And they left because they wanted to create a more radical group of their own. They've been acting clandestinely for the past months, maybe years, gathering names of Communists and Jews they want exterminated once their goals have been achieved.'

Harris and Sarah's laughter died down.

'Yes,' Harris said. 'I think they would provide an excellent source of sub-agents.'

In a matter of moments they had dreamed up the organisation, the name and the motives for their wanting to help the enemy. Now they needed to create the characters who would become Garbo's agents within the group itself.

Pujol picked up a paper and pencil lying on his desk and started to scribble down notes as Harris and Sarah watched. His hand moved quickly over the page as, in a matter of minutes, he built up a list of members, complete with how each one had been recruited, physical characteristics and their relationships to one another.

'This would be the first one,' Pujol said, looking up. 'A man called David, about thirty years old. He was an old schoolmate of Stanley and was released from military service because of his asthma, which was also the reason why he left the Merchant Navy six years ago.'

Sarah Bishop sat down at her desk to listen, while Harris remained standing.

'Stanley found David after searching around the Swansea area for sub-agents of his own,' Pujol continued. He pointed at Agent 7's file. 'As we already instructed him to. Stanley was nervous when he approached David, as he thought he might already be working for the Germans through some other organisation, given his politics. But once he realised that was not the case and they got talking, David told Stanley about his small radical group and how they've been working for years, building up a dossier of information in the hope of one day passing it on to the Germans.'

'That's good,' Harris said. 'David can be the first of the group to be recruited.'

'Stanley already has one sub-agent,' Sarah Bishop said. 'Agent 7(1), the soldier in the notional 9th Armoured Division. David can be Agent 7(2).'

Pujol outlined other members of the group for them. It was straightforward from there, he said, to get more Welshmen from within the Brotherhood to act as sub-agents. But while the next three characters were all Welsh and more or less of the same type, Pujol had a surprise for them when he mentioned the fifth member.

'There is also an Indian,' he said.

Harris tried to stifle his laughter. At her desk,

Sarah Bishop was shaking her head.

'Are not Indians also considered Aryans?' Pujol asked.

'They are,' Harris said.

'This man,' Pujol said, 'is a dreamer, a poet.'

'I know!' Sarah called out. 'We'll call him Rags, or something.'

'Rags it is,' Harris said.

'Right,' Pujol continued. 'Rags joined the Brotherhood to uphold his fanatical belief in the superiority of the Aryan race.'

'Naturally,' Harris grinned.

'And what's more, he's fallen in love with the group's secretary.'

Sarah Bishop threw him a glance.

'Who is . . . ?' Harris asked.

'An Englishwoman.'

'English?'

'She's become Rags's mistress,' Pujol explained. 'And now she's joined the Brotherhood because she's attracted to Indian men.'

'All Indian men? Or just Rags?' Sarah asked.

'Something about the physical and moral supremacy of the Aryan races,' Pujol said.

'She'd be very useful,' said Harris. He knew that someone like this could be sent to India. There was an opportunity here to spread the Garbo network into Asia.

'She needs a name, too,' said Sarah.

'Theresa Jardine,' The name had popped spontaneously into Harris's head.

There was a moment's pause before they all nodded. Yes, it worked. It was so mad there was no chance that it could not work.

'We might want to conscript her into the WRNS.' Harris looked across to Sarah and she began taking notes. 'And on account of her predilection for Indians, she should do everything in her power to get a posting to the subcontinent.'

Harris checked the time: he had a meeting to attend. He left Pujol and Sarah in the office to flesh out more details. The Allied invasion of France was only months away — their new additions to the Garbo network could come in handy. He would mention them to Tar Robertson and Masterman when he saw them. His superiors would welcome the new recruits, he felt sure. David, Rags and Theresa Jardine were typical Garbo characters, existing in some borderland between the unbelievable and the credible, so odd that they had to be real. Or at least in the Germans' minds.

And was it really so strange to dream up something like the Brothers in the Aryan World Order? Real life could throw up equally curious organisations. In fact it was almost as if the Garbo team had clairvoyant powers. Later, in his offical report, Harris would write the following conclusion to his chapter about this particular episode of the Garbo story:

Lest the reader should consider these recruitments too fantastic he should be reminded that the truth is often stranger than fiction. This was subsequently to be proved to us, for several months later the activities of a Welsh seaman who had been arrested were brought to the notice of *M.I.5*. It transpired that he had been detained for spreading subversive propaganda among his fellow seamen. He had been circulating subversive typewritten leaflets and had spread anti-Semitic propaganda in the name of a small organisation which, from the material discovered amongst his property, ornamented with swastikas and other Nazi emblems, was the 'ARYAN WORLD ORDER'.

PART FOUR

'It's no wonder that truth is stranger than
fiction. Fiction has to make sense.'
Mark Twain

14

Germany and the Eastern Front, July 1942–March 1943

Far from Jermyn Street, the war on the Eastern Front ground on.

After guard duties on the Azov Sea came to an end in July, the men of the Leibstandarte Adolf Hitler — LAH — were sent to France, where their swelling numbers were converted into a Panzergrenadier Division — motorised infantry equipped with armoured personnel carriers and half-track fighting vehicles.

Jochen Peiper did not rush to rejoin his men, spending time with his wife in Germany and visiting his mentor, Reichsführer Himmler, at his headquarters. It was an important moment for the head of the SS. His leading subordinate, Obergruppenführer Reinhard Heydrich, the architect of the Final Solution, had recently been wounded in an assassination attempt in Prague by Czechoslovak resistance fighters. Heydrich had not been killed in the attack itself, but debris had been blown into his abdomen and he would later die from his infected wounds.

It was a questionable victory for the Czechoslovaks. Nazi retribution for Heydrich's death was massive and brutal, and, if anything, his murder sped up the process of the Holocaust. In the May of 1942 the gas chambers at

Auschwitz became fully operational and Himmler spent part of the summer visiting the site to ensure that his new installations were running as efficiently as possible.

Staying close to the centre of these developments, Peiper did not make it to France to join his unit until August. There, in September, he was made commander of the III Battalion — a fighting unit comprising almost a thousand men organised into five companies. It was an important step in his already rapid rise through the ranks.

One of his first acts as commander was to forbid his men from having relationships with French girls or visiting the local brothels. It made a poor initial impression and later, on the recommendation of a medical officer concerned, perhaps, by the consequences of imposing monastic rules on fighting men, Peiper rescinded the order.

The autumn was spent getting used to the division's new military equipment. The armoured personnel carriers came with machine guns or anti-tank guns, and could travel off-road, transporting an entire squadron and protecting it from enemy infantry fire. By the winter, they were ready to be used.

Things were developing rapidly in the east. The situation in the southern sector of the front, in and around Stalingrad, was becoming desperate: it was time for Hitler's crack troops of the SS to be brought in to show their worth. On 30 December, the LAH received orders to prepare for deployment to the Ukraine.

The first units were already heading east when, still in France, Peiper was promoted to

Sturmbannführer — the equivalent of major. It was 30 January, the tenth anniversary of Hitler's coming to power, and Peiper's twenty-eighth birthday. The next day his battalion caught the train and headed east, just as, in Stalingrad, General Friedrich Paulus surrendered the German 6th Army to the Soviets.

The defeat at Stalingrad was a shocking blow for the Germans. The 6th Army, a fighting force that had once numbered 300,000 men, had been destroyed and the Wehrmacht's air of invincibility, earned after years of spectacular victories across Europe, had been lost.

The LAH — now also known as the 1st SS Division — was joined by the 2nd SS Division, Das Reich, on the southern sector of the Eastern Front, and together with the 3rd SS Division, Totenkopf (Death's Head), they made up the SS Panzer Corps. Their objective was to retake territory lost in the wake of the Stalingrad defeat.

Peiper and his men were in action as soon as they got off the train, arriving near the city of Kharkov. It was cold and many Wehrmacht units were demoralised. The German 320th Infantry Division — which had once numbered some 20,000 men — had become trapped behind enemy lines. Peiper's III Battalion was given the job of rescuing it, and with only a few hundred soldiers under his command he completed the job in less than two days, destroying the Soviet forces he encountered and fighting his way back to the German lines the long way round because the river ice could not hold the weight of his equipment.

The action won him the German Cross in Gold, one of the highest honours in the Wehrmacht. But as if rescuing an entire infantry division was not enough, Peiper continued over the coming days and weeks with more heroic and daredevil exploits, punching deep into enemy territory and inflicting heavy losses. He gained a reputation for leading from the front, issuing orders calmly and with tactical precision.

Yet there was a price to be paid for his style of leadership — Peiper was becoming known for suffering high casualties among his troops. He admired commanders like Georg Preuss, a first lieutenant who became company commander under him. Preuss not only obeyed orders to the letter, he also used to comment with a grin that the more of his men were killed 'the more women will be left for me'.

Peiper's scant regard for human life was extended many times over when it came to the enemy — both soldiers and civilians. The Germans had abandoned Kharkov on 15 February, yet fighting around the city continued as they tried to retake it. On 3 March, Peiper's battalion invented a new weapon designed for combat in enemy-held villages: the blowtorch.

Taking the heaters that were used to warm the engines on their vehicles in the sub-zero temperatures, Peiper had them modified and turned into flame-throwers that could spew out a jet of fire of up to 15 metres long. He soon had a chance to test them out. The next day they were used for the first time when the village of Stanichnoye, and anyone left inside it, was reduced to ashes. The nearby village of Staraverovka soon suffered the same fate. Anything — and anyone — that got in the battalion's way was incinerated.

The SS was no stranger to atrocities, but this was eye-catching even by their standards. Peiper's cachet was raised even more by his innovation and his unit earned itself the nickname the 'Blowtorch Battalion' — a moniker his men were proud to bear, painting blowtorches on their vehicles as an unofficial symbol.

Meanwhile, Peiper continued in his relentless progress, often reaching his daily objectives early in the morning and then continuing further into enemy territory on his own initiative. Such an action won him another medal — this time the highest in Germany: the Knight's Cross of the Iron Cross.

His greatest moment, in the Third Battle of Kharkov, was yet to come.

Again on his own initiative, by 9 March Peiper's Blowtorch Battalion had reached the western outskirts of the city as the Germans pushed to retake it and the stage was set for a full assault against the Soviet positions, using all three SS divisions available. At the start of the offensive, Peiper was ordered to advance along the main street and reach Red Square in the centre. After seizing a small bridge of the River Lopan, he used his new heavy Tiger tanks with their powerful 88mm guns to achieve his objective. Fighting was fierce and the losses, again, were high, with over 4,500 LAH casualties, but by 14 March Peiper's men had pushed through and the defenders were beaten. Kharkov was back in German hands and the Waffen-SS had achieved one of its greatest victories.

The city may have been recaptured, but Peiper wanted more. Acting independently, and turning off the radio so as not to hear the orders calling him back, he continued to push repeatedly against Soviet positions, breaking through with no protection on his flanks or to the rear. He did not care: Peiper was racing north from Kharkov at breakneck speed, pushing through towns and villages without stopping.

The result was that, at 1135 hours on 18 March he was able to declare that he had single-handedly taken the nearby city of Belgorod as well. The Third Battle of Kharkov had ended.

The Germans were ecstatic. After the disaster at Stalingrad only weeks before they now had something to celebrate on the Eastern Front. And victory had come thanks to the fearless efforts of the three Waffen-SS divisions of the SS Corps. Of these, the LAH, the 1st SS Division, received the largest share of the medals that were subsequently handed out.

Triumphant, they carried out a massacre of Soviet prisoners, murdering hundreds of wounded soldiers in Kharkov's hospitals. Officers and commissars were also executed as a matter of course.

Jochen Peiper, meanwhile, the glorious commander of the III Battalion and the victor of Belgorod, was now a hero of the Reich and one of the most dangerous men in the German armed forces.

15

London, March–June 1943

After months of hesitation, Kühlenthal finally gave permission for Garbo to communicate with Madrid by wireless in March 1943. Pujol was sent the Abwehr cypher table — one that Bletchley had already broken — and was able to put the machine he had 'bought on the black market' into operation. A friend of Fred the Gibraltarian acted as wireless operator, thinking, as Garbo explained to the Germans, that he was sending secret messages on behalf of a clandestine Spanish Republican group. In fact, the man tapping away in Morse code was a real, not fictional, new member of the Garbo organisation: Charlie Haines, a former bank clerk who had failed to get into the armed services owing to a limp brought on by polio.

Harris and the Twenty Committee were pleased: the transmissions and codes that the Germans provided were a clear indication of the value they put on Garbo's material. And the more they trusted him, the greater the opportunities for MI5 to use the channel to deceive the enemy.

The Garbo operation appeared to be going very well. A plan for the Germans to pay Garbo through Spanish fruit merchants as intermediaries was up and running, and several thousand pounds had already been received. By June the

161

figure had reached £7,000, with the added irony that the Abwehr was effectively paying to be deceived.

Meanwhile the Germans had fallen for a new story that Garbo had been working on — a secret arms depot being set up in the Chislehurst Caves, in the south-eastern suburbs of London. From his waitering duties, Fred had been transferred to a job helping to dig and expand the underground chambers as 'all Gibraltarians should have a natural aptitude for tunnelling'. The arms and ammunition stored there would, according to the story, be used once the Allies opened up the Second Front, and by the speed at which the caves were opened and filled, it was hoped that the Germans would come to an erroneous conclusion as to the date of such an operation. The fact was that there were no weapons being kept in the Chislehurst Caves. The tunnels had served as an arsenal during the First World War, but were now acting as a large-scale air-raid shelter.

Towards the end of May, an even greater success came for Garbo. Some weeks earlier, suspecting that the British might have broken them, the Abwehr had changed their Enigma codes. The code-breakers at Bletchley thought they could crack the new ones eventually, but that it could take some considerable time. In the meanwhile they were temporarily blind, unable to read the Abwehr traffic. Help came, however, when Kühlenthal sent Garbo seventeen miniature photographs containing the new cypher tables. These were sent to Bletchley and within a couple of months — a far shorter time than it would have taken otherwise — the code-breakers were back in, reading the Germans' messages once more.

On sending the cypher tables, the Germans wrote to Garbo: 'We trust that you will be able to guard all this material which we confide in you conscientiously and prevent it at any time from ever falling into the hands of the enemy.'

The word came back from a delighted Bletchley — it was the highest-grade cypher used thus far by the German secret service. Harris was in no doubt that it was 'the most important development' yet in the Garbo case.

Garbo was proving useful in other areas as well. On 1 June a KLM plane on the civilian route from Lisbon to Britain was shot down by the Luftwaffe over the Bay of Biscay, killing all seventeen people on board. One of the passengers was the actor Leslie Howard, who had starred in films such as *Gone with the Wind* and *The Scarlet Pimpernel*, and was returning to Britain after a lecture tour in Spain and Portugal.

There have been many theories about the shooting down of Flight 777, including that the Germans mistakenly thought that Churchill was on the plane and were trying to assassinate him. From Garbo's point of view, however, the event was significant — his fictional courier, taking his letters back and forth to Lisbon, worked on that route. He had not been on Howard's flight — luckily — but he might have been.

The Germans were putting a line of communication with Kühlenthal at risk. There could be no more attacks on these civilian planes, Garbo told his spymaster. They had to stop.

And stop they did. Whether or not because of Garbo's intervention is not certain — the planes were re-routed after the attack and henceforth only flew at night. Garbo's message, however, may well have influenced the German decision to leave the planes alone.

It was clear that within a year of arriving in Britain, Garbo had become a star player in the double-cross system. Some of those involved were even beginning to think that Prime Minister Winston Churchill might be interested to hear about this new, very useful agent of theirs. But then, just as the operation was starting to show real promise, a crisis emerged.

Araceli was unhappy. Brought over to London shortly after her husband had finally been taken on by MI5, she struggled to settle in her new home. She had two small boys to look after now — Juan and Jorge — and was forced to live largely isolated from the Spanish community for fear of inadvertently giving the Garbo secret away. The language, the weather, separation from her mother back in Spain, the domestic arrangements at their house in sleepy Hendon, her husband's long hours — all these became sources of tension and stress.

She and Harris did not get on; in fact they disliked each other intensely. From being her husband's collaborator in Spain and Portugal, Araceli had now been reduced to the role of supporting housewife, Harris taking over her position as Pujol's partner in deceit. For his part, Harris appreciated that Araceli was intelligent and astute, but also condemned her as 'hysterical, spoilt and selfish'.

Deeply homesick and unhappy with her new life, Araceli longed to go back to Spain, even for a short visit. MI5 refused, fearful for the security of the Garbo operation.

After many arguments and tense words, things came to a head on 21 June 1943.

Pujol and Araceli used to spend time occasionally with one Spanish couple, known to MI5 as Mr and Mrs Guerra. They were members of a social group called the Spanish Club, and invited the Pujols to join them one evening at one of their functions. There was a problem, however: staff from the Spanish Embassy would also be there for the dinner — people who worked directly for Franco, neutral yet still friendly with the enemy. It would be far too dangerous for Pujol to show his face in such company and he had to insist that they could not go.

It was too much for Araceli — she was perfectly aware of her husband's real work and therefore of the dangers, yet, lonely and isolated, she felt that this was a refusal too far. A violent argument began during which she threatened to go the Spanish Embassy and tell officials there all about Pujol's work for the British. Such a move would not only have brought the Garbo operation to a swift end, but also most, if not all, of the double-cross system itself.

Trying to avoid a crisis, Pujol managed to get out of the house for a few minutes and dashed to

165

a phone box to put a call through to his office. His wife was in a highly excited frame of mind, he said. If she rang up and was offensive they should not take any notice.

As he predicted, later that night Araceli called Harris at his home. Harris made a note of what she said:

'I am telling you for the last time that if at this time tomorrow you haven't got me my papers all ready for me to leave the country immediately — because I don't want to live five minutes longer with my husband — I will go to the Spanish Embassy. As you can suppose, going to the Spanish Embassy may cost me my life — you understand? It will cost me my life — so by telling you that I am telling you everything . . . I shall have the satisfaction that I have spoilt everything. Do you understand? I don't want to live another day in England.'

Years later, Harris was able to write with English aplomb: 'Whilst we were not unaccustomed to such outbreaks the present crisis seemed particularly serious.'

The fact was, Araceli's threat was a major problem for MI5 and they had to come up with a plan quickly. Unfortunately, in their view, there was no way that they could lock her up as the law at the time would not allow it. As a first step, Tar Robertson went over personally to Hendon the next morning to give her an official ticking-off, warning her that she had already committed 'an act preparatory to an act' with her threat.

Meanwhile, two proposals were discussed

within MI5. The first was intended to distract Araceli and give her something to do: a bogus side-story to the Garbo set-up would be arranged, involving a notional Gestapo officer wanting to get in touch with her husband. They would let her run this mini-operation in the hope that it would cure her of her obvious boredom. The second plan was to warn the Spanish Embassy that a woman of Araceli's description was planning on assassinating the ambassador — the hope was that she would be thrown out of the building before being able to tell anyone about her husband's espionage activities.

In the end, however, both these ideas were shelved when Pujol himself came up with a very Garbo-esque solution.

Araceli had been stalled for a while by being told that an answer to her request for travel papers would come the following evening. Shortly before the appointed time, however, after the Spanish Embassy had closed for the day, two police officers knocked on her door. They told her that her husband had been arrested and that they had come to collect his pyjamas and toothbrush.

Araceli reacted exactly as expected. Her husband was loyal to Britain, she insisted. There was no way that he could have been detained. In tears, she called up Harris to find out what had happened. Harris told her the story that Pujol had concocted for them:

Pujol, he said, had been asked to meet section chief Guy Liddell that afternoon. Liddell had told him that he was agreeing to give Araceli and the children their travel papers, but that Pujol would have to go with them as well, and that the Garbo operation was being henceforth shut down. Liddell asked Pujol to write a letter to the Germans explaining away the suddenness of his disappearance.

Pujol, according to the story, refused. He had come to Britain to carry out this work, and his wife could leave if she wanted to, but he wanted to stay. But Liddell explained to him that his wife had threatened to betray everything and so they needed the letter from him to protect themselves.

At the word 'betrayal' Pujol had lost his temper. It was impossible, he said, for Araceli to do such a thing. He refused to believe it. The discussion had become heated, Pujol had become aggressive, and the police had been called to take him away to Camp 020, where he was now being held.

Araceli listened to Harris's tale, believing every word of it. Pujol, she said, had acted exactly as she would have expected — defending her honour, preferring to go to prison rather than write their letter for them.

She seemed a little pacified, and the conversation ended. A short while later, however, she called Harris back, this time in a more belligerent mood, threatening to take the children and disappear. Putting down the phone, she called Charlie Haines, the Garbo wireless operator, in a desperate state, asking him to come round to the house. When he got there, Haines found a distraught Araceli sitting in the kitchen with the gas taps on.

168

She was incoherent, and a little later she made a second attempt on her life.

Haines concluded that she was mostly play-acting. But with a 10 per cent possibility of an accident, he and Harris arranged for Harris's wife Hilda to go and spend the night with her.

The following morning, weeping, Araceli was taken to see Tar Robertson. She was more repentant now, and told Robertson that she was to blame for the situation, that her husband was not at fault and pleaded that he be pardoned. In exchange she promised never to interfere with his work, misbehave or ask to return to Spain again. Agreeing, as per the plan, Robertson made her sign a statement to that effect and told her she would be allowed to visit her husband later that afternoon.

At 4.30 she was taken under escort to Kew Bridge. There she was blindfolded and driven in a closed van to Camp 020. When she arrived an officer told her in no uncertain terms that she had escaped being arrested herself by only a hair's breath.

Pujol was allowed to appear before her wearing prison clothing, and clearly unshaven. He asked her to tell him on her word of honour whether she had been to the embassy. She swore that she had not and that she would never behave like this again, or make any threats.

Pujol was taken back to his cell, to await a 'tribunal hearing' the following morning. Araceli was taken home, 'more composed but still weeping'.

The following morning she was summoned to a further meeting to be ticked off by MI5 staff, this time at the Hotel Victoria on Northumberland Avenue. She was told that the 'tribunal' had cleared her husband, but she was warned once again never to repeat her recent behaviour. As a sop, she was informed that Harris had been taken off the Garbo case. This was untrue, but the plan was that henceforth Araceli and Harris would have as little contact with each other as possible.

The plan had worked. Pujol returned home later that evening for a reconciliation with his wife, shaken by the whole episode, even though the means of resolution had been his own idea. It was, he told Harris, one of the most distasteful things he had done in his life.

Within MI5 there were sighs of relief. The crisis, which had been playing on everyone's minds for the past couple of days, had been 'liquidated' and things across the entire double-cross system could go back to normal.

Thanks to Pujol, they learned that Araceli had never intended to carry out her threat to go to the embassy, that it was merely a ploy to make them take her request to return to Spain more seriously.

And Pujol had risen even higher in their estimation. He had placed his work with the British above his marriage, playing out on his wife the kind of ruse that he usually concocted for the Germans. Surprisingly perhaps for someone who knew him and his ways so well, Araceli never twigged that she was being duped.

The relationship had received a body blow and problems in the marriage continued, but after the crisis of June 1943, as Harris wrote somewhat wearily in his report, Araceli gave MI5 'no parallel trouble thereafter'.

16

Britain, Summer 1943

For generations brought up on war films depicting great British espionage triumphs, it is easy to conclude that the Germans were a bit dim when it came to spying. *The Man Who Never Was* and *I Was Monty's Double* show brilliant, creative Brits consistently outwitting the more powerful yet not-so-bright Boche.

This is not simply a rosy take on events years after the Allies won the war. Even at the time, members of the secret establishment were labelling the Abwehr officers as 'the most inefficient, credulous gang of idlers, drunkards and turncoats as ever masqueraded as a secret service'.

In the immediate aftermath of the conflict, Tomás Harris and John Masterman, separately and secretly writing up their accounts of the Garbo case and the double-cross system, portrayed an enemy that had been no match for British secret services. In hindsight, they both concluded, much more could have been done to fool the Germans given their gullibility.

Easy to say, perhaps, in the initial glow of victory. The truth was that the Germans were no easy opponents in the secret war, and the British were cautious throughout precisely because they knew how formidable they could be. The Venlo

Incident, towards the start of the conflict, when German spies had fooled and captured two MI6 agents on the Dutch border, had demonstrated that. Subsequently the limited success of SOE operations in occupied Europe, and the capture by the Gestapo of many of their operatives, continued to make the point.

German expertise was not limited to counter-espionage. They could carry out deception plans of their own, as the Soviets had discovered in the summer of 1942. Operation Kremlin fooled the Red Army into thinking that the Germans would repeat their push on Moscow that year, having failed to take the city the previous winter. The Luftwaffe increased its reconnaissance flights over the Soviet capital, and maps of Moscow were distributed within the Wehrmacht in preparation for the supposed offensive. All this filtered back to Stalin and his generals, who readied themselves for the attack. When, instead, the Germans launched Operation Blau and pushed south towards Stalingrad and the oil fields of the Caucasus, the Red Army was caught by surprise.

Over the summer of 1943, once the crisis with Araceli had been dealt with, the Garbo network also had a taste of disappointment.

August 1942 had seen the disaster at Dieppe, when Jack Poolton and most of his comrades had either been killed or captured. That attack had been launched with neither surprise nor deception, and with inevitably poor results. 'It is sad, but interesting,' Masterman wrote, 'to speculate whether the Dieppe Raid might not have been

173

more successful, or at least less costly, if it had been effectively covered [by a deception plan].'

In September 1943, a year later, the Allies attempted the reverse: a plan to deceive the Germans into thinking that an attack was coming when there was none at all.

In the east, Stalin was still urging for the Second Front to be opened, but the British and Americans were holding back, waiting until they were fully prepared to launch an assault on what Hitler described as 'Fortress Europe' — the vast network of defences being erected on the coasts of France and other occupied countries. In the meantime, however, in an attempt to take some of the pressure off the Soviets, fake landings would be staged at various points to keep German troops tied down, thereby preventing them from being sent to the east.

The plan was called Operation Cockade and it marked a shift in the Garbo story, in which the network moved fully into what Masterman described as 'deceiving the enemy about our own plans and intentions' — the final and culminating reason for running the double-cross system.

The idea for the operation came from the London Controlling Section (LCS), the highly secret committee based in the underground Cabinet War Rooms that was now coordinating all deception plans. Headed by former stockbroker Colonel Johnny Bevan, the LCS was using MI5's double-cross system directly to influence enemy thinking, with Garbo as one of its main players. The Spanish double agent, Bevan already foresaw, would 'have a very important role to play in the future'.

It was August 1943. Pujol-as-Garbo had been in Britain for almost a year and a half, but for the Germans, as Arabal, he had been spying for them for two whole years. True to character, he sent Kühlenthal a long, moody letter to mark the anniversary of his arrival:

A few days ago [he wrote on 2 August] I completed the second anniversary of my stay here, fulfilling from the start the sacred duty of defending the ideals which inspire me so profoundly against our common enemies, disturbers of justice and social order. I have accomplished a great deal since then, always without thought for the dangers through which I must pass, leaping all obstacles which they put in my way . . .

Don't you realise that this is a sacrifice for me to write these long letters? My work weighs on me, God alive! But I know, although at times you smile at my humour, you appreciate the contents as more valuable than if you read a hundred English newspapers and heard a thousand Anglo-American radio transmissions, because through those you would only hear lies, and my writings only tell you concrete realities . . .

My cool head and effrontery with which I defend the democratic-Jewish-Masonic ideology have opened many doors to me, and from there I have drawn opinions . . . I am not therefore generally taken by surprise by all the moves of our enemy. He is cunning

175

and has ambushes fit for bandits . . .

England must be taken by arms, she must be fallen upon, destroyed and dominated, she must be sabotaged, destroying all her potentialities . . .

I love a struggle which is hard and cool, difficult and dangerous. I am not afraid of death, because I am a madman convinced by my ideals. I would rather die than see myself called democratic . . .

With a raised arm I end this letter with a pious remembrance for all our dead.

Masterman always emphasised the need for double agents to live a life as close as possible to that of their supposed characters. Whether or not Pujol, standing in his tiny Jermyn Street office, actually did a Hitler salute as he wrote out the final lines of his letter to Kühlenthal is not known.

Over the following weeks Garbo's letters to Madrid focused almost exclusively on the build-up to Operation Cockade.

The principal agents used for the deception plan were Senhor Carvalho (Agent 1), Pedro the Venezuelan (Agent 3), Fred the Gibraltarian (Agent 4) and Stanley the Welsh nationalist (Agent 7).

Carvalho and Stanley got things started in August by separately reporting to Garbo on military exercises in southern Wales in preparation for a landing, probably in Brittany (Operation Wadham). Thus the two reports confirmed each other and Garbo was able to pass their information on to Kühlenthal.

Next came reports in support of a supposed

attack on Norway — Operation Tindall. Garbo himself travelled up to Glasgow to consult with Pedro, learning that commandos in Scotland were training in mountain warfare, while new camps were being built near aerodromes for airborne troops who would be used in the attack. Other observations included the use of new cranes and unloading equipment at the docks, an increase in RAF personnel, as well as a general rise in the amount of troops and materiel from his previous visits to the area.

To give a sense that the Garbo network was sending over more information than the Germans were actually receiving, the envelopes were painted with the censor's stripes, indicating that they had been tested for secret inks in Britain before being sent on. The letters that 'got through' were numbered in a way to make the Germans think that some of them had indeed tested positive for secret inks and been confiscated. In that way the Garbo network was seen to be doing a good job, while leaving gaps in what it actually reported. The result was that the Abwehr began to rely even more on Garbo's wireless transmissions — something they had been reluctant about for security reasons, but which MI5 were keen to encourage.

Towards the end of August, the network began passing on reports to back up Operation Starkey, the main plank of Cockade, involving an 'attack' on Calais. Troops were reported to be amassing on the south coast. As a result, Garbo told the Germans that he had called Stanley and Pedro urgently to London with a view to sending them south to find out what was happening.

Meanwhile, Fred the Gibraltarian, digging away in the Chislehurst Caves, had enjoyed a lucky break, and had been transferred to canteen duties in the NAAFI — the armed services recreational organisation. Sent down to Dover for a while, he was able to report that a large number of assault craft and troops were grouping in the area. Over the next few days and weeks, Carvalho, Pedro and Stanley confirmed this with more reports on forces and equipment amassing along the Kent coastline. Everything was set, it appeared, for an attack of some kind against the Pas-de-Calais.

It was around this time that Garbo introduced a new source of information in his expanding network of agents, a character whom Pujol later described as 'without a doubt the most important' in the network. Known only as J(5), she was a secretary in the Ministry of War, 'far from beautiful and rather dowdy in her dress', as Garbo described her (Kühlenthal christened her 'Amy'). She was, however, in need of attention from the opposite sex, a role Garbo was happy to play in exchange for her unwitting indiscretions about things she had heard and seen at work.

'You must let me know', Garbo wrote to Kühlenthal shortly after meeting her, 'whether I have carte blanche with regard to expenses incurred in her company, for it is natural that whenever I take her out I have to invite her to dinner and drinks and give her presents. I am certain that with this girl I can obtain information.'

Imagining Garbo to be an exiled Spanish

Republican, J(5) became his mistress and began passing over more information about the troop movements on the south coast. They were, she said, intended to probe the coastal defences, and if possible, penetrate into enemy territory, but only using a small force. Either that, she told him, or there was a larger force elsewhere preparing for the attack as well.

It was a clever move, designed to cover Garbo's back once the operation had been carried out. For Starkey was never going to be a full-scale invasion and Garbo would need something to keep his reputation intact once that became clear to the Germans.

Finally the day for the 'attack' came. In a further boost to his reputation as spymaster, Garbo actually reported the night before that it was going to take place. That evening, Pedro had come up to London from the coast to report that soldiers had been given iron rations and confined to barracks. The operation would begin that same night.

Hours later, on 9 September 1943, Operation Starkey finally took place. The battleships and troopships sailed out, complete with a large escort of RAF fighter planes, towards the Calais coast. There they waited, expecting the Germans to react in some way, particularly to send over the Luftwaffe so that they could be engaged in battle. But over in France the Germans merely got on with their day, untroubled by the armada sitting impatiently on the horizon.

They had not fallen for any of it.

All the build-up, the troops, equipment, the

ships and fighters, and the deception plan, had come to nothing. The boats and planes were obliged to turn around and head back home.

German High Command did not believe that the Allies were going to invade in the summer of 1943, and they were right. The only exception was Field Marshal Gerd von Rundstedt, the commander-in-chief of the Wehrmacht's western forces. He did think an invasion was coming, but had been overruled. In the build-up to Starkey, German High Command had even taken ten divisions out from France for duties in other areas. The Allies' plan to get the Germans to concentrate forces in France and thus keep them away from the Eastern Front was a complete failure.

Cockade was inevitably renamed 'cock-up'.

Important lessons needed to be learned, and fast, because the Allies were now committed to launching a proper invasion of France the following spring. If their lack of success with Starkey was anything to go by, D-Day was going to be a disaster.

For the Garbo network, all energies were engaged in damage-limitation. There was a danger not only that Garbo would lose credibility with Kühlenthal, but that Kühlenthal himself would go down in his masters' estimation. Rejecting official Allied statements that Starkey had merely been an exercise, Garbo insisted that a full attack had been envisaged from the start, but that it had been called off at the last minute owing to the recent armistice in Italy. The Italians, now that US and British troops in Sicily threatened the mainland, had deposed Mussolini back in July

180

and on 8 September announced their surrender. According to Garbo, officials in London were now speculating whether something similar might not happen in Germany, hence the last-minute decision to call off the Calais attack.

The story appeared to have the desired effect. Kühlenthal reported this to Berlin, who came back with messages, picked up by Bletchley, that they were very happy with Garbo's intelligence.

In Jermyn Street, the Garbo team could heave a sigh of relief. It was clear that despite the lack of Cockade's success, they still had a channel for passing over deception to the Germans. In the postmortem, though, there were many mistakes to be picked over.

Militarily, it was clear that all sections of the armed forces needed to be working in closer harmony — the Royal Navy and RAF had only played reluctant parts in the plan.

As far as MI5 were concerned, other conclusions were reached. The first was that being overly subtle, trying to make the Germans reach their own conclusions, was not always a benefit in the Garbo traffic sent to Madrid. In fact, it became clear that the more specific and sensational they were, the more attention they were given. By tracking how the Garbo material trickled through to the Abwehr via the Bletchley intercepts, Harris could see that extremely urgent messages from Garbo reached Berlin within an hour. This was a useful observation for the more important deception plans to come.

Another problem was the bureaucracy involved in drawing up a message that Garbo could send.

So many authorities needed to check and double-check the bogus reports that it slowed the process down considerably, to the extent that some messages had to be cancelled as events on the ground changed and rendered them out of date. This would be amended to some degree in the run-up to the invasion, but continued to be a problem, much to Harris's frustration. These difficulties, he later wrote, 'always constituted by far the most strenuous and exasperating work in the running of the case.'

A final lesson from Cockade was the need for coordination with the media. Just a few days before Operation Starkey, the BBC French Service had been about to broadcast a coded message to the Resistance that the coming attacks on the coast did not concern them and that they were not to rise up in response. The text could have seriously undermined Garbo's credibility had it gone out, and was only exchanged at the last minute and after much wrangling for something less compromising to the deception plan.

In general, Operation Cockade might have been a mess and a failure, but, like the Dieppe Raid a year before, it afforded the Allies important lessons for the real invasion nine months later.

They were still quite unprepared, their armies manned largely by inexperienced conscripts. Against them, on the other side of the Channel, stood a vast force of hardened soldiers, many of them with a fanatical belief in their cause.

Would the Allies be able to learn those lessons?

Would the lessons in themselves be enough?

PART FIVE

'. . . I expect the reader to expand his concept
of truth to accommodate what follows.'
Anthony Burgess

17

London, Early 1944

After more than two years nurturing and expanding his fake Nazi spy network, strengthening the Germans' trust in their 'man-in-London', the time had come for Garbo's most important task.

From February 1944 onwards Pujol and Harris focused exclusively on deception preparations for Operation Overlord — the code name for the full-scale Allied invasion of German-occupied France. Across southern England, British, American and Canadian soldiers, sailors and airmen were preparing for the amphibious assault on the Normandy coastline, waiting to take part in 'the greatest combined operation in history'. On the first day of the invasion alone — D-Day — 150,000 men and 1,500 tanks were scheduled to be landed on the beaches by a fleet of almost 5,500 ships, escorted by 12,000 planes. Almost 3 million more servicemen would then join them over the following weeks as subsequent waves were expected to punch deep into Nazi-held territory and finally open up the much-awaited Second Front.

Deception was vital for the success of Overlord. Without it, the US, British and Canadian troops landing on the Normandy beaches were likely to be massacred, and the invasion would fail. Amphibious operations were extremely risky and nothing had been tried on this scale before.

The Normandy coast around Caen had been chosen for the invasion because of its wide, open beaches and gaps in the sand dunes through which the Allies could — in theory — pour men and arms without too much opposition. Yet the failure of the Dieppe Raid was uppermost in people's minds, as were the painful memories of Gallipoli in the First World War — an amphibious assault that had ended in defeat and over 200,000 casualties. Since Dieppe, the Allies had launched amphibious landings in Sicily in July 1943, and at Anzio and Salerno on the southern Italian coast in January 1944. In both instances the invasions had been chaotic and had nearly ended in disaster. At Anzio, Allied troops were stuck in a confined area for months as resilient German forces counter-attacked their positions.

These experiences weighed heavily on the Allied commanders, particularly the British, who were reluctant to launch a full-scale invasion of France. At best, it was feared the human cost would be very high. At worst the Allies might even be defeated. This at a time when the Soviets were making clear, if bloody, progress in the east.

In theory the success of a seaborne assault depended on 'the ability of the attacker to sustain a more rapid rate of reinforcements by sea than the defender is able to do by land'. The words 'sea' and 'land' are key here. Unless the defender was hampered by difficult terrain, he would always have an advantage over the attacker. The flat plains and gently rolling hills of Normandy, where the invasion was to take place, in no way constituted a problem for the Germans. The pressure was always going to be on the Allies to send over troops and materiel fast enough over the often turbulent waters of the Channel before the Germans could concentrate their own forces in the area of the landings.

On the face of it the Allies had much to be worried about. For centuries Britain had boasted of the natural defences provided by the sea; now it was preparing to turn the tables, to cross the waters and invade at the very point — Normandy — from which the last successful invasion of Britain had been launched, 900 years previously.

Geography and the technicalities of an attack from the sea were not the only considerations. A major worry, particularly for the British, was the German Army itself. The collapse of the British Expeditionary Force and the evacuation from Dunkirk in 1940 had caused something of a trauma for the British armed forces. The Wehrmacht, with its modern blitzkrieg techniques, had clearly demonstrated what Max Hastings describes as its 'institutional superiority'. A sense of military inferiority towards the enemy had developed, which victory at El Alamein in 1943 had only partially cured.

Despite reverses against the Soviets and in North Africa, the German Army was a mighty opponent, one which few looked forward to engaging in open field. It had better discipline and motivation and, apart from its artillery, was also better armed: German Panther and Tiger tanks were greatly superior to the Shermans and Churchills of the Americans and British.

The Americans were slightly less nervous about engaging the Wehrmacht — they had more men available, could absorb more casualties, and had suffered less at the hands of the Germans in the war so far. Nonetheless, no one in either the US or British commands was under any doubt as to the scale of the risk that the Normandy landings would entail.

It was to make up for some of the Allies' military weaknesses that the deception plan was conceived. It was called 'Bodyguard', after a comment Churchill made to Stalin at the Tehran Conference in November 1943 that 'In wartime, truth is so precious that she should always be attended by a bodyguard of lies.'

Within Bodyguard, the deception relating specifically to Overlord and the invasion of Normandy was called 'Operation Fortitude'. This was then divided in two: 'Fortitude North' and 'Fortitude South'. The first dealt with plans to fool the enemy into thinking that an invasion of Norway was imminent and thereby hold German troops in Scandinavia; the second was to deceive them over when and where along the French coast the main assault was to take place.

The key to a successful invasion would be to prevent the Germans from quickly sending reinforcements to Normandy from other parts of western Europe once the landings began. Largely stationary infantry divisions were dotted in and around the coast in preparation for the coming assault. They would be relatively slow in responding. The real danger came from the reserves — the highly mobile Panzer, or armoured, divisions — which would be able to descend on the Allied forces at great speed. Particularly feared were the Waffen-SS Panzer divisions, filled with true fanatics, brutal and ruthless defenders of Nazi ideology armed with powerful mechanised weaponry. 'They were convinced of Germany's rightful dominance and in 'final victory',' historian Antony Beevor writes of them. 'It was their duty to save the Fatherland from annihilation.'

The Waffen-SS divisions had already shown their capabilities in various theatres during the war, not least in the Balkan campaign in 1941 and in the German recapture of Kharkov on the Eastern Front in 1943. Slowing them down in their response to the Normandy landings would be crucially important.

The Allied deception plan, therefore, needed to achieve three things: firstly, to keep the enemy guessing about when the landings would take place; secondly, to make them think that the invasion would occur along the Pas-de-Calais coastline; and thirdly, once the assault had begun in Normandy, the Germans needed to be convinced that this was a feint, intended to draw their best forces away from the Calais area so that the Allies could subsequently launch the main force of the invasion there.

The first of these objectives was relatively straightforward, a case of fooling the Germans about the Allies' state of readiness. The other two were more complicated.

The deception planners were assisted, however, by the fact that the Germans themselves thought that the invasion would come in the Pas-de-Calais. Militarily it made sense: providing a shorter distance to cross by sea, and a chance for greater cover from air forces. It was also a better position for striking into Germany itself once a foothold had been established.

Calais was also the obvious site for a landing because of its major sea ports. The Germans knew that one of the Allies' main difficulties would be to send in men and materiel fast enough once the invasion had started. Which was why, they reasoned, they would have to attack and capture a port.

But here the Allies had a major secret up their sleeve: the Mulberry harbours.

Another of the many lessons learned from Dieppe was the near impossibility of capturing a port from the Germans. Even if one could be taken, the thinking went, it would suffer so much damage in the attack that it would take months to repair and be ready for use. The answer, therefore, was to make a floating harbour in various pieces, drag it over the Channel and construct it off the Normandy beaches ready for disembarking the men and equipment needed for continuing the invasion after the initial attack. In the end, two such secret harbours were made, and they were given the code name 'Mulberry'.

The existence of the Mulberries meant that

the Allies could launch the invasion where the Germans did not expect them. The Normandy coast from Caen stretching west towards the Cherbourg peninsula is a sleepy, rural stretch of shoreline dotted by a handful of villages. Most of it is quite flat, while a section in the middle rises up to cliff faces with grassy fields tumbling down behind them. It lies roughly 100 miles from the southern English coastline. There are no ports and, apart from Caen, no major cities to speak of.

The Germans had built powerful defences along the entire French coastline, even in Normandy: they knew that the invasion was coming. The strongest of these defences, however, were in the Pas-de-Calais.

Again, convincing the enemy of something which they are already convinced of, while having its own complications, is relatively easy. The real success or failure of Bodyguard would depend on the accomplishment of the third objective: making the enemy think that Normandy was a feint.

Deceiving the Germans about the timing and the place of the invasion was, in effect, about creating the surprise. But once the landings had begun, the questions of where and when would be answered, and the Germans could then respond. Surprise itself was not enough. The enemy's strength and capability was such that they could still beat the Allies once their powerful Panzer reserves had been mobilised and brought in to deal with the invasion.

For Normandy to succeed, the surprise had to

continue well beyond D-Day, which was where deception really came in. How could the Allies keep the Panzer divisions and other units from descending on them once the assault had begun? The answer, they hoped, would be to make them think that the invasion was a trick.

It was, in fact, a trick within a trick, a deception within a deception. The Germans needed to believe that the Allies were trying to fool them. Which indeed they were. But not in the way the Germans thought.

18

Britain, Winter–Spring 1944

Over the course of the war, MI5 ran almost forty double agents. Many of them were reluctant collaborators, fooling their German masters to save their skins. Others were in it for the money or the sense of adventure, or were just barking mad. A good number had to be 'liquidated' — their cases closed — before the end of the war owing to weaknesses in their cover stories, or because they had been compromised in some way. In the end, of the dozens of such agents, only three were to play a critical role in the D-Day deception — the crowning moment of the double-cross system. Their code names were 'Brutus', 'Tricycle' and 'Garbo'.

Brutus was a diminutive Polish former fighter pilot called Roman Czerniawski who had escaped Poland after the German and Soviet invasions in 1939 and made his way to France, where he independently set up an intelligence-gathering organisation known as the Interallié. Betrayed by an associate, he was imprisoned by the Germans in November 1941. He led them to believe, however, that he would be willing to change his allegiances, so in the spring of 1942 he was released — the Germans pretending that he had escaped — and sent to Britain. Soon after he arrived, he got in touch with British intelligence, offering to work for them, and was taken on by MI5 under the code name Brutus.

Tricycle was a gregarious, womanising Yugoslav lawyer named Dusan 'Dusko' Popov who was recruited into the Abwehr in August 1940. His sympathies, however, always lay with the Allies and he immediately told the British that he had been taken on by German intelligence. From then on he acted as a double agent, passing between Lisbon and London, telling the Germans that he was working on an escape route for Yugoslav airmen, when the truth was he was handing over their secrets and passing back deception material dreamed up in London. He was given the code name 'Tricycle' because, it has been claimed, of his fondness for *ménages à trois*. MI5 regarded him as their second-most valuable double agent; he has been named as one of the possible inspirations for Ian Fleming's James Bond.

Of the three agents, however, Brutus's loyalties were always first and foremost to Poland, while Tricycle had effectively been taken off Fortitude in the months before D-Day owing to doubts over his cover. Garbo was the most important.

'Garbo was the man who developed into our real star,' wrote Ewen Montagu, 'probably out-doing even Tricycle.'

The official historian of MI5, Christopher Andrew, agrees: 'The double agent who contributed most to the success of the Fortitude deceptions was . . . Garbo.'

A fan of cricketing analogies, John Masterman described Garbo in the following terms, comparing him with one of the earlier — and ultimately disappointing — double agents, 'Snow': 'If in the double-cross world SNOW was the W.G. Grace of the early period, then GARBO was certainly the Bradman of the later years.' International cricket was suspended during the war, but Australia's Donald Bradman was the leading batsman of the day. Today, he is not only regarded as the finest cricketer ever, but possibly the greatest athlete of any sport. Masterman was describing his double agent in the most flattering terms he could think of. The Garbo case, he concluded, was nothing short of 'the most highly developed example' of the art of deception.

By early 1944 the Germans knew that some kind of Allied invasion would be forthcoming over the course of the year; what they did not know was where or when. In January they instructed Garbo to find out as much as he could about the Allied plans, suggesting he send sub-agents from his network to cover areas around the south coast. Which was just as well, because that was precisely what Harris and Pujol were intending to do anyway. Not in order to tell Kühlenthal what was really going on there, but gradually to feed disinformation that would seep into the German military command structure.

Harris later described the process: 'The procedure at the beginning was to ensure that the percentage of checkable truth should be high, so that the falsehoods inserted into the reports would, on the principle of all Intelligence appreciation, have to be accepted. Gradually we were to increase the percentage of false in our mixture until the entire substance of our reports would be based on the false or the notional.'

And there were now plenty of fictional sub-agents to send around the country to keep an eye on the relevant patches of coastline. In Scotland, Garbo's deputy, Agent 3 — Pedro the Venezuelan — was keeping an eye on movements in and around the Clyde. One of his sub-agents — Agent 3(3), a Communist Greek seaman who thought Pedro was working for the Soviets — was looking after the eastern Scottish coast. Between them they reported material to back up Fortitude North — the supposedly imminent invasion of Norway that was holding down around half a million German armed forces personnel in Scandinavia — a figure that never dropped below 400,000 during the rest of the war.

Meanwhile, the bulk of the Garbo network was based in southern England, backing up the deception for Fortitude South. Agent 4 — Fred the Gibraltarian — was sent to work in a canteen in a sealed military area around Southampton.

By this time Fred had recruited some sub-agents of his own. The most important — Agent 4(3) — was an American sergeant in the US Army Service of Supply. Fred had met him in Soho, where they had ended up talking about the Spanish Civil War. The American was described as 'sociable, jocular and fairly talkative' and was virulently anti-Communist. He was also an admirer of Franco, and he and Fred had established a friendship based on their shared anti-British sentiment. Never given a name by the British — although the Germans referred to him as 'Castor' — Agent 4(3) would be the main source through which Garbo passed on misinformation about the US military — even details that a mere sergeant would almost certainly never have been privy to. The Germans, thankfully, never questioned this.

Garbo himself stayed in London as the head of the network, where he was also gathering intelligence from his unconscious collaborators: J(3), Garbo's supposed boss, was still a source from the Ministry of Information, while Garbo's mistress, J(5), continued unwittingly to give him material direct from the War Office itself in their pillow talk.

The final part in the Garbo jigsaw puzzle was played by members of the recently created Brotherhood in the Aryan World Order. Stanley — Agent 7, the man who had recruited them originally — was moving back and forth between south Wales and London, acting as a contact. Agent 7(2) — David — was stationed in Dover to cover Kent. Agent 7(3) — Theresa Jardine, the group's secretary — had been transferred to Ceylon to cover the war effort in the east. Her lover, Rags the Indian poet — Agent 7(4) — was now in Brighton covering the Sussex and Surrey coasts. Agent 7(5) — an unnamed Welshman — was sent to cover Exeter, Devon and Cornwall. Agent 7(6) — also unnamed — was stationed in Swansea to cover south Wales. And Agent 7(7) — the group's treasurer, unnamed but known to the Abwehr as 'Dorrick' — was in Harwich covering the coasts of Essex and Sussex.

By this time Agent 5 — Agent 3's brother — was working for Garbo from Canada, a part that was being played by Cyril Mills, Pujol's first MI5 case officer, who had gone to liaise with the intelligence agencies on the other side of the Atlantic.

Agent 3 — Pedro (a role played by Harris) — was now acting as Garbo's deputy and sending in reports of his own in English directly to Kühlenthal. Written in a much more concise style than Garbo's, they often detailed supposed troop positions and movements around southern England.

A typical Pedro message of the time went like this:

Area west of Stifford closed to civilians, including Grays by pass. Very large vehicle park at Belhus Park, has special new road built to it . . . Hordon-on-Hill, saw large NFS HQ and depot. At Gravesend, saw men, vehicles of 47 London Division, 61 Division, East and Southeastern Command, and men, 9 Army Division.

Kühlenthal could not get enough of this kind of thing. He still had one eye over his shoulder, and needed good intelligence to strengthen his position within the Abwehr — a hotbed of professional jealousy and back-stabbing at the best of times. Ambitious and hard-working, by early 1944 he had become the head of the Madrid station in all but name, but his Jewish blood meant that there remained the threat of being sent back to Germany to join one of the workers' group battalions supporting front-line troops. He replied to Garbo, praising his Venezuelan sub-agent:

We are very satisfied with the way messages have been set out by [Agent] Three. They are very clear and efficient.

A recommendation from his direct opponent, the same man he was deceiving — Harris must have allowed himself a smile.

Communication by this point was almost exclusively through wireless transmissions — a set-up that MI5 was happier with, and had managed to arrange by making the Germans think that most of their cover addresses in Lisbon had been blown. The amount of material being sent over was now very high, with five or six messages being broadcast every day. From January to D-Day on 6 June 1944, some 500 wireless messages were exchanged between Garbo and Kühlenthal in Madrid. The only letters were the few that Garbo wrote accompanying those that he forwarded from Agent 5 in Canada and Theresa Jardine in Ceylon, a role played by Peter Fleming, the elder brother of author Ian.

Kühlenthal would immediately retransmit to Berlin any information on military matters. At times Garbo would add a personal appreciation to the messages, a kind of exegesis on the information that he was receiving from his sub-agents. In the past these might have been dropped or reworded before being sent on to Berlin, but from now on they would be broadcast over word for word. The Germans were not only relying on Garbo's information; they were also starting to value his opinions on the Allied preparations for the invasion of France.

And as ever, thanks to the material from Bletchley, MI5 were fully aware of these developments. When the time came they would prove to be very important.

As luck would have it, the Germans sent in requests for information on precisely what MI5 and the deception planners were intending to give them. One of the key pieces in the puzzle was the Allied Order of Battle for the landings. These were largely supplied by the US sergeant, Agent 4(3). Unfortunately for the Germans, the details he gave of the Allied formations — the divisions, their commanders and how they would all fit together — bore only a passing resemblance to reality.

A central plank of Fortitude was making the Germans think that the Allies had far more troops available to them than they actually did. This was necessary for pulling off the stunt of pretending that the main force of the invasion would come over the Pas-de-Calais, even after the Normandy landings had taken place. To this end dummy tanks and landing craft were built, dotting the English countryside and port areas to fool German spy planes. Meanwhile phantom divisions were created, with fake insignia and other paraphernalia. The biggest element of all in this was the creation of an entirely fake army group — the First US Army Group — or FUSAG, based in the southeast of England and supposedly headed by General Patton.

Patton was the Allied general that the Germans feared the most, with his ivory-handled pistol and ruthless military vision. Controversial and confrontational, he had been temporarily suspended from duty after slapping a battle-weary soldier in Sicily in the face. There was, he had asserted, no such thing as shell shock; it was an invention of the Jews. No wonder Hitler admired him.

The deception planners knew that the Germans held Patton in high regard, so he was the obvious choice to command what was meant to be the main invading force. FUSAG, centred around Kent, was made up of the Canadian First and US Third Armies, but was fictitious. Garbo and the other double agents sent in reports — such as Pedro's quoted earlier — giving details of the various formations of FUSAG that were supposedly stationed in the area. Meanwhile, up and down the south-east coastline went radio transmission trucks, simulating the volume of traffic that such a large military formation would have created, which was picked up by the Germans listening in across the water.

Dover, meanwhile, was filled with ships and landing craft, which were easily visible from German spy planes. The spotters were allowed to fly high over the port to take their shots, but were immediately attacked if they tried to get better-quality photos from lower down. Had they managed to do so their images might well have shown that those 'battleships' in the harbour were no more threatening than pleasure cruisers: almost all were dummies made to look as though the Allies had more weaponry and resources than they actually did. Dover, during this period, rather than a military HQ, was more like 'an enormous film lot'.

All this, and the hundreds of other details, required enormous cooperation. The centre of it was the area around St James's, in central London. General Eisenhower was now the overall commander of Overlord and his HQ — the Supreme Headquarters of the Allied Expeditionary Force, or SHAEF — was set up in Norfolk House in St James's Square. His deception group was known as Ops (B) and worked in close and sometimes informal collaboration with MI5, the Twenty Committee and the London Controlling Section, which was the coordinator of the deception plan as a whole. It was a small group of people, all working in offices a short walk from one another. The fact that so many different bodies were involved in the planning and executing of the deception might have caused serious bureaucratic problems. Thankfully it did not, largely, as one historian of the time has put it, 'because responsibility still lay with a handful of men who knew each other intimately and cut corners'.

Tar Robertson, John Masterman and Tommy Harris were in constant touch with Noel Wild and Roger Hesketh at SHAEF and Johnny Bevan and Ronald Wingate of the London Controlling Section, allowing them to conduct business 'with speed and informality'.

And in the middle of all these scuttling feet pacing up and down the streets of London's secret heart, sat Pujol in his Jermyn Street office, dreaming his dreams and writing his stories.

By now Garbo's disinformation was being used, often verbatim, in the Daily Intelligence Reports sent out by German High Command.

Everything was set for him to help carry out the greatest act of military deception in history, one that could decide the outcome of the war.

What could go wrong?

19

Britain, Spain and Algeria, 1936–44

It was a time of suspense, expectation and excitement. People were intent on having fun while they could.

The first sign that the long wait might be coming to an end came when Monty visited to give his set-piece pep talk. It was early in 1944. The 23rd Hussars had only been in existence for a few years, an armoured regiment born by 'the stroke of a pen' in the War Office in late 1940. Cecil Blacker had joined shortly afterwards, a junior officer and veteran of Dunkirk brought in to help turn a collection of civilian men — farmers, businessmen, the unemployed, cobblers, clerks and carpenters — into soldiers, keen operators of the US-built Sherman tanks with which they were now carving up the English countryside on manoeuvres.

During his officer training at Sandhurst, Blacker had been given the nickname Monkey — one of the wits there thought he looked like an ape and scratched his armpits, shouting 'Monk, Monk', whenever Blacker appeared. It was part of a custom of giving new officers embarrassing nicknames — 'Ugly', 'Crackers', 'Splosh' — and Blacker thought he had got off lightly. But the name stuck, perhaps on account of his smiling, circular face, and he was

'Monkey' thenceforth.

His passion was horses. Brought up in Oxfordshire, where his father had been secretary of the Bicester Hunt, Blacker had enjoyed the world of stables and livery yards, of cubbing and the thrill of the chase from a young age. Now an officer in the 23rd Hussars, commander of its C Squadron and with sixteen tanks under him, he did his best to combine his duties with his first love. But it was getting harder now: the moment was soon coming when the years of training would show as they were sent into battle.

Tanks, of course, were not horses, but it had fallen to the lot of the former cavalrymen of the British Army to take on board this still relatively new weaponry. The British may well have invented the tank in the First World War, but the Germans had taken the technology on much further. The British Mark VIB light tank, which Blacker had been fighting with in France in 1940, being rapidly pushed back to the Channel, was little more than a truck with thin armour plating nailed on the sides. Uncomfortable and offering little protection, it had been no match for the German Panzers and the blitzkrieg tactics of the Wehrmacht.

Now, veterans of the desert campaign and Monty's victory at El Alamein were swanning around, full of themselves and talking condescendingly about how to win a tank battle. Blacker and his men had their doubts as to whether the sands of North Africa were really comparable with the mud and fields they could expect in northern Europe. No one knew exactly where they would be going when D-Day finally came, but it would not be Egypt, that was for certain.

And then Monty himself showed up. They had read the same speech several times in the newspapers as he travelled around the country addressing the troops. But Blacker found it interesting to see him in the flesh.

'The performance was impressive, mainly for the remarkable self-confidence and bounce which the little man exuded,' he remembered.

Monty performed his usual ritual, looking at the men intently, then summoning them to form a square around him while he stood up on his jeep to give them an address.

'I wanted to have a look at you,' he said, 'and for you to have a look at me — we have a job to do together — hitting the Boche for six . . . '

Blacker's sergeant, a Yorkshireman, commented drily that 'the general seemed to have a very good opinion of himself'.

The 23rd Hussars had been shunted around the country several times, from Whitby to Sussex to Norfolk, Newmarket, Bridlington . . . Now came the final change before being sent over to France: Aldershot. It was convenient for getting into London and they took advantage of the pleasures that the capital offered. Blacker was in his late twenties and had a girlfriend, but the atmosphere was licentious and sexually charged, many living to the motto of 'eat, drink and be merry' with the spectre of sudden death hanging over them. The Berkeley Hotel in Piccadilly acted as an officers' club where champagne cocktails fuelled the revelry. Other party venues included the Four Hundred, the Embassy or the Café de Paris, where couples could dance cheek to cheek in semi-darkness.

'Emotional stress was by no means confined to the single. Many married couples became infected by the prevailing mood of 'anything goes' and danced off into the night with a new partner, for good.'

For Blacker, the mood was summed up by the Cole Porter song 'Just One of Those Things' with its message of quick, uncomplicated sexual encounters and one-night stands.

Once the parties ended, however, and lovers pulled themselves free of each other's embrace, the sense of purpose across the country to defeat the Germans and see the war through to the end, was almost palpable.

'Although we were on the threshold of what might be a terrible and for many a terminal experience, we felt uplifted and carried away by the mood of the moment. There had been so much suffering, so much heartbreak, so many tragedies and sacrifices, so much disruption, and now the time was at hand when we were to rise up and strike the blow which could end it all. The British people, for once totally united, held their breath and waited.'

* * *

The men of La Nueve company liked and respected Lieutenant Amado Granell; he had been a soldier for longer than most. Now, very soon, the Spaniards under his command would be heading for France to fight alongside other Allied troops. It was the next step — perhaps the first of many — but the dream of a Spain free from fascism kept them going. Hitler, Mussolini, Franco — they would all fall in the end. And now they had American guns and tanks to get the job done.

Granell liked soldiering: as a young man, in the 1920s, he had joined the Spanish Legión — a force based in Spanish Morocco and modelled on the French Foreign Legion. Its founder, Colonel Millán Astray, was a one-armed, one-eyed maniac and devotee of the Japanese 'samurai way'. His 'legionarios' were expected to embrace a heroic demise; not for nothing were they dubbed the 'bridegrooms of death'. Tough conditions and harsh punishments for misbehaviour were the norm — unlike other units, the members of the Legión were often bearded, wearing their shirts unbuttoned to the belly and sniffing at the way other soldiers marched — a legionario always ran.

Millán Astray's second-in-command in the 1920s was a young major — Francisco Franco. Millán Astray revered his protégé and thought he was destined to be the saviour of Spain. Franco, a conservative Catholic, did not disagree. Amado Granell had different politics from his commanding officer, however, and once his service in the Legión came to an end, he returned to civilian life in his native Valencia and joined the Republican Left Party, becoming an active member of the socialist UGT trade union.

When the Spanish Civil War started, Granell joined the Republican army to fight the rebels — or the Nationalists as Franco's coalition of monarchists, fascists and Catholics came to be known. Within a short time Granell had risen up the ranks to become an officer, and commanded a unit equipped with armoured cars and motorcycles — shock troops to be used at various key points of the shifting front lines. He spent much of the Civil War defending Madrid, riding up and down the streets where, only three years later, his compatriot Juan Pujol would meet at cafés with his Abwehr controllers to discuss plans for spying in London.

But after two and a half years of fighting, and half a million deaths, the Republicans lost the Civil War. As Franco's troops, helped by his German and Italian allies, conquered the remaining areas of Republican territory, in late March 1939 Granell was one of the last left-wingers to get out of the country, securing a place on HMS *Stanbrook* as she sailed out of Alicante towards Algeria. Many of his comrades left stranded on the docks committed suicide where they stood.

The French in Oran were uncomfortable with so many armed Spaniards turning up. They stripped the new arrivals of their weapons, put them in concentration camps, ordered some to join the French Foreign Legion. Granell held on for over three years. A new world war started, France fell to the Nazis, and the French soldiers now watching over him shifted their allegiance to Pétain and the regime collaborating with Hitler.

Granell and the other defeated Spanish

209

Republicans never stopped dreaming that a moment of redemption might come.

And then, in 1942, at long last the Americans landed in Oran. As they were being shot at by French defenders, Granell took his chances and helped the GIs move around the city, giving them directions, telling them where the defenders were staked out. He had been waiting for this moment. Now other kinds of French — the Free French — were in control. He and the others quickly joined up to help, and they became soldiers in the French 2nd Armoured Division, led by General Philippe Leclerc.

Spaniards were scattered throughout the unit — over 2,000 of them. The largest concentration, however, around 150 men, was in the 9th Company, which soon became known as 'La Nueve' in Spanish. The commander was Captain Dronne, a Frenchman. Under him, and the effective company commander, was Lieutenant Granell. His years in the Legión and then the Spanish Republican Army counted for much.

Granell handed out Spanish Republican tricolour flags of red, yellow and violet to sew on to his men's uniforms. They were under French orders, but they knew who they were, and what they were fighting for.

They had been stationed in Rabat for a while, where they had been fitted out with US Sherman tanks, armoured cars and Jeeps. The Spanish gave each vehicle a name, often the name of a battle from the Civil War — words like 'Brunete' or 'Teruel' would be painted in white on the side. A group of anarchists wanted to call their armoured car Buenaventura Durruti after their charismatic leader, killed during the siege of Madrid in 1936, but the French would not allow it. They called it Les Pingouïns instead. Granell's car got the name Los Cosacos — 'the Cossacks'.

In the run-up to D-Day, La Nueve was transferred along with the rest of Leclerc's division to Britain as part of the troop build-up. Billeted in Pocklington, west of York, the company waited for the moment when the invasion would begin, itching to be a part of the new chapter in the war.

20

Britain, France and Germany, Spring 1944

On the eve of the Normandy landings Germany had over a million men available to fight in France. Even after three years of heavy fighting in the east the Wehrmacht was still a large, powerful and well-equipped military force. Many on the Allied side were anxious about the success of the landings. Just hours before D-Day British Chief of the Imperial General Staff Field Marshal Sir Alan Brooke wrote in his diary of his concerns. 'At the best', he said, 'it will fall so very very far short of the expectation of the bulk of the people, namely all those who know nothing of its difficulties. At the worst it may well be the most ghastly disaster of the whole war.'

On the German side, by contrast, many thought they would win once the Allies finally landed. Generalleutnant Fritz Bayerlein, commander of the Panzer Lehr Division, was convinced that what had happened at Dieppe in 1942 was 'proof that we could repel any invasion'.

Hitler himself was confident of success, betting on the destruction of the Allied forces in France so that he could get on with fighting the Soviets. He had adopted a defensive stance in the west, which went against the grain of

212

German military thinking. A vast 'Atlantic Wall' of reinforced coastal positions had been erected from Norway down to the French border with Spain. Dunkirk, Calais, Boulogne, Le Havre, Cherbourg, Brest, La Rochelle and Bordeaux — all ports — had been designated 'fortresses' which would be defended to the last man.

Along the northern French coast — the most likely target for invasion — the German 15th Army, with a total of eighteen divisions, and the best men and materiel that the Wehrmacht could muster, was stationed around the Pas-de-Calais. To its left was the 7th Army, less well equipped, set to defend the Normandy sector.

Despite the optimism of some, there was a degree of nervousness about the coming invasion on the German side, however. Overall command was held by Field Marshal Gerd von Rundstedt, based at St Germain just outside Paris. He was unimpressed by the coastal defences, regarding them as 'just a bit of cheap bluff'. The main assault, he was convinced, would come over the Pas-de-Calais, hence the positioning there of the 15th Army.

Von Rundstedt was not a lone commander in total control of his forces, however. The German command structure in the west was complicated, following Hitler's liking for arrangements where more than one agency was performing the same task — a competitive set-up, according to Nazi post-Darwinian thinking, brought out the best in people.

Under von Rundstedt, in nominal control of the Panzer forces, was General Leo Freiherr

Geyr von Schweppenburg. Meanwhile, in command of Army Group B, the German forces grouped across northern France and the man responsible for the coastal defences, was Field Marshal Erwin Rommel. Rommel wanted the Panzer divisions to be kept close to the seaboard for a quick response to the invasion. He was, however, only given control over three of the total six Panzer divisions available. Of the remainder, two were of the Waffen-SS: the 12th SS Panzer Division made up of boys of the Hitler Youth and with an average age of about 18; and the 1st SS Panzer Division LAH. Rommel had no say over how these key, crack formations would be deployed.

The three-way split of authority between von Rundstedt, von Schweppenburg and Rommel was further exacerbated by the fact that Hitler himself insisted on having final command over the Panzer divisions, convinced that the Allied landings would be 'the sole decisive factor in the whole conduct of the war'.

Rommel and Hitler agreed, unlike von Rundstedt, that Normandy might be a target for the invasion. In the weeks leading up to the assault, Rommel reinforced his units there, his intuition, like the Führer's, telling him that landings of some sort might happen along these beaches.

This confusion at command levels might favour the Allies' chances come D-Day, but on the ground at least German soldiers were better equipped and in general more experienced than any of the 'citizen soldiers' that the Allies could send against them. A key element in this superiority was that of the Germans' tanks.

By this point in the war the basic German workhorse tank was the Mark IV. It had a 75mm gun, armour up to 80mm thick and a top speed of just under 40 kph. In terms of numbers produced, it was the most important German tank in the conflict, and was equal, if not considerably superior, to the Shermans and Cromwells of the Allies. The Mark IV was already being superseded by an even better tank, however, one that is commonly regarded as the best produced by any country in the war: the Panther. This tank had a 75mm gun like the Mark IV, but also had three machine guns, armour up to 110mm thick and a top speed of 46 kph.

In addition, the Germans had Tiger tanks — heavier and slower than Panthers, but with thick armour and a massive 88mm gun that could easily take out any Allied opponent.

By comparison, Shermans, which were produced in great numbers by the Americans and were set to be used by all Allied forces in Normandy, had a short 75mm gun, armour only 51mm thick at its strongest point, and a top speed of just 38 kph. They were also tall, which made them relatively easy targets. Soldiers used to call them 'Ronson Lighters' owing to their unfortunate habit of catching fire once they had been hit.

After the landings had begun, Allied tank crews became all too aware of the superiority of the Germans' tanks.

'There was, I think, no British tank commander', one officer wrote, 'who would not happily have surrendered his 'fringe benefits' for a tank in the same class as the German Panther or Tiger.' Once a Sherman, Churchill or Cromwell had been hit by one of these steel monsters, the results were commonly fatal.

Even in lighter weaponry, the German soldier enjoyed a clear advantage. The MG42 machine gun — the 'Spandau' — could fire 1,200 rounds per minute, compared to an equivalent 500 rpm from a British Bren or BAR. Meanwhile, the German anti-tank weapon, the *Panzerfaust*, was also superior to the American bazooka or British PIAT.

Only in artillery and air power could the Allies claim superiority.

Battle hardened from the Eastern Front, the best fighting unit within the German military forces now based in the west — the 1st SS Panzer Division LAH — was regrouping in Belgium having finished its tour of duty in the Ukraine. Fighting the Soviets it had been reduced to a mere *Kampfgruppe* — an ill-defined 'fighting group' — after heavy losses had reduced it from a full division. Now, however, its numbers had swelled once more to around 20,000 men, and it had been re-equipped, reaching a near-capacity 103 Mark IV tanks and 67 Panthers.

The LAH was part of the 1st SS Panzer Corps, which also included the 12th SS Panzer Division Hitler Youth. The Corps was led by former LAH commander General Sepp Dietrich, a one-time petrol-pump attendant and Hitler's erstwhile chauffeur and brutal sidekick. His place in the LAH had been taken by General Theodor 'Teddy' Wisch.

216

At the age of twenty-eight, Jochen Peiper had been promoted to Obersturmbannführer — Lieutenant Colonel — in charge of the 1st SS Panzer Regiment. His brutality had continued in the same vein after the victory at Kharkov. In one encounter with Soviet forces his men killed a total of 2,280 Red Army men and took only three prisoners. The complete annihilation of the village of Pekarshchina using the now famous blowtorches was also added to his tally.

Hitler himself awarded Peiper his latest decoration and the following notice was published in German newspapers: 'In grateful recognition of your heroic actions in the struggle for the future of our people, I award you the Knight's Cross of the Iron Cross with Oak Leaves as the 377th member of the German Wehrmacht so honoured. Adolf Hitler.'

The fighting in the east was taking its toll on Peiper. Fuelling himself with coffee, cigarettes and Pervitin, a German-manufactured amphetamine, had caused his heart to suffer, leading to exhaustion and fainting spells. At the start of 1944 he began a lengthy period of leave, staying with his wife and two young children at their home in Bavaria. Sigi was heavily pregnant with their third child.

Late April saw Peiper back with his regiment, stationed in the Belgian town of Hasselt. The new recruits brought in to fill the LAH's numbers needed to be trained up to the high, fanatical standards demanded by the Waffen-SS. As well as the hard training and familiarisation with weaponry, two one-hour education sessions were held each week to teach the troops about the American forces they were expecting to face. The USA, Peiper's men were told, was a decadent country ruled by Jews, made morally corrupt by Jewish artists and Black music.

Peiper took this seriously and upheld the 'moral' values of the SS more than other commanders. Sexual relations were only for breeding purposes, to preserve the race. For Peiper there was none of the 'Jewification' — *Verjudung* — of the soul by giving in to the sex drive. He was even abstemious towards drink, following Himmler's example of avoiding alcohol and prostitutes. The Reichsführer had trained as a young man in a Jesuit seminary and had taken many of the ideas of the Society of Jesus and applied them to his 'Black Order'.

But the pep talks and air of monasticism were not enough for Peiper. Some of the new recruits were not up to standard. They needed teaching a lesson, an experience that would turn them into the ruthless, brutal and indoctrinated fighters that the SS expected them to be. An opportunity arose in May. Five young new soldiers were caught shirking their duties. The boys admitted, in addition, that while away from their posts they had stolen food, including some chickens and a ham. It was a relatively minor offence.

Nevertheless, a court martial found them guilty, and Peiper was merciless. On 28 May he had the five recruits executed by firing squad in front of the entire regiment. Afterwards, every man in the unit was forced to walk past the dead bodies where they had fallen to the ground.

Some of them, then still in their teens, never forgot the experience.

It was an important moment for Peiper. When the war had started five years earlier, he had witnessed mass shootings in Poland. Now he was giving the same lessons to his men. The boys who had been shot were, in his mind, mere *schlechtes Menschenmaterial* — 'bad human material'. They could be dispensed with. Meanwhile he had shown his soldiers the kind of mentality that was expected of them now that they were in the Waffen-SS, now that they were Peiper's men.

Fully armed and psychologically prepared, the 1st SS Panzer Regiment, the leading tank formation within the LAH, with Peiper at its head, was now ready for anything that the Allies could send its way.

PART SIX

'A lie gets halfway around the world before
the truth gets a chance to put its pants on.'
Winston Churchill

21

London, Lisbon and Berlin, Spring 1944

In the spring of 1944 Pujol and Araceli were keeping their marriage going, but only just. Sexual fidelity had become a problem, with Araceli forming an attachment to an Allied naval officer later captured in action and made a prisoner of war. Pujol himself may also have been unfaithful. Real people were now playing the roles of some of the Garbo network's fictional characters: Harris was effectively Pedro, Agent 3; Cyril Mills was Agent 5 in Canada; and Charlie Haines was Agent 4(1) the radio operator. Was there any parallel between Garbo's mistress Agent J(5) and Sarah Bishop? Both of them were former War Office secretaries. Certainly Pujol had never had any difficulty finding girlfriends before meeting Araceli. His wife's letters from Lisbon showed a jealous side to her — did Pujol give her reason to suspect him?

The complications of their sex life aside, Pujol and Araceli were no longer living in Hendon. In December 1943, after rumours had circulated of new secret German weapons designed to terrify Allied civilian populations, Kühlenthal warned his London agent to move out of the capital. No reason was given, but MI5 assumed that it was a

223

reference to the imminent arrival of whatever the Germans had been cooking up over the past months. Pujol packed his bags and took his wife and two boys down to a hotel in Taplow, Buckinghamshire.

Others took the hint, and moved out of the centre, including Harris, who left his Mayfair home for Logan Place, a house with a large garden in Earl's Court. But so far, no mysterious new bombs had fallen on London, and everything appeared set for Operation Fortitude.

Something was bothering Harris, however, a niggle in the back of his mind that refused to go away. There was a weak link in the Garbo chain, indeed in the entire double-cross system. In a bizarre role reversal, in 1943 Dusko Popov — MI5's agent Tricycle — had asked his own Abwehr case officer, Johannes 'Johnny' Jebsen, to work for the British with him. Jebsen was an old friend of Popov's, based in Lisbon, a chain-smoking, champagne-drinking devotee of P.G. Wodehouse who shared Popov's penchant for the high life.

Like Popov, Jebsen was also anti-Nazi. It was becoming increasingly evident by this stage which way the war was going, so he agreed to Popov's proposal — he too would become a double agent, still working for the Abwehr, but in reality acting for MI5 with the code name 'Artist'.

It seemed a good idea, but brought a new problem: Jebsen's recruitment meant that for the first time a fully paid-up member of German intelligence knew that Popov was a double agent.

In addition, Jebsen had given indications to MI5 through Popov that the Abwehr in Madrid had a large spy network operating across Britain with its head — a Spaniard — based in London.

This was a clear reference to Garbo. Yet MI5's failure to act on Jebsen's intelligence meant that Jebsen would now have deduced that Garbo as well as Popov — Tricycle — was a front man for a British scheme to fool the Germans. In March 1944 he told the British that he thought that all of Kühlenthal's 'spies' were in reality British double agents.

Jebsen knew too much. He might have changed sides by this stage, but he posed a threat. Could he really be trusted? What if he let slip a piece of information that led the Germans to unravel the vastly complex deception puzzle that MI5 had built up? His own position was under threat at times. What if he were suspected by the Germans themselves and forced to talk, perhaps under duress?

The British had to limit any potential damage, but there was not much they could do. They tried telling Jebsen that Kühlenthal was the kind of spymaster who frequently made up much of his 'intelligence'. It was not MI5 who was feeding disinformation to him, but the Abwehr official himself who was liberally peppering his reports to Berlin with 'facts' drawn from his own imagination.

It worked, to a degree, but there was no guarantee that Jebsen would believe them. Harris in particular was nervous about the threat Jebsen posed.

'Unless steps are immediately taken to cease contact with Artist completely or evacuate him forthwith from Spain, then grave risks of blowing the Garbo case are inevitable.'

So much was riding on the success of Garbo and the double-cross system as a whole, that he even suggested 'liquidating' the Garbo case before it was too late, otherwise all the double agents might be in danger.

The men in charge of double-cross — John Masterman of the Twenty Committee, Tar Robertson of B1A, and the head of MI5's B section Guy Liddell — refused. They should wait and see, they said. Best not be too hasty.

The blow came in early May.

Jebsen was not feeling comfortable with his Abwehr masters. Doubts had been raised about some of his financial dealings while he had also been putting his nose into internal affairs that they thought did not concern him. So when he was asked to travel to Biarritz to meet a superior officer for a meeting about Popov's expenses, he smelt a rat and made his excuses.

Soon after, however, still in Lisbon, Jebsen visited the German Embassy to collect a medal for his war work — the Kriegsverdienstkreuz First Class. This was meant to be a moment of vindication, when all doubts about him within the service were expelled. Instead, once inside, he was punched unconscious, sedated and thrown into a trunk placed in the back of a car with diplomatic plates. The car was then driven over the border, across Spain to France. From there he was taken to Berlin, and placed in the

226

Gestapo prison on Prinz Albrecht Strasse for interrogation.

MI5 first became aware of Jebsen's disappearance on 6 May, when Bletchley transcripts showed that the other German intelligence agency in the city, the SD, was getting worried about the fact that they could not find him. The following day, the British learned that he had been kidnapped and taken to Berlin.

For MI5 it was a crisis: their worst fears had come true. Johnny Jebsen, the man who knew too much, was now in the hands of the Gestapo, almost certainly being tortured to make him talk. The question was, would he blow Tricycle, Garbo and the entire double-cross operation?

Harris was beside himself. After years of preparation, and less than a month before D-Day, everything hung in the balance. He suggested liquidating Tricycle immediately. That way, he said, a cut-out could be placed between Popov and Garbo. The assumption was that Jebsen would betray Tricycle at the very least. And once the Germans started comparing Tricycle and Garbo's intelligence, they would quickly see that the two agents were saying virtually the same thing — namely that the build-up of Allied troops in south-east England was for a major assault on the Pas-de-Calais. The natural conclusion, according to Harris, would be that if Popov was feeding them misleading information, then so was Garbo.

There was a long meeting in St James's Street involving John Masterman, Tar Robertson, Guy Liddell and Harris. Harris put forward his act-now proposals, but Masterman and Liddell were more circumspect. Better, Masterman said, to carry on as if nothing had happened. Only if and when concrete evidence came through that either Tricycle or Garbo had been blown should they close those agents down. In the meantime, it was better to leave them alone. Liddell agreed. There was a strong chance that Tricycle might be blown by the Germans, but then again Jebsen may simply have been taken in for questioning about his irregular financial dealings.

But, Harris countered, Bletchley had not been able to warn them that Artist was about to be arrested; the code-breakers might not give them any forewarning that he had told his interrogators what he knew either. Artist had informed the British that he thought all of Kühlenthal's spies in Britain were double agents. Everything, the whole of double-cross, was at stake. They could not wait for Jebsen to break under torture and for the Germans to work things out for themselves; MI5 had to act now.

Harris had overstepped the mark. He was Garbo's case officer, but now he was making suggestions about the running of other double agents. Liddell told him as much.

'Don't endanger your position by poking your nose too much in other people's affairs,' he said.

Carry on like that and he would be sacked.

Harris could do nothing. This time his famed powers of persuasion were not enough. He was outnumbered and outranked. All they could do was continue as before, monitor the information from Bletchley for any sign that Jebsen might

228

have talked, and then take things from there.

MI5 would adopt a calm, steady British approach to the problem.

But Harris was still concerned.

What if the Germans started playing games with the Allies? If they extracted the truth from Jebsen, they might keep running Pujol as their agent in London, now aware that he was working for the British. Then they would simply take what he said and believe the opposite.

The potential for damage to Overlord was immense. If Garbo was telling the Germans that the Pas-de-Calais was the main target for the invasion, the Wehrmacht would inevitably end up taking its best forces, including the feared SS Panzer divisions, away from the area to make them available for action in Normandy. The future of Europe and tens of thousands of lives hung in the balance, yet the deception plan on which the Allied assault depended was under threat.

D-Day was imminent. Everything now lay with Johnny Jebsen. Would he be able to withstand the horrors that his torturers would inflict?

22

England, Northern France and Southern Germany, 5 June 1944

Mavis rarely read the full texts of the messages that she deciphered at Bletchley Park. A sentence, or half-sentence — that was enough to break into the coded text and then the rest would be passed on to the analysts. And she did not ask questions: it was not how things were done. But she saw enough to get some idea of what was going on — aspects of the war that ordinary civilians and even the majority of fighting men were unaware of.

It was the first week in June and the weather had been nice over the weekend, although storms were predicted for the coming days. She was on a train, heading to London from the station that sat at the bottom of the hill from Bletchley Park.

Dilly Knox, her beloved mentor, had died a year before, shortly after Mavis had married. Keith Batey was one of the code-breakers in Hut Six working on the German naval Enigma. She and Keith had tried to hide their relationship from the others at Bletchley for as long as possible, until some sharp-eyed colleague noticed that, mysteriously, the two always managed to coincide for mealtimes in the canteen. Dilly had joked that mathematicians were not much fun, but Mavis had gone ahead with the wedding anyway. She was Mavis Batey now, sharing a passion for crosswords and puzzles with her husband.

There were plenty of people in the carriage that Monday, gazing out at the budding green countryside through the grimy windows: mothers, businessmen in suits, servicemen and women in uniforms of many shades, from many parts of the globe. The war was now in its fifth year and the world had changed — even here, rolling over the quiet fields. The Luftwaffe was not dropping quite so many bombs over English cities as it once had, but there were rumours of a new terrifying Nazi weapon to come. She worried about her parents; their house to the south-east of London was in the direct firing line of whatever it might eventually turn out to be.

The Germans were no longer triumphant as they had been, however. In North Africa, on the Eastern Front, and now in Italy, they were slowly being pushed back.

But there was more than enough fight left in Hitler's forces. The call from Moscow for a Second Front — a real second front; what was happening in the Mediterranean did not count — was finally being heard. Britain was awash with US soldiers, shipped over the Atlantic to help fight the Nazis. A new attack was imminent, almost certainly in France. What no one except a very, very few could say, however, was where in France the attack would come, or more importantly, when. Certainly nothing was being given away on the radio or in the newspapers.

But judging by the numbers of GIs around, and the endless manoeuvres and exercises, even the least observant would conclude that it could not be too far off. Some time over the summer, perhaps.

Mavis did not get to read entire messages, but she did know things, important things. It was part of her work.

As she looked around the carriage at her fellow passengers she realised, with a jolt, that she was almost certainly the only one there who knew the actual date of D-Day. This quiet corner of England was soon about to be drawn much closer to the actual fighting of the war; the battlefields would no longer be in distant lands but just across the sea on the beaches of France.

And it was coming much sooner than anyone thought. Tomorrow, in fact.

Would it be enough? Would these young men in uniform be up to the job? Before too long, some of the soldiers now sharing the carriage with her might be dead.

The train heaved its way down to London. Once again, everything was about to change.

★ ★ ★

Field Marshal Erwin Rommel was an early riser. Dawn had broken and the clear, hot weather of the previous few days was turning into a storm over northern France and the Channel. The commander of German Army Group B, with special responsibility for the coastal defences against an Allied attack, was confident that he

232

would not be missed for a few days. Eisenhower would be insane to attempt a crossing in the face of so much wind and rain. The waves breaking on the beaches that morning were well over two metres high.

Rommel had decided to take some leave and head back to Germany. It was his wife Lucie's birthday the following day, and he also wanted to go to Berchtesgaden, in the Alps, where Hitler was staying at his mountain retreat. There were matters that he needed to discuss face to face with the Führer — a strengthening of the Atlantic Wall defences along the French coastline, and an appeal for two more Panzer divisions to help fight off the Allies when eventually they came.

Not that any such move was imminent. The Luftwaffe meteorologist had predicted that the bad weather was to continue for the next few days at least, with winds in excess of force 6, thus preventing an Allied landing while the tides and moon cycle suited them. It would be another fortnight before the conditions would once again be favourable.

Rommel was anything but complacent. He knew, like everyone, that an attack was coming. Only the day before he had urged for more reconnaissance flights over southern England to gather new information on the enemy's intentions. But the storm meant any such action would now be impossible. The Allies had also imposed radio silence — as they had done previous to all their actions in North Africa, when Rommel had fought the British across the sands of Libya and Egypt. Yet there had been other instances of radio silence since March that year — attempts to throw the Germans off guard, no doubt.

And so, at 6.00 in the morning, he set off from his headquarters at La Roche-Guyon, an eighteenth-century chateau built into a cliff face overlooking the Seine. Accompanied by his aide and his driver, he began the long journey to his home in Herrlingen, a small village outside the southern German city of Ulm. It would take him most of the day.

He was happy for others to lower their guard that blustery Monday morning. As he sped away in his open-top Horch car, his chief of staff told the German armies in France and Belgium that they might stand down in the light of the bad weather. They needed a break after so much time spent on alert, watching for signs of the Allies approaching from over the northern horizon.

Officers and commanders of the German 7th Army, stationed in Normandy around the Cherbourg peninsula, decided to go ahead with some war-game exercises in Rennes the following day, 6 June. They did not consider themselves to be in the main firing line in any case. If Allied air operations were anything to go by, the target for the landings was almost certainly the Pas-de-Calais, where the bombing in preparation for an assault was heaviest.

Field Marshal Gerd von Rundstedt agreed. On 5 June he wrote a report on the prospects of an Allied landing: 'The main front between the Scheldt [River in Belgium] and Normandy is still

234

the most probable place of attack.'

Like Rommel, he foresaw no imminent danger. 'As yet there is no immediate prospect of the invasion.'

★ ★ ★

There is a cloying beauty about Berchtesgaden. Set near the Alpine Austro-German border, it is a place of wide green valleys banked by high mountain walls, sweeping pine forests of uniform perpendicular trees and spotless timber-framed houses with overbearing roofs and carved wooden eaves. According to legend, Frederick Barbarossa is buried inside the nearby peak of Untersberg, waiting to return, Arthur-like, to save the German peoples at their hour of need.

Hitler adored it, and turned this corner of southern Germany into both a playground and a spiritual homeland for the Nazi elite. His own home, the Berghof, was a grand villa commanding impressive views over the surrounding landscape, while Goering, Himmler, Goebbels, Bormann and other dignitaries also had retreats built there to be close to the Führer.

This was no mere holiday resort. Hitler spent a great deal of time at the Berghof, and as head of state and commander-in-chief, whenever he decided on an Alpine sojourn the machines of government and the military had to travel south with him. As the war raged on the Eastern Front, he was usually to be found at the Wolf's Lair, his military headquarters in modern Poland. On 5 June, however, he was back where he felt happiest, deep in the southern German mountains, now filled with the delights of spring.

The day had been devoted to dealing with a number of matters. Rome had fallen to the Allies just the day before, although the German 10th Army had managed to withdraw successfully, abandoning the Eternal City with little fighting. Meanwhile there was the matter of Portuguese tungsten imports to deal with, as well as a meeting with Albert Speer to discuss plans for creating smokescreens on bridges along the Rhine. Then he had a medical examination with his personal doctor: the Führer's flatulence was causing him problems again and a stool examination was performed. He was in bad shape by this stage, both physically and psychologically.

It was a starlit night, and after the matters of state had been attended to, Hitler listened to some music and chatted with Eva Braun and Goebbels about cinema late into the night, before taking a sleeping potion and going to bed.

In the early hours of 6 June, having finally reached his home in Herrlingen and dined with his wife and son, Rommel was busy writing a memorandum to Hitler about the need to bolster the defences in France with more Panzer divisions.

Meanwhile, in Normandy, British gliders carrying paratroopers of the 6th Airborne Division circled over bridges crossing the Caen canal and River Orne in preparation for landing.

As the first shots of D-Day were being fired, Hitler was falling deep into a drug-induced sleep.

23

London, 1 May–5 June 1944

People who worked with him commonly regarded Harris as one of the most talented officers involved in double-cross. Ewen Montagu dedicated his book *Beyond Top Secret U* to the memory of his colleague, describing him as 'the greatest deceptioneer of us all'. Today, a sense of his genius comes across from the movements and messages of Garbo around D-Day.

It was clear to those involved that Garbo's greatest importance as a double agent and purveyor of false notions to the Germans would come once the Allied troops had actually landed on the beaches of Normandy and established a bridgehead. Getting ashore would be hard in itself, but their vulnerability would continue for several days thereafter. There was every chance that if the Germans hit back hard, using their best troops and Panzer reserves, thousands of British, US and Canadian soldiers would be pushed back into the sea, and the much-needed Second Front would die with them. Keeping those crack German troops away from Normandy, therefore, was of paramount importance, and Garbo was to play the most vital part in attempting to hold them at bay.

Harris knew, thanks to the Bletchley decrypts, that Garbo was held in high regard by his

Abwehr masters in Madrid. Only a few weeks before, as part of his supposed work for the Ministry of Information in London, Garbo had 'signed' the Official Secrets Act, meaning that he was now in a position to receive information unavailable to ordinary civilians — and of course pass the contents over to the enemy.

Much had been achieved with the set-up for Fortitude. Enigma traffic showed that the Germans thought there were a total of eighty-nine divisions in Britain on 1 June, while in actual fact there were only forty-seven — the fictional troops that largely made up Patton's FUSAG in southeast England were very real for the enemy. But the plan's success rested on the misinformation that Garbo would be sending once the Normandy campaign had actually begun, so it was vital to cement his reputation in *all* German eyes — not just the intelligence gatherers in Madrid, but all echelons of the secret service as well as the military commanders. They were the ones whose decisions the Allies needed to influence.

The question was, how? How could they turn Garbo from being simply a respected master of a spy-ring based in Britain to someone whose reports and analyses from inside enemy territory would be read and trusted by all concerned?

The answer came to Harris one fine May morning as he sat in the garden at his new home in Earl's Court. D-Day was a month away. The only way the Allies could ensure that Garbo would be listened to by everyone once the invasion had begun, Harris realised, was to give him an incredible scoop as a spy. While every effort had been made to conceal the actual date of the attack from the Germans, Garbo would go on air some time before the first soldiers hit the Normandy beaches and warn them that the assault was on. It would be a spectacular coup, and raise him so highly in the Germans' esteem that they would subsequently hang on his every word.

Needless to say, it was a controversial idea. Warn the Germans that we're coming? Some baulked at it. But unlike many US commanders, General Eisenhower was in favour of deception: he had seen how useful it could be while campaigning in the Mediterranean the year before. In the end he gave Harris's plan the go-ahead. Yes, get Garbo on the air to tell the enemy the attack was under way, but only so late in the day that it could not have any real effect on their defences. The first landing crafts of the assault, carrying men of the US 4th Infantry Division, were due to hit Utah beach, at the western end of the invasion front, at 0630 on 6 June. Garbo's message could go out no sooner than three-and-a-half hours beforehand, at 0300.

Harris and Pujol were satisfied, but there was a problem: the German radio transmitter in Madrid went off air just before midnight. How could they engineer it so that Kühlenthal was listening at the other end in the middle of the night without alerting him that it was something to do with D-Day?

The Germans themselves provided the answer. On 22 May Kühlenthal told Garbo that he was particularly interested in the movements of Allied troops in Scotland, whose manoeuvres

Garbo's sub-agents had reported a few days earlier. This had been part of the Fortitude North deception plan, aimed at making the Germans believe that an attack of some sort was imminent against Norway. Any developments, Kühlenthal insisted, should be radioed through to him as soon as possible.

Harris and Pujol therefore set up the following story. The only remaining sub-agent in Scotland at that point was Agent 3(3), the communist Greek sailor who thought he was helping the Soviets. He got word to Garbo that the Clyde fleet was about to set sail at any moment and that he would phone through with a code word once this occurred. Garbo therefore told the Germans on 5 June that they should be listening at the agreed emergency night-call hour of 0300 in case he had urgent news to pass on.

Everything was set: without having an inkling of what was really in store, the Germans were due to be on air at the appointed time to receive news — not about the Clyde, but about the beginning of Operation Overlord and the invasion of France.

There are two accounts of the Garbo team's activities on the night before D-Day. Years later, Pujol himself described how he, Harris and Charlie Haines had been stuck all night in their little office, having forgotten to bring sandwiches or even a flask of tea to keep them going, as Harris popped back and forth from the Cabinet War Rooms bringing news of developments on the ground.

The author Sefton Delmer, however, who

(*Above*) Private Jack Poolton was lucky to survive the disastrous Allied strike against the Normandy coast.

(*Left*) Juan Pujol, aged 21, during his military service in 1933.
His commanding officer in the light artillery regiment used to beat Pujol until he learnt how to ride a horse.

(*Below*) Barcelona was one of the first European cities to suffer major aerial bombardment. Here, bombs explode over the Eixample and Raval districts during a Civil War raid in 1938.

(*Left*) Pujol and Araceli married in April 1940, having met in the Francoist capital Burgos during the final weeks of the Spanish Civil War.

(*Below*) The German Embassy in Madrid, from which Kühlenthal and other Abwehr officers used to operate during the Second World War.

(*Above*) The cottages at Bletchley Park, where Dilly Knox had his team. This was where Mavis Batey and Margaret Rock first broke into the Abwehr Enigma in December 1941.

(*Above*) Half-Spanish half-Jewish, Tomás (Tommy) Harris was a talented artist and MI5 officer. He took over the running of Pujol as a British double agent in the spring of 1942 and they became close friends.

(*Above*) Pujol collaborated enthusiastically with the British. By the summer of 1942 Araceli had joined him in London and they lived with their two boys in Hendon.

(*Left*) 35 Crespigny Road, the MI5 safe house in Hendon run by Mrs Titoff, where Pujol was taken to be debriefed.

(*Left*) 55 Elliot Road, a two-minute walk from Crespigny Road. Pujol and Araceli lived here until early 1944.

(*Above*) Pujol's handwriting was almost as flamboyant as his prose style. This is a letter he wrote supposedly from Madrid to Araceli in London as part of his elaborate cover story towards the end of the war.

(*Above*) A young Joachim Peiper on an official visit to Spain as Himmler's adjutant in October 1940. Peiper is to the left of Himmler, glancing over towards Franco's group.

(*Above*) Joachim ('Jochen') Peiper in 1943 wearing the Knight's Cross of the Iron Cross that he won on the Eastern Front.

(*Right*) Tiger Tanks of the 1st SS Panzer Division LAH on manoeuvres through northern France, March 1944. Allied tank commanders feared and envied the Panthers and Tigers that their inferior machines had to face.

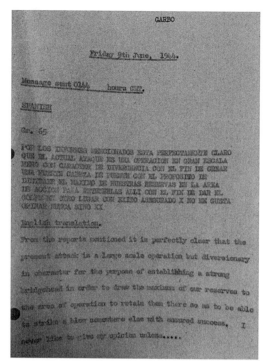

GARBO

Friday 9th June, 1944.

Message sent 0144 hours GMT.

SPANISH

Gr. 65

POR LOS INFORMES MENCIONADOS ESTA PERFECTAMENTE CLARO QUE EL ACTUAL ATAQUE ES UNA OPERACION EN GRAN ESCALA PERO CON CARACTER DE DIVERSION CON EL FIN DE CREAR UNA FUERTE CABEZA DE PUENTE CON EL PROPOSITO DE DISTRAER EL MAXIMO DE NUESTRAS RESERVAS EN LA AREA DE ACCION PARA RETENERLAS ALLI CON EL FIN DE DAR EL GOLPE DE JURO LUGAR CON EXITO ASEGURADO X NO ME GUSTA DE DAR MI OPINION SINO XX

English translation.

From the reports mentioned it is perfectly clear that the present attack is a large scale operation but diversionary in character for the purpose of establishing a strong bridgehead in order to draw the maximum of our reserves to the area of operation to retain them there so as to be able to strike a blow somewhere else with assured success. I never like to give my opinion unless......

(Above) The text of Garbo's crucially important D+3 message.

(Below) The Berghof, Hitler's Alpine home. Here Hitler read the intelligence report based on Garbo's disinformation. His decision to reroute his Panzer reserves changed the course of the Battle of Normandy.

(Below left) V-1. The first V-1 flying bomb hit London on 13 June 1944. As more rained down on the capital, Pujol's German handlers asked for information about where they were landing.

(Below right) In Madrid, Kühlenthal was using very out-of-date maps to chart the V-1 strikes. It took several days for the Garbo operation to find something that both sides could use, which bought them valuable time.

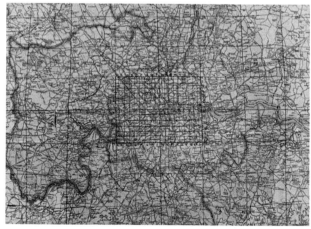

(*Below right*) Sherman tanks of the 23 Hussars set off to attack enemy lines during Operation Goodwood, 18 July 1944. Large numbers were 'brewed up' by Peiper's forces and the operation ended two days later having only advanced seven miles.

(*Below left*) As part of his cover story, Pujol had to pretend that he was in hiding from the British, and changed his appearance. This is how he appeared for the secret ceremony awarding him an MBE in December 1944. Guy Liddell of MI5 thought the beard made him look like Lenin.

(*Above*) The front page of the Paris newspaper *Libération* announcing the arrival of the first Allied forces in the capital. The soldier on the right is the Spaniard Amado Granell.

(*Left*) One of Tomás Harris's self-portraits showing a mysterious and imaginative side to Garbo's case officer. Harris was as much a story-teller as Pujol, and 'Garbo' was a double act where each man was as important as the other.

(*Right*) After the war, Harris moved to Spain, where he returned to his artwork and collecting. Pujol and other friends remembered Harris as 'always smiling'.

(*Right*) Pujol died in October 1988 and was buried in Choroní, Venezuela.

worked in intelligence during the war, gives a slightly more colourful account. He relates how, on the evening of 5 June, Pujol, Harris, MI5's double-cross chief Tar Robertson, and SHAEF deception planner Roger Hesketh, all met at Harris's house for dinner. It was a modest affair, according to Delmer, but in light of the historic moment they drank the last remaining magnum of Chateau Ausone 1934 from Harris's famous wine cellar (today, ordinary-sized bottles from that vintage sell for over £800).

As H-Hour and the official start of D-Day approached, they poured out into an official car and drove across blackout London to 35 Crespigny Road in Hendon — the house where Pujol had first been interviewed by Harris and Bristow on his arrival in Britain two years previously. It was here that the Garbo radio had been set up, manned by telecoms operator Charlie Haines.

The usual evening traffic with Madrid was coming to a close. There had been nothing unusual to report — just some messages from Kühlenthal to Garbo's sub-agent in Canada. There was no indication from the Germans that this was anything more than an ordinary night — no sign that they knew what was to be unleashed on the northern shores of France in just a few hours' time.

Around midnight the German radio operator in Madrid signed off. The agreement was that they would be back on air at 0300, when Garbo would send his D-Day warning.

For the next few hours, the group of deceivers

wrote out and then enciphered the message that was to be sent. British and US airborne troops had already landed at either end of the invasion beaches, and a vast armada of over 5,000 ships was powering over the Channel towards Normandy by the time Pujol and Harris had finished.

Agent 3(3) was now out of the picture. What Harris and Pujol had to say had nothing to do with troop movements in Scotland. The person — the sub-agent dreamed up from Pujol's imagination — who would warn the Germans that one of the most momentous occasions in history was about to begin was none other than the Gibraltarian waiter Fred.

Garbo had not had any contact with Fred since earlier in May, when the former Chislehurst-cave digger now working for the army canteen staff had been given twenty-four hours' leave. After a meeting with his spy chief, he had returned to his job at the military's Hiltingbury Camp, on the south coast, to which all communications with the outside world were closed.

On the night of 5–6 June, however, Fred suddenly and unexpectedly reappeared with vital fresh information. Garbo's message told the Germans what Fred had said, without spelling out what exactly it meant. They could work that out for themselves.

The text read as follows:

Still no word from 3(3)[the Greek sailor in Scotland] *but meanwhile Four* [Fred] *has hastened to London having broken camp* together with two American deserters who had arrived in the camp last Sunday. Discovering the plans of the two men he decided to join them in view of the important news which he would otherwise have been unable to communicate in view of the complete sealing of the camps for the last week. En route he tried to communicate by telephone, using the password prepared in case of emergency, but found that only official calls were being accepted. He therefore continued his journey clandestinely to London in order to report to me personally. He arrived after a difficult journey created by the steps he took to slip through the local vigilance. He states that he wrote to me three days ago announcing anew the distribution of cold rations and vomit bags, etc. to the Third Canadian Division. This letter has not yet reached me due to the delay in the mail. Today he says that after the Third Canadian Division had left Americans came in, rumours having reached him that the Third Canadian Division had embarked. The American troops which are now in the camp are a mixed formation belonging to the 1st US Army. The two Americans who escaped with him through fear of embarking belonged to 926 Signals Corps.

On reading this, Kühlenthal could have no doubt. The references to 'cold rations' and 'vomit bags' made it clear that the Allied forces camped in southern England were on the move

243

and already sailing for France. D-Day, the beginning of the Second Front, was under way.

By 0300 British and US airborne troops were already fighting German troops in Normandy at the eastern and western end of the invasion area. Meanwhile, out to sea, minesweepers were clearing a path for the thousands of vessels now waiting over the horizon.

As Alaric, Pujol had earlier encrypted the message and given it to the Widow to hand on to Agent 4(1), the Radio Operator, to be transmitted to the Germans at the agreed time. In reality, Pujol, Harris, Tar and Hesketh stood around at 35 Crespigny Road as Charlie Haines tapped out the calling signal to Madrid. They were on time, the agreement had been made. At the other end, Kühlenthal and his radio man would be listening.

The Garbo team waited, but there was silence. Haines tried again, but still no answer.

'I don't get it,' he said. 'Normally Fritzy answers right away.'

The five men were puzzled. They had thought the whole thing through so carefully, and had depended on German efficiency and punctuality to allow them to pass the vital message over.

'I'll try again in fifteen minutes,' Haines said.

After a quarter of an hour, however, there was still silence at the other end. Then after half an hour and an hour as well. Whatever they had agreed, there was no one in Madrid to hear their momentous news.

Whether they were out drinking in the late-night bars of the Spanish capital or had simply gone to bed, the Germans had lost their chance to hear a calculated pre-warning of the Overlord invasion.

As a German spy, Garbo was outraged. How on earth could his own side have let him down like this?

As a British double agent, however, Pujol, along with Harris and the others, was delighted. Not only would the Allied troops now land with total surprise on the Normandy beaches, but Garbo could still tell his German masters that he had tried to warn them.

The element of surprise for Overlord had been protected, Kühlenthal would be shamefaced, and Garbo could bask in the glory of being the only German agent who had known the truth about D-Day.

Kühlenthal was not going to miss a single message in the future.

The set-up for the next few days was perfect.

24

Northern France and Southern Germany, 6 June 1944

As Pujol and Harris caught a few hours' sleep in Hendon, 150 miles to the south, 'the most complex and daring military operation in the history of modern warfare' finally got under way.

To the east of the designated landing areas the British 6th Airborne Division successfully attacked and held bridges north of Caen over the River Orne and Caen Canal, strategically vital to hold up any German counter-attacks on that flank. The US 82nd and 101st Airborne Divisions performed a similar, if more chaotic, operation to the west, carrying out a large-scale parachute drop in the Cotentin peninsula. Then, at 0630, came H-Hour — the moment of the first landings. Amphibious craft carried infantrymen of the US 1st Army to the beaches of Utah and Omaha, their arrival timed to avoid German mines and defences exposed by the low water tide. An hour later, British and Canadian troops from the British 2nd Army began landing further east at Gold, Juno and Sword beaches.

Four years had passed since the evacuation from Dunkirk. In that time the sea had helped impede any German invasion of Britain. Now, however, the same defensive advantage had to be overcome to stage an attack in the other direction.

There was much heavy fighting and loss of life as over 150,000 men poured over the Channel in a vast armada. As many as 3,000 Allied soldiers were killed, many from the 1st US Infantry Division landing at 'bloody' Omaha, and the 3rd Canadian Infantry Division, which ran into heavy resistance at Juno. Elsewhere, on the beaches of Utah, Gold and Sword things went relatively well for the Allies, although the British, pushing inland, were unable to capture the nearby city of Caen — one of their main objectives for the day. That failure would cost them heavily over the coming weeks, but Eisenhower and the Allied commanders could be satisfied that by midnight on the first day the five invasion beaches — precious toeholds in the sand — had been secured.

German casualties were high as well that day — perhaps even double those of the invaders. Yet despite offering pockets of determined resistance, the Wehrmacht failed to launch a decisive counter-attack against the Allies before nightfall. In some cases it was down to luck, but the inability of the Germans to coordinate a proper defence strategy owed much to Garbo and the Allied deception plan as a whole, serving to confuse the enemy as to what was actually happening on the day. The vast majority of Allied soldiers were unaware of the umbrella of deception that was easing their progress against the enemy, but Fortitude was already paying important dividends.

Rommel, the man whose presence in France could have made a difference, had only arrived in southern Germany the evening before. He was informed early in the morning that the landings had begun: General Hans Speidel, his deputy, called him once the sightings of the invasion fleet had finally been confirmed. Confusion reigned as to what exactly was happening, however. Others in the German military were reporting at that very moment that the Allies were invading but that the attack was coming in the Pas-de-Calais area.

'How stupid of me. How stupid of me,' Rommel said quietly into the phone.

Ending his call with Speidel, he quickly rang through to Berchtesgaden to cancel his meeting with Hitler, and raced outside, where his car was waiting for him. It would take him most of the day to get back to his command post. As tremendous events unfolded in Normandy, he had to sit in the back of an open-top car, uninformed and unable to issue orders.

Rommel was not the only commander crucially absent from the scene, however. Others had seen the bad-weather reports and decided it was the right moment to take some leave. The nearest armoured division to the Normandy beaches was the 21st Panzer, led by General Edgar Feuchtinger. Close to Hitler and the Nazi party, Feuchtinger had had no combat experience before D-Day and owed his position to his political connections. On 5–6 June he was away from his post, having travelled to Paris to entertain a mistress. When, crucially, his tanks

248

might have rattled the nascent invasion force, he was not in a position to give orders.

Problems on the German side went beyond absent commanders. Arguments over strategies for dealing with the Allies meant that there was no coordinated plan. General Geyr von Schweppenburg insisted on allowing the enemy to land and establish a footing, effectively drawing them in, before launching a full-scale counter-attack, using all the armoured units available.

Meanwhile Rommel countered that they had to be stopped in the first hours or days of landing. They could not be allowed to get a toehold because once they pushed inland their control of the skies (what remained of the Luftwaffe at this stage was concentrated in Germany, defending the country against Allied bombing raids) would make it difficult for German armoured units to move about unscathed. The Panzer formations, with their powerful tanks and superior equipment, had to be sent in quickly, he said, to deal with any threat.

That Rommel was convinced the early stages of the invasion would be crucial made it particularly ironic — and fortunate for the Allies — that he was away when the landing actually began.

Neither side had won in this dispute: neither Geyr nor Rommel's reasoning had prevailed. In the end Hitler himself decided to take control of the armoured Panzer divisions — the units that would make the difference in the battle for France. No one could deploy them anywhere without his approval.

What with the Germans' misreading of the weather, disputes over strategy and a confused command structure, the Allies already enjoyed some much-needed advantages on 6 June. The deception plan of Fortitude South — convincing the Germans that the main attack was going to come over the Pas-de-Calais — was the crucial added ingredient.

As reports — often confused and contradictory — flooded into von Rundstedt's headquarters at St Germain-en-Laye in the early morning hours, the head of the German forces in the west issued an order: the two Panzer units near the Normandy beaches, the Panzer Lehr and the 12th SS Hitler Youth Division, were to move at once towards the invasion zone to repel the Allies.

It went against Hitler's instructions that only *he* could order the armoured reserves to move. No matter, von Rundstedt reasoned. Give the order now and later they could get clearance from Hitler and High Command, currently based in Berchtesgaden with the Führer.

Von Rundstedt sent a message explaining what he had done. 'If [the Panzer Lehr and 12th SS Panzer divisions] assemble quickly and get an early start they can enter the battle on the coast during the day.'

It was still early and the Führer was asleep. Not only that, his underlings refused to waken him, despite the fact that his forces were now fighting the largest amphibious invasion force in the history of warfare. Furthermore, from Berchtesgaden, Colonel-General Jodl of High Command, who had woken by this point and seen the message from France, called back to insist that the Panzer reserves could not be moved. Von Rundstedt's order had to be rescinded immediately and the tanks stopped. Jodl even rang von Rundstedt personally to make sure that his word got through.

The field marshal did as he was told: the armoured units were halted.

Other commanders in France came to the same conclusion as von Rundstedt and tried to free up the Panzer divisions over the course of the morning, all with the same result. Adolf Hitler was still sleeping, and no, the armoured reserves could not be deployed.

'Why?' came the call.

The word from Berchtesgaden was unequivocal. Those on the ground were in 'no position to judge'. High Command enjoyed a clearer view, could see the bigger picture. Normandy was only a sideshow.

'The main landing was going to come at an entirely different place.'

And besides, only the Führer could make the decision.

When, finally, he woke, late in the morning, Hitler was informed of the developments in France. His first reaction was one of glee.

'It couldn't be better,' he said. 'As long as they were in Britain we couldn't get at them. Now we have them where we can destroy them.'

It was time to review the situation and start issuing orders. He was pleased that Jodl had countermanded von Rundstedt's decision to send in the Panzer Lehr and Hitler Youth divisions.

Word from military intelligence assured him even further that the right decision had been made. Colonel Alexis Baron von Rönne, the head of Fremde Heere West (FHW), whose job it was to assess the Allies' military capabilities, sent a report through for Hitler's midday conference.

'While the Anglo-Saxon enemy landing on the Normandy coast represents a large-scale operation,' von Rönne wrote, 'the forces employed comprise only a relatively small portion of the [Allied forces available]. Of the sixty divisions held in southern England only ten to twelve . . . appear to be participating so far . . . Not a single unit of the First United States Army Group [FUSAG] . . . has so far been committed.'

As far as the Germans were concerned, Patton, the Allied general they most feared, was not taking part in the events in Normandy. He was still in Dover with his superior troops waiting for his moment to cross over to Calais. Operation Fortitude was paying important dividends.

Finally, after lunching with the Hungarian prime minister, at 1500 hours, over nine hours after the first Allied soldiers landed on the beaches, Hitler gave word: the Panzer divisions in Normandy — the Panzer Lehr and 12th SS Hitler Youth — could move in and attack the invasion force. It was precisely what commanders in France had been pleading for since first light.

It was too late to inflict significant damage that

day. But the Allies had only just made it onto land and were still highly vulnerable.

Much would depend on how hard the Germans could hit them over the following few days, and how many other Panzer divisions would be sent in.

Tens of thousands of Allied soldiers were now pressed into tiny, liberated patches of Normandy. They had artillery and tanks, air cover from the RAF and USAAF, and the backing of thousands of ships behind them in the Channel. Yet they would be helpless if the Germans rapidly sent in their best forces to engage them.

Success now depended on the deceivers back in London, with the Garbo team poised to act. Would the months of preparation, of lying and hoodwinking, be enough?

25

London, 6 June 1944

Pujol, Harris and Haines took turns to sleep during the night of 5–6 June. After their D-Day message had failed to get through, one of them would check the radio at regular intervals to see if there was any signal coming back from Kühlenthal in Madrid. The sun was rising and Pujol began to reflect on his work, on his family back in Spain, and on the lives that were being lost across the Channel at that very moment on the beaches of France.

The new day was a Tuesday. There was a traditional Spanish saying: *Martes — ni te cases ni te embarques.* It was meant to be the worst day of the week for getting married or setting sail. Would the Allied soldiers crossing the Channel be fortunate or unfortunate that day?

Moments later Harris woke up and they exchanged a few words. Harris was as optimistic as ever, and now he had to head back to St James's Street: it had been a busy night but the days ahead would be even busier.

Despite the failure to communicate with the Germans during the night, the deception plan was still alive. There had been no word over the fate of Johnny Jebsen: MI5 were working on the assumption that the double-cross system had not been blown, that the Abwehr man had given little, or perhaps nothing, away. Although for how much longer was not certain.

The person who did put a spanner in the works at this most crucial moment, however, was the least expected — Prime Minister Winston Churchill.

All concerned knew that the idea behind Fortitude was to convince the Germans that Normandy was a feint, and that the main thrust of the invasion would come later over the Pas-de-Calais. It was a deception about a deception. As such all efforts had to be made to avoid references in public to any possibility of a second invasion force — otherwise the Germans might suspect that this was just a ruse. If not, why talk about it? Blurting out the 'secret' made it no secret at all.

But that was precisely what Churchill did in his morning speech to the House of Commons on 6 June. Harris had seen a copy the day before, but there was nothing MI5 could do to have it changed. Despite knowing everything about the deception plan, and being aware that all ministers and commentators had been asked not to speculate on any other possible landings in France, Churchill went ahead and effectively let the cat out of the bag.

After talking at some length about recent developments in Italy, and the fall of Rome, the Prime Minister finally commented on the events of the previous night, and the fierce fighting that was taking place on the beachheads as he spoke.

'I have to announce to the House that during the night and the early hours of this morning the

255

first of the series of landings in force upon the European continent has taken place ... There are already hopes that actual tactical surprise has been attained, and we hope to furnish the enemy with a succession of surprises during the course of the fighting ... All this, although a very valuable first step — a vital and essential first step — gives no indication of what may be the course of the battle in the next days and weeks, because the enemy will now probably endeavour to concentrate on this area, and in that event heavy fighting will soon begin and will continue without end, as we can push troops in and he can bring other troops up.'

On hearing this, the Germans might be expected to wonder why, if the Allies were secretly preparing for a second attack, Churchill was openly talking about such a possibility. What if the whole thing was just a hoax?

The problem was exacerbated by Eisenhower's radio broadcast that same morning to the people of Western Europe, in which he talked of the Normandy landings as an 'initial assault'. Clearly the implication was that more were to come. Which again begged the question.

The Normandy campaign had begun, and Garbo's most important work was still ahead of him. Now, however, the very foundations of the deception plan were being shaken. Harris and Pujol had to limit the damage as quickly as they could.

In theory Garbo still did not know that his message of the night before had not gone through in the early hours as planned. His reaction on learning of the Germans' lapse would come later. In the meantime, in preparation for that evening's reports to Madrid, Harris and Pujol concocted a story about Garbo heading off in the morning to his job at the Ministry of Information.

I arrived to find the Department already in a complete state of chaos, everyone speculating as to the importance of the attack which had started this morning against France.

At the Ministry, Garbo received a copy of a special directive issued by the Political Warfare Executive, the British propaganda agency, which he passed on to the Germans. It clearly stated that 'care must be taken to avoid any reference to further attacks and diversions', and that 'speculation regarding alternative assault areas must be avoided'.

The plan was, Harris argued, that the Germans would read this 'directive' in reverse, and therefore come to the conclusions that the Allies wanted them to. The only problem was that Churchill and Eisenhower were busy undermining the scheme.

The Garbo solution was to attack it head on, and try to bluff his way through.

In his message, Garbo said that he brought this very discrepancy up with his boss at the Ministry — his unwitting agent J(3) — pointing out that the directive was in complete contradiction to the Prime Minister and Supreme Commander's speeches. He had told J(3):

It was inevitable that these speeches would be quoted and used as the basis of propaganda by the World Press.

As was often the case with Garbo, the job of explaining away difficult truths was given over to someone else, someone who did not really exist.

J(3) told Garbo that he had seen the one flaw in the directive plan. Eisenhower, he said, was in a bind: he needed to stop people from rising too soon against the Germans in areas where there was yet to be any fighting, but he had to keep that information from the enemy at the same time. Hence the broadcast. As Harris later wrote, they needed to convince the Germans that sometimes great men were bound to tell 'the truth' to their people, even if that truth went against security interests.

In the end, J(3) tried to shrug the matter off.

He said he did not think the enemy would be able to draw any definite conclusions from these speeches.

Pujol and Harris had to leave it at that and hope for the best. At least they might sow some doubt in the Germans' minds about the meaning of the two speeches, and what the Allies' real intentions were.

In the meantime they had to carry on as normal, and prepare for a more important message to come over the course of the next few days: before finishing and handing over the text to be enciphered and sent over the airwaves to

Madrid, Garbo mentioned that he had called all his active agents to London for an urgent conference.

There was, of course, the business of the message of the night before — the warning about D-Day in the early hours, which the Germans had failed to pick up at the scheduled time.

Pujol and Harris knew that the message had not finally been sent until 0800, when the German radio operator in Madrid finally came back on air. But the Germans did not know that they knew that. So they had to pretend. One can only imagine the smiles on their faces as they wrote out the final paragraph of their evening message.

The Allies, Garbo wrote triumphantly, had been

robbed of the surprise which they wished to create through the information from [Agent] Four [Fred the Gibraltarian], as from the hour at which the assault is said to have started I am able to prove with satisfaction that my messages arrived in time to prevent the action coming as a surprise to our High Command. There is no doubt that Four has accomplished through this action a service which, though it will make it impossible to use his collaboration in the future, has justified a sacrifice by his last report.

Except that the Germans had not been listening when they were supposed to.

Continuing with the drama that was put on for

Kühlenthal, moments after handing his evening message over to his radio operator, Garbo then hurriedly scribbled down a further text to be sent immediately afterwards. It was only now, he said, that the Widow had told him that his message had not gone out at 0300 after all, and was not able to be sent until much later. He had been robbed of his great coup, his moment of glory.

This makes me question your seriousness and your sense of responsibility. I therefore demand a clarification immediately as to what has occurred . . . I am very disgusted as in this struggle for life or death I cannot accept excuses or negligence. I cannot masticate the idea of endangering the service without any benefit. Were it not for my ideals and faith I would abandon this work as having proved myself a failure. I write these messages to send this very night though my tiredness and exhaustion due to the excessive work which I have had has completely broken me.

The tiredness was almost certainly real — Pujol and Harris were working very long hours at this point. Yet everything else — the indignation, the sense of victimhood — was all vintage Garbo. It was a trick he had used before: acting like a jilted lover, slapping his supposed masters down until they effectively became his playthings. Harris and others in MI5 laughed out loud when they read what Pujol had written: it was like something that Hitler himself might have said.

If anything, it was the best possible outcome. Not only could Garbo claim to have had prior knowledge of the D-Day landings, thus raising his status to a super-spy in the Germans' eyes, but he could now also berate them for their failures.

When it came, Kühlenthal's reply was suitably grovelling.

I have read your two messages of yesterday, and I perfectly well understand your state of morale ... It would be difficult if not impossible to find out who is to blame if a culprit really exists, with regard to the delay in the transmission of the message of Four.

He went on to suggest that perhaps Garbo's radio operator was at fault. He was, after all, unaware of what Garbo's messages really contained, believing him to be a Spanish Republican sympathiser. As such, not understanding the importance of that particular message and its need to go out at 0300, he might have gone to sleep and not sent it until later on.

Kühlenthal's attempt to cover up for himself was risible, as Pujol, Harris, Tar Robertson and Roger Hesketh had all been standing over Charlie Haines at the given hour when the message was supposed to have gone out.

Still, the German spy chief recognised that there had been a mistake, and made efforts to soothe his prize agent's wounded pride.

261

*I reiterate to you, as responsible chief of the
service, and to all your collaborators, our
total recognition of your perfect and cherished work and I beg of you to continue with
us in the supreme and decisive hours of the
struggle for the future of Europe.*

'Perfect and cherished work' . . . Kühlenthal
was now both repentant and malleable — putty
in Harris and Pujol's hands.

26

Northern France, Southern Germany and Belgium, 6–9 June 1944

Their weathermen had let them down and their best commanders had been absent at the crucial hour, but the Germans did have a certain amount of good luck on their side on 6 June.

As night fell over the western, US sector of the landing area, German infantrymen near Omaha beach made a discovery. Floating in the waters of the River Vire was a little boat. Inside, the soldiers found the body of a US officer who had been killed in action earlier in the day. And chained to his body was a briefcase.

It did not take long for the briefcase to reach the division's operations officer, and when he opened it he could not believe his eyes. There in front of him were the operational orders of the US units that had landed at Utah beach. Almost all the details that he could have wanted about which American divisions had landed and their scheme of manoeuvre were laid out for him. It was highly valuable information for the battles in the days ahead, particularly as stamped on the cover of the documents it clearly said, in English, 'Destroy Before Embarkation'. For whatever reason, the US officer had failed to do so, bringing the valuable pieces of paper along with him. And now they were in the hands of the enemy.

Amazingly enough, the next day, 7 June, soldiers from the same German division also found a very similar document — which again should never have been brought as far as the landing beaches — on the body of another dead US officer in the Omaha sector, giving similar details.

Both sets of papers were soon in the hands of Generalleutnant Max Pemsel, chief of staff of the German 7th Army, which was tasked with defending Normandy. As he pored over them, noting the US divisions that were now involved, and the vast numbers of men and equipment being shipped over the Channel to what had previously been a quiet little corner of France, he came to a chilling conclusion: the Normandy landings that had started the morning before must actually be the real thing.

'The great expansion of the American bridgehead', he said, 'led to the conclusion that this operation required such a large number of American forces that a second landing at another point [e.g. the Pas-de-Calais] was not likely at all.'

Operation Fortitude, and the carefully laid-out plans to convince the Germans that Normandy was just a feint, had been rumbled. Thanks to a couple of officers who had disobeyed orders and carried operational plans with them into battle, not only were tens of thousands of Allied lives at stake, but the future of Operation Overlord and the liberation of France from the Nazis now hung in the balance.

News of the documents, and the intelligence

they contained, moved higher up the chain of command and arrived at La Roche-Guyon early on the morning of 8 June. Rommel was delighted. Finally he had what he needed to get Hitler to release the Panzer divisions that he had been holding back the day before. This was it — Normandy was the real Second Front. There was just time to hit the Allies hard with everything the Wehrmacht had available.

Von Rundstedt agreed, and quickly got on the phone to High Command in Berchtesgaden.

There were doubters: General Blumentritt, von Rundstedt's chief of staff, wondered if the documents might not be a plant. What if the Allies had deliberately left the papers on the officers for the Germans to find, in order to confuse them? It would not have been the first time they had carried out such a stunt . . .

Rommel was adamant, though. The Normandy landings were strategic, no mere diversion. There was not a moment to lose.

High Command took von Rundstedt's request to Hitler, who by now had seen copies of the documents found on the US officers. He did not reply immediately, but when the call came back the news was good: the Führer agreed.

The Panzer divisions were now in Rommel and von Rundstedt's hands. They wasted no time.

As Allied soldiers on the ground were painfully discovering, the 21st Panzer, Panzer Lehr and 12th SS Panzer Hitler Youth divisions were already in Normandy, doing all they could to halt their advance. To their number were now to be added 2nd Panzer, 116 Panzer, and the 2nd SS Panzer Division, driving up from their base in Toulouse.

Not only that, Hitler had ordered that his best fighting unit, the 1st SS Panzer Division Leibstandarte Adolf Hitler (LAH), which was now stationed in Belgium, should attack as well.

It was known as 'Case Three' — the Allies' nightmare scenario in which all the Germans' available armoured reserves were sent into Normandy to crush the invasion. This was now happening. Almost as soon as it had begun, Operation Overlord was in danger of being snuffed out.

★ ★ ★

In Hasselt, northern Flanders, the waiting was over. After months of refitting, training his new recruits and rebuilding his Panzer regiment into a fearsome fighting unit, Jochen Peiper was ready to go. The nights spent reading quietly in quasi-monastic abstinence while his fellow officers went out drinking and cavorting with the local girls had ended.

The LAH was put on alert, and during the night of 8–9 June the SS men prepared for the order to move out at first light, readying their combat and supply vehicles for the journey across northern France to the battle zone.

The division itself now numbered around 20,000 men, of whom 12,000 were considered to be 'bayonet', or combat, forces. Peiper's regiment had already been equipped with over sixty tanks — including the deadly Panthers — and more were on the way. Under the command of Teddy Wisch, the LAH was a crack force, battle-hardened from its brutal experiences on the Eastern Front.

As dawn broke on 9 June, the first tanks and armoured cars fired up, and the LAH started moving out.

Jochen Peiper was on his way to Normandy.

PART SEVEN

'We must be practical. The important bee to deceive is the Queen Bee. Can you see which is the Queen Bee from down there?'
A.A. Milne, *Winnie-the-Pooh*

27

London, 9 June 1944

It was Harris's idea to wait until the Germans had actually started sending their armoured reserves into Normandy before making a move. That way, he argued, if they could be made to turn around, German High Command was less likely to change its mind again in a hurry, and as a result they would keep the dangerous SS Panzer divisions away from the Allied troops for longer.

It was a good theory. But would it work?

Some of the deception planners in MI5, SHAEF and the London Controlling Section had their doubts. What if the Germans did not fall for the idea of a second landing in the Pas-de-Calais? What if, once the tanks and heavy weaponry had set off on their journey towards Normandy, they could not be stopped? Surely it would be better to prevent them from moving out in the first place?

It was a huge risk, and everything hung in the balance. Sufficient evidence to give Harris's plan the green light eventually came from an unusual source, however.

On 27 May, the Japanese Ambassador to Berlin, Baron Hiroshi Ōshima, had met Hitler at Berchtesgaden. A fluent German speaker, Ōshima was a lieutenant-general in the Japanese Imperial Army and had become a confidant of the Führer over

271

the course of his postings to the Third Reich. Ōshima was an avid supporter of Nazism, and he diligently reported back to Tokyo every conversation and observation as he toured Germany and the occupied countries. Thanks to his keen military eye, these even included troop positions and movements. What Ōshima did not know — and up to his death in 1975 he remained ignorant of this — was that his communications with the Japanese government were being tapped and deciphered by the Americans in a project known as 'Magic'. So good was the intelligence that he unwittingly passed over to the enemy that US General George C. Marshall declared after the war that Ōshima had been 'our main basis of information regarding Hitler's intentions in Europe'.

The US decrypts were being shared with the British, and it was thanks to the reported conversation that Ōshima had with Hitler just over a week before the Allied invasion of France that the deceivers in London were able to see with their own eyes that Harris's idea had a chance of success.

The seeds of Fortitude, it appeared, had fallen on fertile ground.

Speaking of the Second Front, [Ōshima told Tokyo in his 27 May report] *Hitler said that he, himself, thought that sooner or later operations for the invasion of Europe would be undertaken. He thought that about eighty divisions had already been assembled in England . . .*

There were in fact only forty-seven.
Ōshima continued:

I then asked him in what form he thought the Second Front would materialise, and he told me that at the moment what he himself thought was most probable was that after having carried out diversionary operations in Norway, Denmark and the southern part of the west coast of France and the French Mediterranean coast, they would establish a bridgehead in Normandy or Brittany, and after seeing how things went would then embark upon the establishment of the real Second Front in the channel.

Hitler was thinking what the Allies wanted him to think. He had successfully fallen into the trap of assuming that Normandy (or Brittany) would itself be a diversion before a bigger assault at the narrowest stretch of the Channel — from Dover to Calais.

It was enough for Harris to be given the permission he needed: he could go ahead with his plan. The SS tanks could set off for Normandy first before Garbo attempted to have them sent back.

On 8 June, two days after the landings had begun, the news the Allies dreaded came through. German armoured reserves, including the 1st SS Panzer Division LAH, had been ordered to Normandy. 'Case Three' was a reality. RAF Typhoons, bombing the German columns as they travelled along French roads by day, could slow them down to some extent, but the Panthers and Tigers could move relatively easily by night. It was a question of hours, days at most, before these hardened Nazi troops would be attacking Allied soldiers on the ground.

It was at this very moment, as Jochen Peiper and his men began to move out from their positions in Belgium, that Garbo sent Kühlenthal 'the most important report of his career'.

The message went out, as usual, from the radio set in Hendon. But just to be certain that the Germans would be listening, Garbo sent them a taster earlier in the evening.

I have had an extremely agitated day today. But I have the satisfaction of being able to give you the most important reports of my work. As I have not got all the messages ready I hope you will be listening tonight.

The last line was a clear reference to the German no-show of three nights before. This time there could be no excuses: for the Allies, this was a message that Kühlenthal absolutely must read.

Garbo came back on air with his news a few hours later, at seven minutes past midnight. It was now 9 June.

Everything — the outcome of the Second Front, the outcome of the war itself — depended on how the Germans reacted to what he had to say. The months of preparation, the lessons learned from the mistakes of Operation Cockade, and the painstaking and detailed work that had gone into creating Garbo — from the fear and anxiety of Pujol sweating over his false

274

reports from Lisbon, to the great network of fictional sub-agents and collaborators dreamed up with Harris from a cramped office off Piccadilly — now focused on this one moment, this one message. And to be absolutely clear, so that there could be no doubt in the Germans' minds about what he was trying to tell them, he broke almost every rule in the spy's guidebook.

He began slowly, almost low-key. But then Garbo was not only a master double agent, he was a master storyteller. Move in gently, and save the best for last.

There was, he told Kühlenthal, an argument brewing between neutral embassies in London and the British government over lifting the ban on diplomatic communications that had been imposed in the run-up to D-Day. The information came from Garbo's mistress, J(5), with whom he had spent the previous night. Why continue to prevent diplomats from reporting back to their respective governments now that the landings had actually taken place? went the argument. There was no need for any more security, any fear that the date and place for the invasion might inadvertently leak out now that operations had begun. But the word from the top came that the ban had to remain. The only logical conclusion was that there were more landings to come . . .

Stepping things up a little, Garbo then reported the lunch he had had that day with a friend of Fred the Gibraltarian. Agent 4(3) was a pro-Franco member of the US Service of Supply based in London who had been recruited to the

Garbo network in late 1943. Now, just a couple of days after D-Day, he passed on 'an interesting bit of information'.

He told me that FUSAG had not entered into the present operation.

General Patton's First US Army Group (FUSAG) was the large fictional unit which Garbo had helped conjure up in the enemy's mind. The fact that this powerful force was still in south-east England now that the invasion had begun was suspicious.

Charlie Haines had been transmitting for half an hour by this point, but the real meat of Garbo's message was still to come.

Racheting up the tension, Garbo then moved to the detailed information that his sub-agents had brought in from various points on the south-east coast. It was here that the Brothers in the Aryan World Order came into their own: Sub-agent 7(2), David, the founder of the movement, now based in Dover, known to the Germans as 'Donny'; Sub-agent 7(4), Rags, the Indian poet and lover of group secretary Theresa Jardine, based in Brighton, known to the Germans as 'Dick'; and Sub-agent 7(7), group treasurer based in the Harwich and Ipswich area. Garbo never named him, but Kühlenthal referred to him as 'Dorrick'.

These fanatical Nazis had passed on to Pedro, Garbo's deputy, news about the various Allied divisions that were *still* stationed in their respective areas.

Garbo began forwarding long lists from each of the sub-agents detailing these units.

7(2) reports that the following divisions are to be found in his area without any indications that they are to embark for the moment: the 59th Division, the 43rd Division . . .

7(4) reports that the following divisions are to be found in his area without indication of embarking at present: South Eastern Command, 1st Canadian Army . . .

7(7) reports that the activity in his area has greatly increased, giving the following divisions stationed without indication of embarking for the moment: 28th US Division, 6th US Armored Division . . . He furthermore said that he had learned through a well-informed channel that there are more than a hundred tank transport barges capable of transporting about five hundred tanks.

Garbo had now been transmitting for over an hour and a half. If he had been a real German spy he almost certainly would have been caught by this point, as by staying on air for so long he would easily have been picked up by the Radio Security Service as they homed in on unauthorised signals and their source. As it was, Kühlenthal did not suspect anything: the information that his Arabal network was providing him was first class.

Garbo was about to break another rule, however, as he moved into the final and most important section of his message. Spies were meant to pass on hard information, not speculate or give their opinions. But Garbo was no ordinary spy; he was, in the Germans' eyes, a spymaster, the head of a valuable and widespread ring of agents running around enemy territory. He was on the ground and could give them a much-needed eyewitness view of how things looked from the other side. As such he was a man whose opinions, they had learned over time, had to be listened to and respected.

And besides, experience had shown that trying to get the Germans to work things out for themselves was rarely successful. This time everything would be spelled out for them, in black and white.

It was 0144 hours. Time to move in for the kill.

Charlie Haines tapped out the most important part of his message.

From the reports mentioned it is perfectly clear that the present attack is a large scale operation but diversionary in character for the purposes of establishing a strong bridgehead in order to draw the maximum of our reserves to the area of operation to retain them there so as to be able to strike the blow somewhere else with ensured success.

Garbo knew that he was crossing a line here, so his next sentence was carefully chosen.

I never like to give my opinion unless I have strong reasons to justify my assurances. Thus

278

*the fact that these concentrations which are
in the east and south east of the island are
now inactive means that they must be held
in reserve to be employed in the other large-
scale operations.*

So far so good: everything pointed to another
Allied assault subsequent to Normandy. The
question was, where?

*The constant aerial bombardment which the
area of the Pas de Calais has suffered and
the strategic disposition of these forces give
reason to suspect an attack in that region of
France which at the same time offers the
shortest route for the final objective of their
illusions, which is to say, Berlin.*

To underline his point, Garbo returned to
another piece of information he had gleaned the
night before from his mistress.

*From J(5) I learned yesterday that there
were 75 Divisions in this country before the
present assault commenced. Supposing they
should use a maximum of twenty to twenty-
five Divisions they would be left with some
fifty Divisions with which to attempt a second
blow.*

The message was clear, nothing more could be
said.

The only thing was to make sure that the
intelligence Kühlenthal was now receiving went

straight to German High Command.

Like a puppetmaster, gently pulling strings from faraway Hendon, Garbo urged his supposed spymaster in Madrid to act:

I trust you will submit urgently all these reports and studies to our High Command since moments may be decisive in these times and before taking a false step through lack of knowledge of the necessary facts they should have in their possession all the present information which I transmit with my opinion which is based in the belief that the whole of the present attack is set as a trap for the enemy to make us move all our reserves in a hurried strategical disposition which we would later regret.

It was done. It was ten past two in the morning. Charlie Haines and the rest of the Garbo team could finally go to bed.

Would the message get through? Even assuming that Garbo's words got passed up through German intelligence to reach High Command, would anyone be listening? Could the Panzer divisions now tearing down to Normandy be stopped?

All Pujol and Harris could do was wait.

28

Madrid, Germany and the Pas-de-Calais, 9–10 June 1944

Garbo's message had successfully been radioed across to the German intelligence station in Madrid — this time they had been listening . . . So far, so good. Everyone in Allied deception now waited on tenterhooks to see if his words would filter through the enemy's secret service all the way to German High Command. Even if it made it that far, however, there was the question of whether it was enough to halt the enemy's tank reserves.

Having been received overnight, Garbo's message had to be decoded into clear script at the other end before anyone could read it. It was long, and the process took some time. It would have been mid-morning on 9 June by the time that Kühlenthal finally read the last lines, and the warning that the Normandy landings were a trap.

He wasted no time, quickly writing a report based on Garbo's text — using whole phrases verbatim. This was then encoded once again and sent via Enigma machine to the German secret service HQ in Berlin.

Kühlenthal had performed his part; his link in the chain had held firm. This fact alone, however, was little short of remarkable. Only a short time earlier his own mentor, Admiral Canaris, had been deposed by Himmler and the Abwehr had effectively been closed down. Long suspicious of the diminutive spymaster and his true loyalty to the Nazi regime, Himmler had built up a dossier of mistakes and treacherous behaviour by members of the Abwehr, using it to get rid of its chief. Canaris was given an insignificant desk job, and the SD — Himmler's parallel Nazi intelligence agency — took over the running of the Abwehr stations and machinery.

It was a personal blow to Kühlenthal: the man who had mentored and safeguarded his position was now removed from power. Kühlenthal was working directly for the very people who would persecute him over his Jewish blood.

Somehow he had managed to survive — not because of any lack of zeal on the part of the Nazi ideologues. The extermination of Jews was accelerating at this stage in the war, unaffected by the military reverses of the Wehrmacht on the battlefields. His certificate of 'Aryanisation' was a legal fig leaf. He was still vulnerable — now more than ever. The number of secret service staff at the German Embassy in Madrid was reduced to only a hundred and twenty-nine. Of these, forty-two were forced out into offices dotted around the city, losing the diplomatic protection that the embassy afforded them. Kühlenthal survived because he was allowed to, because of his worth to the whole German intelligence and military system.

What saved him was Arabal — Garbo.

No one was about to remove an intelligence

chief with an entire network of agents working for him from inside enemy territory. Take Kühlenthal away, the trusted link and case officer, and the whole enterprise might unravel. Kühlenthal might be quarter-Jewish, but he was useful. With much of his intelligence system dismantled, the Arabal traffic was practically all he had left.

And now he had just been handed a message from his top man in London that might change the course of the war. He had to get it to the right people as quickly as possible.

The intelligence men in Berlin were the next link in the chain. With all the recent changes since the SD takeover of the Abwehr, the operation was not running as smoothly as it might. It posed a danger at this critical moment — not only for the Germans, but for the Allies, who were relying on the flow of communications within German intelligence in order to feed misinformation.

With Canaris gone, the man in charge of foreign intelligence was Walter Schellenberg, a thirty-four-year-old Nazi and Himmler protégé. Bright, hard-working and ambitious, Schellenberg had masterminded the Venlo Incident that had so out-foxed MI6 at the start of the war. He kept a list of over 2,000 people who were to be immediately arrested after an invasion of Britain, had a desk in his office with machine guns built into it that could be fired at the press of a button, and was rumoured to have been the lover in Paris of the fashion designer Coco Chanel.

Busy with his reorganisation of the German

secret services after Canaris's fall, commonly working twenty-hour days, he had removed many Abwehr men from their foreign postings and replaced them with SD members — true believers. The Abwehr itself ceased officially to exist on I June, just days before D-Day. Kühlenthal, however, was still in his post. And when his message reporting Garbo's text came through, Schellenberg's organisation quickly and unquestioningly passed it on to the relevant bodies within the Wehrmacht.

Miraculously, the next step had been successfully completed.

The first intelligence man within the armed forces to read Garbo's message was Colonel von Rönne, the head of Fremde Heere West (FHW).

Owing to the intensive Allied bombing of Berlin, much of the military command structure had moved to the town of Zossen, just to the south of the capital. It was here that Schellenberg and von Rönne both had offices in the headquarters of the German High Command.

Von Rönne was not a Nazi. In fact he was a member of the movement now plotting to remove Hitler from power. But he came from an aristocratic German family and was loyal to the German military. Not only that, he was quick and extremely competent — some of his colleagues regarded him as something of a genius when it came to military and intelligence matters. More importantly, Hitler himself — unaware of von Rönne's political sympathies — trusted his judgement.

Tall, slim and with round spectacles perched on his large hooked nose, von Rönne now pored over the report from Madrid. The FHW's job was to evaluate the Allies' strength in the west, basing their conclusions on all sources of evidence available: intercepted military communications, interrogations with POWs, photographs from spy planes, and reports from spies working behind enemy lines.

Garbo's message fell clearly into the last category: because of the difficulty of flying over Britain at the time, information from agents in the field had now become the main source of information for the FHW's assessments. In general, owing to the bad name that the Abwehr had earned itself over the previous years, there was suspicion in German military circles about spies' reports. They had shown themselves too often to be unreliable. But this particular agent in London had proved his worth — his earlier material had been good and von Rönne had come across his reports before.

The latest message came complete with eyewitness sightings of Allied divisions based in south-east England from three different sub-agents. The London spymaster's conclusions were therefore backed up by evidence. He was surely right — Normandy was a trap into which they must not fall. Besides, it made better military sense to invade the Pas-de-Calais, the closest point to the British coast.

Von Rönne's immediate response was to call the two generals closest to Hitler at that time: the head of German High Command, Field Marshal

Wilhelm Keitel; and his chief of operations Colonel-General Alfred Jodl. Both were in Berchtesgaden with Hitler, and both agreed with von Rönne's assessment of this new, highly valuable report from the London-based spy. They had to act quickly before it was too late.

Subsequently, and with the clearance of High Command, von Rönne issued an initial warning from FHW to all commands in the west:

In all probability major landing by enemy on the Belgian coast is to be expected on June 10. Withdrawal of our forces from 15th Army sector [Pas-de-Calais and Belgium] untenable.

The second line was a clear reference to Hitler's order the previous day that the Panzer reserves could be sent into Normandy. From that moment the Führer's best troops of the 1st SS Panzer Division LAH had begun to move from Belgium westwards towards the invasion area. And they were making steady progress. If this armoured force was allowed to carry on much further it would be difficult to haul them back to Calais in time for the expected second prong of the Allied invasion. Added to the other formations that had been released for Normandy by Hitler's order, a total of 50,000 soldiers with around 500 tanks were falling into the trap that the Allies had so carefully laid, and which the Germans' spy network in London was now warning them about, just in time.

Garbo's message had already worked its way

close to the top of the German military hierarchy, unhindered and virtually unchanged from the original words first shaped by Harris and Pujol, encrypted and then transmitted by radio by Charlie Haines in the middle of the night from a modest, rather drab north London house.

But von Rönne's assessment alone was not enough. The Panther tanks of Jochen Peiper's Panzer regiment were still rumbling along the roads of northern France towards the Allied invasion force in Normandy. Only one man could stop them now, make them turn around and head back the other way.

Already that morning Hitler had ordered the 9th and 10th SS Panzer divisions from their rest posting in Poland to Normandy. Together they numbered 35,000 men and had 350 tanks, but they would take weeks to cross the Reich from east to west and reach their destination. Rommel and von Rundstedt in France needed armoured reserves immediately if they were successfully to snuff out the Allies while they were still vulnerable. Hitler's order of the day before had given them just what they needed.

But now, with Garbo's message and von Rönne's subsequent warning of a new and imminent Allied attack, there was a dilemma. Allow the Panzer reserves to carry on to Normandy and risk weakening the defences around Calais? Or send them to Calais, and thereby weaken the response to the Normandy landings that had already taken place?

Von Rönne had made up his mind. The

question was whether the Führer could be made to change his.

Just before midday von Rönne called the intelligence liaison officer at Berchtesgaden, Colonel Freidrich-Adolf Krummacher. Krummacher was Hitler's personal intelligence officer, the link between intelligence and High Command. He was also a former Abwehr man, and as such had a greater trust for reports sent in by spies.

Von Rönne explained the situation quickly to Krummacher, reiterating the fact that he had evidence that suggested a new invasion of France was about to be launched from eastern England, and that therefore the Panzer forces had to be stopped at all costs and sent up to Calais.

Krummacher was about to go into the midday conference, where Hitler discussed military matters with his commanders and staff. He told von Rönne that he would pass on the information to the Führer and rang off.

But Hitler was not in the mood just then to change his mind. Listening to both von Rönne and Jodl make the point, he agreed that an attack on Calais made sense, that it was what he had expected all along. Had he not told Japanese Ambassador Ōshima that just such an eventuality would occur?

Nonetheless, he could not be sure. He would not, he said, change the order. Or at least not yet. He would think about it and make up his mind at the midnight conference later on.

Peiper's tanks kept moving towards Normandy.

Before the midnight meeting took place, however, the actual text of Garbo's message to Kühlenthal reached Berchtesgaden itself, and Krummacher was able to read almost the exact words of the Germans' top spy in London, as reported by the head of the Madrid station:

After personal consultation on 8th June in London with my agents Jonny [this was a misprint for 'Donny'], Dick and Dorrick, whose reports were sent today, I am of the opinion, in the view of the strong troop concentrations in South-East and Eastern England which are not taking part in the present operations, that these operations are a diversionary manoeuvre designed to draw off the enemy reserves in order then to make a decisive attack in another place. In view of the continued air attacks on the concentration area mentioned, which is a strategically favourable position for this, it may very probably take place in the Pas de Calais area, particularly since in such an attack the proximity of air bases will facilitate the operation by providing continued strong air support.

The text came complete with an evaluation from German intelligence in Zossen:

The report is credible. The reports received in the last week from the Arabal undertaking have been confirmed without exception and are to be described as especially valuable. The main line of investigation in future is to be the enemy group of forces in South-Eastern and Eastern England.

Had Harris and Pujol been able to read the assessment of their message at this moment, and the high esteem in which Garbo was now held by the Germans, they might well have danced for joy.

As it was, Krummacher underlined the passage in the text about a 'diversionary manoeuvre designed to draw off enemy reserves in order to make a decisive attack in another place'. He then wrote his own comment at the bottom: 'Confirms the view already held by us that a further attack is to be expected in another place (Belgium?)'

The midnight conference was approaching. Krummacher showed Garbo's message to Jodl, who underlined the words 'in South-East and Eastern England', and then took it in to show Hitler.

It was precisely what the Führer needed to see. Reading Garbo's actual words put paid to his earlier indecisiveness. There were other reports as well that added to its impact — that US General Marshall was soon to be visiting Patton's FUSAG HQ, while a message to the Belgian resistance had been decrypted on the 8th which called for guerrilla action to start the following day.

It all pointed to the Pas-de-Calais area, where Hitler's superior fighters — the LAH — had been stationed only the day before, and from which he himself had ordered them away.

There was still time. They could be turned back. He needed his best troops in the right place to receive the most threatening Allied forces — Patton and his FUSAG poised just over the Channel for a second assault.

Garbo's message, straight from London, had tipped the balance and given Hitler the evidence he needed to reach his decision. He issued new orders immediately.

Keitel telephoned through to von Rundstedt in France. The next morning, at 0730 on 10 June, von Rundstedt issued the following message:

As a consequence of certain information, C-in-C West has declared a 'state of alarm II' for the 15th Army in Belgium and North France. The move of 1st SS Panzer Division will therefore be halted.

Jochen Peiper and the tanks of the LAH were on the road. Now news came through that they had to change direction. Not to Normandy after all, but to the area just east of Bruges, behind the infantry of the German 15th Army, where a second, bigger and more important Allied invasion was expected at any moment.

Following their orders to the letter, they halted and turned around as quickly as possible to head to their new posting.

They were the right men for the job: ruthless vanquishers of the Reds on the Eastern Front, equipped with the best tanks in the world, lovers of fighting for its own sake and with a cause they

291

were prepared to die for. They could take on the best that General Patton could throw at them and hurl the Allies back into the Channel.

Within hours, the new orders had been carried out, and the LAH took up its defensive positions around the Scheldt River.

Settling down in his new command post, Peiper kept his eyes trained on the horizon, and waited.

29

London, 10 June 1944

In London, military commanders, politicians and deception planners waited nervously to see if their great hoax had worked. A whole community of men and women working in numerous departments now sat on their hands, watching for news that their top double agent's ploy had paid off.

Over the next few hours the Bletchley decrypts would tell them whether it had been a success or a failure. Would Hitler's order for the Panzer units to move into Normandy — the 'Case Three' scenario — remain in force, or would the Führer's mind be changed?

Ronald Wingate of the London Controlling Section was there, an eyewitness at government offices in Whitehall, where US and British chiefs of staff wandered around in an atmosphere 'heavy with tension and pipe and cigarette smoke combined with a faint aroma of good whisky'.

Their card had been played, yet still, according to their information, the Panzer divisions were moving towards the Allied landing areas.

'It was a frightful moment — there were these big red blobs on the war maps moving towards Normandy all the time . . . Would the [German] tanks have to come round through Paris . . . ? Ought we not to bomb the bridges over the

Seine in Paris? Had Garbo overplayed his hand?'

At that moment, the secretary who looked after the Bletchley reports knocked on the door and came in, saying that a message had just been received that might interest them. The British and US chiefs of staff, General Sir Alan Brooke and General George Marshall, were the first to go over and have a look.

'They were all smiles,' Wingate remembered. 'We looked at the Ultra — and there it was: Hitler had cancelled Case Three. We'd won, and what an astonishing moment that was! We knew then that we'd won — there might be very heavy battles, but we'd won.

'There was nobody more astonished than Bevan [head of the London Controlling Section], for I don't think he thought that we'd really pull it off. Brooke's attitude was the oddest. He said if Hitler was such a bloody fool why had it taken us so long to beat him? Then he stalked off.

'The P.M. came in with [head of MI6] Stewart Menzies and the P.M. said this was the crowning achievement of the long and glorious history of the British Secret Service — or something like that.'

Harris and Pujol's gamble appeared to have worked. From being on the brink of suffering a head-on assault from the Führer's fiercest troops, the Allied forces had won crucial breathing space in which to reinforce their positions. Soon they could start pushing from the beachheads deeper into the Normandy countryside. The battle of the numbers — who could get the most men and armour into the combat zone the quickest — was close to being won. Not only had the 1st SS Panzer Division been turned around, but the 116th Panzer Division, which had also been heading for Normandy from the Paris area, had also been rerouted to the Somme. In total seven German divisions which might have descended on the Allies were moved to or kept in the Pas-de-Calais instead.

There was much work still to be done, but no one on the Allied side could have been happier. The most fulsome praise for Garbo's achievement, however, came from the Germans themselves. A few days later Bletchley Park intercepted a message from the FHW assessors in Zussen to Kühlenthal in Madrid repeating the endorsement they had written on the back of of the Garbo message that had reached Hitler.

The report is credible. The reports received in the last week from the Arabal undertaking have been confirmed almost without exception and are to be described as especially valuable . . .

The most important sign that the Germans were pleased with Garbo's work came from none other than Himmler himself. Georg Hansen, now acting as head of German intelligence after the removal of Canaris, sent a message to Kühlenthal expressing appreciation in the name of the SS chief for the work of the Arabal network in England, urging that further intelligence should try to ascertain when the embarkation of Allied troops in the south-east began and what their destination was.

Not only had the Germans fallen for Garbo's trick, they were also applauding his accuracy and usefulness.

Everything had fallen into place. Now all Harris and Pujol had to do was continue telling the story that had diverted the best German troops away from the Allied forces and keep the deception running for as long as possible.

They had pulled off a tremendous coup, yet much heavy and bloody fighting through the Normandy countryside lay ahead. The casualty figures on both sides were becoming comparable with those on the Eastern Front. The battle was far from over and the Panzer forces still had to be held in check.

At this very moment, though, when things were going so well, Hitler launched his much-feared secret weapons on London. As a result, the Garbo operation was thrown into a new crisis which threatened to blow Pujol's cover . . . and destroy everything.

30

London, 13 June–29 July 1944

Those who heard it said it sounded like a motorbike with the silencer removed, or an old steam train struggling to climb a hill. It was early in the morning on 13 June. Without warning the strange noise in the sky stopped and there was silence. A few seconds later came a loud explosion.

When the first V-1 flying bomb hit London, crashing into the East End where the Great Eastern Railway crosses over Grove Road, six people were killed, a further nine were wounded, and some two hundred lost their homes.

The Germans called them *Vergeltungswaffen* — 'vengeance' or 'retaliatory weapons' for the Allied bombing of their cities. Londoners quickly dubbed them 'doodlebugs'. Over the course of the summer as many as a hundred rained down every day causing over 20,000 deaths, almost all of them civilians.

There had been rumours of a new German weapon since the summer of 1943. In September of that year a Swedish journalist wrote an article in the *Telegraph* about a German 'rocket gun' being established on the French coast with which to bombard the British capital. In the same month Tricycle had brought intelligence warning of the same. Pujol and Harris were

297

instructed to try to find out as much as they could from the Germans about the terrifying new weapon, but Kühlenthal remained silent.

Then, in mid-December 1943, Kühlenthal told Garbo that he should leave London.

Circumstances dictate that you should carry out your propositions with regard to setting up your home outside the capital. This warning is strictly confidential for you . . .

It was a clear warning that the new rocket or gun, or whatever it turned out to be, was soon to enter into operation.

Again, Harris and Pujol tried to find out when the attacks might begin, trying to force Kühlenthal, through a complicated story involving the radio operator and setting up a new transmitter, to give the game away, but to no avail.

Pujol and Harris were already in Taplow and Earl's Court. The Pujols stayed at the Amerden Priory Hotel, run by a couple from Valencia, the Terradas. Another guest was the Spanish vice-consul, to whom Pujol repeated his cover story that he was working in the Spanish section of the BBC. A Czech couple were also there, along with a Jewish woman with red hair who asked Pujol to give her Spanish lessons. In the evenings the guests would hold small parties, with Pujol showing off his paso dobles and foxtrots, of which he was rather proud.

Since the showdown of the previous summer, Araceli had been causing fewer problems for MI5, but the threat of a new, unspecified German

298

weapon about to target London could play on her already fraught nerves. Still, by this point Harris and Robertson trusted her to keep her husband's secret; no one vetoed her being so close to a high-ranking member of the Spanish Embassy, especially in the months leading up to D-Day and the great deception. Pujol himself, one assumes, gave assurances that she could be trusted.

On 6 January, Garbo informed Kühlenthal that he had moved. Over the rest of the winter and into the spring, Pujol and Harris tried again without success to get Kühlenthal to tell them what was to come — and when.

In May Bletchley Park deciphered a message from Berlin referring to questionnaires that Madrid was about to receive with the prefix 'Stichling' ('stickleback'). No one at the time knew exactly what this referred to, but the Berlin — Madrid traffic was put on priority watch for any sign of a Stichling message.

Eventually one came through, on 16 June, three days after the first V-1 bombs had landed on London. From Madrid, Kühlenthal passed the Berlin message on to his top agent.

It is of the utmost importance to inform us about the effects of the bombardments. We are not interested in partial details but wish you to communicate results as follows: Take as your basis a plan of London by the publishers 'Pharus' which I suppose you have in your possession and indicate how many targets or missiles have fallen in the determined squares on the plan, defining these by their 'ordinates' and 'co-ordinates' and the approximate hour.

A couple of days later, living in terror of the new unmanned weapons, Pujol stayed in character and replied with pro-Nazi enthusiasm:

> I am proud that you have been able to try out this fantastic reprisal weapon, the creation of German genius. Although I have not seen the apparatus in flight personally, from what I have heard it must be an object of marvel and when the present trials have finished and when the scale on which it is used is increased I am certain that you will have managed to terrify this very pusillanimous people who will never admit that they are beaten.

As a Nazi spy — Alaric, head of the Arabal network — it was what he might be expected to say. As a double agent working for the British, however, he was in trouble. Through the press reports picked up via neutral diplomatic missions, the Germans would eventually discover where their flying bombs were landing. They were clearly asking Garbo to give them as accurate information as possible so that they could fine-tune their range and direction.

If Garbo gave them what they wanted, he was helping the enemy and putting the lives of thousands at risk. Yet if he sent back false information the Germans would eventually realise, by cross-checking with the newspapers, that his reports were wrong and hence begin to question him as a source.

It was paramount to keep up pretences, not to blow his cover. The success of the continuation of Fortitude depended on it. But to do so at the cost of so many people, almost all of them civilians?

The Garbo operation was in a fix.

For the time being, they tried to stall a little, continuing with reports on troop movements, maintaining the threat to the Pas-de-Calais area. There was a real problem, however, with the German instructions: no one could find a copy of the Pharus map of London anywhere. Eventually one was tracked down in the British Library; it turned out to be from before the First World War and had been out of print in Britain since 1908. German intelligence, it turned out, had been basing all its information on London on a map that was entirely out of date.

Garbo eventually told Kühlenthal that it was unobtainable, asking whether he could use the Stanford map instead. Kühlenthal agreed, telling Garbo to pinpoint Tower Bridge, Wandsworth Bridge and Gospel Oak station on the Stanford map so as to be able to locate them on the Pharus edition and cross-refer between the two.

It was now 22 June and Garbo had managed to pass a few days without giving over important information on the doodlebugs, but he could not stall for ever. On the same day he gave a half-hearted report about flying bombs landing in Bayswater Road, Hyde Park and other areas of the city, without specifying at what time they had hit.

He also wrote a long letter to Kühlenthal marked 'strictly personal'. In it Garbo questioned the usefulness of the new weapon. The bombs were causing minimal damage, he said, while the lowering of morale had only been temporary. Now, almost a week since the first V-1s, far from being afraid of them, Londoners were actually ridiculing them. They were proving ineffective both as a military and a propaganda weapon, he said.

The letter was sent on 26 June. In the meantime Harris and Pujol managed to stall some more by informing Kühlenthal that there were no 'ordinates' on the Stanford's map, so the plan to make it square up with the Pharus one would not work. Further vague reports about the bomb sites were also included in the messages to buy more time.

On 27 June Kühlenthal instructed Garbo to get hold of a Baedecker's *Guide to London*.

I do not think it would be dangerous to purchase. It can probably be found in second-hand bookshops.

The Germans themselves obviously had a copy of the same guidebook, with its own maps of the city. The time for stalling was coming to an end. A more permanent solution was needed.

The V-1 reports were not the only pressure on Garbo. Real Allied divisions which had supposedly been part of General Patton's FUSAG, poised to attack the Pas-de-Calais, were about to arrive in Normandy. Once German troops encountered and identified them, Garbo could expect to be asked all manner of questions. It was a further potential threat to the Garbo operation, one which, like the flying-bomb reports, could lead to the Germans becoming suspicious of their chief spy in London.

The answer to both these problems was neat and ingenious — and typical of Pujol. Getting himself arrested had worked the previous summer to pacify Araceli. Now the same ploy was acted out for the benefit of Kühlenthal.

In early July Garbo sent through a couple of reports about flying-bomb damage based on information which he himself had gathered by travelling to the specific sites. The locations were given along with casualty numbers and time of impact — although the last details were deliberately inaccurate.

Then, on 4 July, there was no evening transmission to Madrid.

The following day Pedro, Agent 3 — Garbo's deputy (the role played by Harris) — signalled to Madrid that Garbo had gone missing, that he had not appeared the previous day, nor had he been at the regular morning meeting. He was worried, he said, that his chief had been hurt in a 'bomb accident'. He was therefore sending 'the Widow' — Mrs Gerbers — down to Taplow to see if she could shed any light on the matter.

But the word the following day from the Amerden Priory Hotel was even more alarming: Mrs Garbo told the Widow that she did not know anything about the whereabouts of her husband. She had thought he was in London with Pedro.

Clearly anxious, Pedro asked Kühlenthal what he should do. 'His wife is in a terrible state.'

Kühlenthal, obviously worried that something untoward had happened to his spy, the man whose valuable information was keeping him safe from Nazi persecution, advised that for the time being Pedro should 'keep calm and quiet'.

On 7 July Pedro radioed again to explain what had happened. Garbo had been arrested! The Widow had just told him, having heard the news from Mrs Garbo. The police had been round to see her that morning to pick up her husband's Spanish Republican identity papers.

The Garbo operation — with Pedro at its head and prompted by Kühlenthal in Madrid — was now on red alert. All contact with the sub-agents had to be stopped, while emergency measures had to be taken in the eventuality of the network being blown by the British authorities.

There was no word about Garbo's fate, or why he had been arrested, but the implication was clearly that it had something to do with the reports that he personally had been preparing on the V-1 damage.

The Germans themselves had forged Garbo's Spanish Republican papers. If the British discovered they were fakes there was every reason to suspect that his whole operation would begin to unravel.

The Garbo operation went off the air. After the intense labour of the past few months, Harris and Pujol had bought themselves a much-needed holiday. Harris travelled to the countryside, where he picked up his easel and painted at the house of Sarah Bishop's parents.

Radio silence could not be maintained for too long a period, however. If Garbo were detained for anything more than a few days the Germans might suspect that he had confessed to being a spy, or even worse that he had turned double agent on them. So on 12 July Pedro sent a message reporting that Garbo had been released on the 10th and that he was safe and well and back in his hotel. Despite looking 'worn out', according to the Widow, his cover was still secure, he said. In the light of events, however, he had decided to give the radio operator a ten-day break and had ordered Pedro back to Glasgow to keep his head down for a while.

Meanwhile he would send a letter to Kühlenthal explaining what had happened.

The letter was duly written on 14 July. Garbo explained that while he was investigating a flying-bomb site in Bethnal Green a policeman had become suspicious of him and taken him to the station. Garbo had tried to swallow a piece of paper with some incriminating notes on the way, which only made the policeman even more inquisitive.

Garbo had insisted on his innocence the entire time, he told Kühlenthal. Then, when his Spanish Republican papers proved his identity, and his boss at the Ministry of Information vouched for him, he was able to clear the matter up.

The Home Secretary himself intervened in the affair, sending Garbo a letter apologising for what had happened and for the zeal of the policeman who had arrested him. This letter and the documents relating to his arrest — which had both been forged by MI5 — were included with Garbo's missive as further proof.

Kühlenthal was delighted that his man in London was safe. Not only that, he could still function as a spy — despite being arrested, he had managed to talk his way out of trouble.

It was clear, however, that investigating the sites of the V-1s was too hazardous a task. It had already brought the Arabal undertaking close to disaster. There was no reason to carry on. Its own survival was the most important thing. From now on no agent in the network was to endanger the operation by having anything to do with pinpointing the bomb sites.

Garbo had pulled it off again. Now he could carry on with the important business of fooling the Germans without having to get sidetracked by the flying bombs.

There was to be one more surprise, however. On 29 July Kühlenthal told Garbo that Hitler himself was awarding him the Iron Cross. He pointed out that the medal was given 'without exception' only to front-line combatants. 'For this reason we all send you our most sincere and cordial congratulations.'

Garbo's reaction was characteristically grandiloquent:

I cannot at this moment, when emotion overcomes me, express in words my gratitude for the decoration conceded by our

Führer to whom humbly and with every respect I express my gratitude for the high distinction which he has bestowed on me for which I feel myself unworthy as I have never done any more than what I have considered to be the fulfilment of my duty.

Pujol was obviously very proud, and it was proof of the success of the Garbo operation. Yet he was aware that he had not been able to achieve this on his own. There was praise as well for his German spymaster Kühlenthal, whom he called 'Carlos'.

I must state that this prize has been won, not only by me, but also by Carlos and the other comrades, who, through their advice and directives, have made possible my work here and so the congratulations are mutual.

Perhaps secretly Pujol was thinking of Harris as well when he wrote these words, the man who had orchestrated the Garbo project. His final comments, however, were for those for whom all this — the lying, the deception, the masterful storytelling — was intended.

My desire is to fight with greater ardour to be worthy of this medal which has only been conceded to those heroes, my companions in honour, who fight on the battlefield.

'Alaric' referring to the troops of the Wehrmacht? Or Pujol thinking of the Allied soldiers now struggling to push on deeper into Normandy? It may have been deliberately ambiguous.

Garbo-Alaric-Pujol — the lines dividing the various characters that he played were becoming gently blurred.

PART EIGHT

'History has shown that the loss of Paris
always means the fall of the whole of France.'
Adolf Hitler

31

Normandy and Belgium, 8 June–18 July 1944

'Monkey' Blacker spent D-Day with the 23rd Hussars in Aldershot waiting for orders to move out. His tank force, intended specifically to tackle the German Panzer divisions, would be needed in the subsequent wave, once the bridgeheads on the French coast had been established. On 8 June, D+2, the word came — they were to join the rest of the 11th Armoured Division and set off for Normandy. The first Allied troops had landed. Now it was the turn of the reinforcements to sail over and take part in the breakout operations — pushing the Germans deeper into France as the area of liberated territory was expected to grow.

The US troops were at the western end of the invasion front. The assault on Utah beach had been successful and Allied gains had been considerable. Omaha beach had been the scene of the heaviest fighting and casualties on 6 June, but now, a few days later, the American positions were consolidated and they were beginning to push inland.

British and Canadian troops had landed at the eastern side of the invasion area, on the beaches code-named Gold, Juno and Sword. Here the fighting had been relatively lighter on D-Day itself, but they now faced some of the toughest German fighters in Normandy — the boys of the 12th SS Panzer Division 'Hitler Youth'. Often no older than sixteen, these soldiers had been trained, and were being led, by commanders transferred from the 1st SS Panzer LAH — Jochen Peiper's comrades. Already the British and Canadians had learned what these lads and their superior weaponry were capable of.

The name Caen comes from an ancient Gaulish word meaning 'battlefield'. Montgomery's objective had been to capture the city by the end of D-Day itself, but this had not been achieved. The Germans were putting up tougher resistance than the invasion planners had foreseen. Now, as the Americans gradually conquered more territory to the west, the British were becoming stuck around Caen, trying to encircle and capture it. In return the Germans were throwing some of their best divisions in to hold them back.

True to its name, Caen, burial place of William the Conqueror, was becoming another killing ground.

Blacker landed on Juno beach on 13 June. The first thing that he saw was a destroyed Sherman tank like his own that had been hit during the first wave on D-Day. There was a large hole where the armour plating protecting the driver was meant to be.

'They don't seem very frightened of these, then,' Blacker's own tank driver — Sam English, a former London bus driver — commented.

The tank crew spent the first few days living

and sleeping as a group, digging holes in the ground and placing the tank over them as shelter at night from the Normandy rain. There were stories that a tank crew somewhere had done this one night and then never woke up as the tank sank in the soft earth and crushed them: Blacker's men always made sure the ground was hard enough to take the tank's weight.

In Bayeux, the first Norman town to be captured on D-Day, they gorged themselves on butter and Camembert cheese — unthinkable luxuries in ration-book Britain — filling the tank with more supplies to take with them as they pushed further inland.

Then, on 26 June, they properly entered battle for the first time. 'Operation Epsom' was the first Allied attempt to go around Caen and outflank the German defenders.

Blacker was in command of C Squadron, his Sherman tanks moving in behind in support of the 15th Scottish Infantry Division as it pushed forward on the morning of the battle. As the tanks started out, they kicked up large amounts of dust and dirt that made for poor visibility, while giving the enemy a clear idea of their positions.

The first things Blacker saw as his company moved forwards were piles of dead bodies: initially of Norman cows caught in the crossfire, their legs pointing stiffly towards the sky; later of Scotsmen from the infantry division that had gone in ahead of them, mown down by German machine guns.

Finally the Shermans came head to head with

Tiger tanks, with their formidable 88mm guns. A shell from one of these soon landed directly on one of Blacker's units and the Sherman went up in smoke. Four of the five men inside managed to get out, but the driver, Lance-Corporal Hogg, was the 23rd Hussars' first fatality.

Other tanks were now being hit, and Blacker's company retreated. They were learning from experience why Sherman tanks were referred to as 'quick brewers'. The Germans were more direct, calling them 'Tommy Cookers'.

The Sherman's short 75mm gun was practically ineffective against the thick armour of the Tiger, particularly at the front, where the Allied shells simply bounced off. A few Shermans had been fitted with larger 17-pounder guns, but even these were only effective if they hit the Tiger at the side, or the turret. Panther tanks, with their sloping armour, were equally hard to take out.

The following days brought more hard lessons. Charging through the village of Mondrainville, Blacker came upon a hill with a small wood growing on the summit. It was clear that whoever controlled the point would have a command of the surrounding area. On his map it was referred to as Hill 112. Blacker was about to suggest that his tanks take the point, but in the fog of battle his plan could not be carried out.

The Germans had also spotted the hill, however, and by the next morning the tanks of the 12th SS Panzer Hitler Jugend had taken up positions there. It would take a month to remove them and Hill 112 would become one of the best-known landmarks in the entire Battle of Normandy, its name etched in the memories of the thousands of British soldiers who fought over it.

On this first day, a detachment of tanks led by Bob Clarke was ordered up to try to dislodge the enemy. 'Cheerful and likeable', Clarke was a former corn-merchant who had recently married a racehorse trainer's daughter from Newmarket. Now he charged into his first battle operation with unfortunate and inappropriate courage.

'He motored up the hill as if on exercise,' Blacker described, 'and innocently allowed his tanks to drive too far over the ridge and expose themselves.'

The result was a disaster: all the Shermans in Clarke's squadron were immediately hit and destroyed by the German Tigers, suffering heavy casualties. A few moments later, manoeuvring his own squadron in an attempt to outflank the SS troops, Blacker caught sight of Clarke lying on the ground. His first thought was that his body looked shorter than usual, until he realised that Clarke's legs had both been cut off below the knee. He died a few minutes later.

Soon afterwards the 23rd Hussars were relieved and pulled out of the battle. In three days they had suffered eighty casualties — around half of them fatal — a figure that constituted 20 per cent of their strength.

Bloodied yet exhilarated at still being alive, Blacker and his men had no idea that their worst day in Normandy was yet to come.

Although on high alert for an imminent Allied invasion across the narrowest part of the Channel, the 1st SS Panzer Division LAH enjoyed its stay in northern Belgium. The city of Bruges offered the usual entertainments for fighting men away from the front, and despite a ban on leave, the officers of Jochen Peiper's armoured regiment would often head off for quick trips to the bars and brothels.

The last party was on 16 June. Werner Wolff was Peiper's former adjutant and was now an Obersturmführer — equivalent to senior lieutenant — in command of the 7th Tank Company. The 16th was the date he had arranged to get married. Owing to the state of alert, however, Wolff was unable to leave his post to join his bride-to-be, and Peiper had arranged for the girl to be brought over from her home in the Baltic states and smuggled over the Belgian border to the chateau of Knesselare for the wedding ceremony.

The castle was bedecked with a giant black SS flag as well as the Nazi swastika flag. An LAH officer married the couple following the quasi-pagan SS rites, the bride touching bread and salt as symbols of life, and the groom touching an SS sword in his role as protector of the family. A flame burned in an urn while the couple swore oaths of loyalty and exchanged SS rings. A copy of *Mein Kampf* was then taken out of a wooden casket decorated with runes and handed to the groom before they passed out through an arcade of saluting SS officers.

At the dinner, Peiper gave a speech at the head table. Then the serious drinking began as the wedding festivities continued into the night.

The next morning, however, on 17 June, the LAH received orders it had not expected.

Thanks to the intelligence reports from its spy network in Britain, German High Command still considered the threat to the Pas-de-Calais to be real and imminent, but a crack force like the 1st SS Panzer Division would not be kept out of the fighting for ever. On the coast further west the Allies were establishing a powerful bridge-head which needed to be crushed as quickly as possible. It was time once again to move out, to where they were meant to have gone a week before.

It was time to go to Normandy.

Had they gone at the start, the journey would have been much quicker and shorter. In the intervening days, however, much had changed in northern France. Bridges over the Seine had been knocked out, making the crossing slower and more difficult. Then there was the Allied air superiority to deal with. RAF Typhoons, with ground-attack rockets, were particularly effective at slowing columns of German tanks from moving around in the hours of daylight.

But another factor complicated the LAH's progress to Normandy: a lack of trains to move men and supplies. Most of the local engines and wagons had been taken over to the east, where, since the middle of May. Peiper's SS comrades were busy rounding up Hungarian Jews and transporting them to Auschwitz. Racial cleansing, the 'ideological war' of the Nazis, was a greater priority at this crucial stage than the logistics of moving men and materiel to the new front opening up in France.

The result was that Peiper did not reach his assembly point south of Caen until 5 July, a month after D-Day.

Garbo had slowed the LAH reinforcements down, and crucially its tanks had failed to make it to Normandy in the early days of the campaign. But they were still dangerous. The Allied advance of Operation Epsom, bogged down around Hill 112, had ground to a halt. The stage was set for another British attempt to encircle Caen, Operation Goodwood, this time striking around the east and south of the city.

Where Peiper and the LAH would be waiting for them.

★ ★ ★

A few days before the launch of Operation Goodwood, Monkey Blacker received news that depressed him: he was being relieved of his command of C Squadron and being made second-in-command of the regiment. No longer in the front line with his tank crew, his job was effectively to act as a replacement for the colonel in case he became a casualty in battle. There was little time to feel sorry for himself, though, and he accepted the decision as best he could.

His replacement as C Squadron leader was Major Bill Shebbeare. A former president of the

Oxford Union and editor of *Isis*, Shebbeare had been a Labour councillor for Holborn and was a Labour parliamentary candidate. Now an officer in the 23rd Hussars, he had written a short book on his military experiences — a manifesto for a democratic army which he called *A Soldier Looks Ahead*, and which he signed anonymously as 'Captain X'. With a rose-tinted view of the Soviet Union, he was a convinced anti-Nazi and secretly — like his contemporary Denis Healey — a member of the Communist Party.

On 8 June Shebbeare had been ordered to stay behind in Aldershot while the rest of the 23rd Hussars set off for Normandy, but now he had managed to get himself over and was keen to see some action.

'Small and slight, with a head that seemed too big for his body, complexion pasty, his full lips could break into a most charming smile which lit up his whole face. He looked very like a garden gnome.'

Despite holding different political views, Blacker and Shebbeare had become close friends.

Now Shebbeare was to take over C Squadron, and one of the first things he did was to scribble a note to Blacker.

'I do indeed believe C Squadron', he wrote, 'to be the best armoured squadron in the army and everything I have seen of the men's spirit here confirms me in this. It makes me feel such a usurper to have taken over ready-made and without any effort on my part, a squadron that you have taken three years to create. I feel that when we go into action again that I need have no worries except my own ability to give them the leadership they deserve.'

Operation Goodwood, the biggest tank battle in the history of the British army, began on the morning of 18 July. At around half-past five over 1,000 Lancasters bombed the German positions. These were followed by American B17s and an artillery barrage. The bombardment lasted for several hours, driving many of the German soldiers that survived it mad. Others committed suicide.

And yet the bombing was not wholly effective, failing to reach the German tanks further back that would later prove so lethal.

The forty-six Panthers and fifty-nine Mark IV's of Jochen Peiper's regiment were practically unscathed. And now they knew what was coming. Peiper's commander used a trick he had picked up on the Eastern Front of putting his ear to the ground to listen for the rumblings of an approaching tank assault. The dust kicked up by the hundreds of Shermans now moving slowly towards them confirmed that this was the beginning of a major Allied offensive. The German tanks moved into position and waited.

Ahead of the British were a number of small villages and hamlets lying in open, flat countryside, while beyond was a low promontory — the Bourguébus ridge, quickly renamed 'Bugger Bus' by the approaching Sherman crews.

After long delays caused by traffic jams of tanks stretching for miles as they tried to squeeze through minefields and over bridges, the battle began. The 11th Armoured Division was at the forefront of the attack, made up of the 3rd Royal Tank Regiment and the Fife and Forfar Yeomanry, with Blacker's 23rd Hussars coming in reserve behind them. Bill Shebbeare, now wearing the helmet and goggles of a tank commander, had waved to Blacker as he set off at the head of C Squadron, with Blacker tagging along in his own tank alongside that of the regimental commander.

As they moved ahead it became clear that the bombing raid earlier in the morning had only had a partial effect. While some German defenders emerged from their dugouts looking shaken by the experience and only too willing to surrender, further on Tiger tanks were waiting in some of the villages. The 23rd Hussars were ordered to deal with them as best they could, before being relieved by another regiment behind them. By the time they caught up with the Fife and Forfar things were already beginning to turn for the worse.

On the German side, Jochen Peiper was working closely with the LAH divisional commander, Teddy Wisch, on how to deal with the British advance. Some of Peiper's tanks were to take up positions on the Bourguébus ridge, while a battalion was to move down and engage the enemy directly and push them back over the railway line that they had recently crossed.

It was Peiper's first proper military engagement since Kharkov back on the Eastern Front. Now, finally, after the delays and changes of order by Hitler himself, he was here in Normandy, fighting against the British. The

Anglo-Americans might enjoy air superiority and have better artillery, but man to man, tank to tank here on the battlefield, their army was no match for the 1st SS Panzer Division. It was time to show what the best forces in the Wehrmacht were capable of.

By the time Blacker and the 23rd Hussars caught up with the vanguard tank regiments, it was too late.

'We could soon see the tail of the Fife and Forfar', Blacker wrote, 'sitting in the middle of an open plain which gave them no more cover than a polo field. But why was there no sign of activity and why in any case were they just sitting there? There was something unreal about their stillness. As we motored closer we realised that they were all dead, burnt out. The only sign of life came from blackened, dishevelled parties on foot, tending wounded or trickling back.'

The Fife and Forfar had become the day's first victims of Peiper's Panthers. In a matter of minutes twenty-nine Shermans, including that of their commanding officer, had been destroyed.

A survivor of the massacre came up and spoke to Blacker.

'I don't think we have more than four tanks left in action,' he said. 'Both the 3rd Tanks and ourselves have been stopped by armour and guns up there on the ridge, and as you can see there's no cover, so I should watch out.'

It was a desperate situation. Already, as they spoke, tanks of the 23rd Hussars were also being shelled. Spewing out a smokescreen for cover, they hastily beat a retreat behind the railway line, which provided some protection.

But the word soon came from command: they had to press on. There was too much at stake. The Bourguébus ridge had to be taken by nightfall.

Both A and B Squadrons had already suffered losses. Now it was time for C Squadron, Blacker's former command, to push ahead. There was no time for thinking about tactics or planning: the situation was urgent. It was only early afternoon on the first day and already Operation Goodwood was turning into a disaster. Bill Shebbeare was told to hurry forwards, capturing a village just ahead of them called Four, and from there proceed towards the ridge.

Eager and excited, Shebbeare set off with the tanks of C Squadron, crossing the railway lines and charging towards the German positions.

Then all at once the firing started, coming, it seemed, from all directions. Blacker had to sit back as his former command was torn apart by Peiper's guns.

The first to go was the tank of Mike Pratt, who had come to the regiment almost straight from school. His Sherman quickly blew up after a direct hit, killing all inside. Next was Jock Addison's tank. Addison, who later in life became an Oscar-winning film composer, managed to get out, but his driver, co-driver and gunner were all dead. His operator was only wounded and Addison managed to pull him out.

Inside Blacker's former tank, the gunner watched in terror as shell after shell targeted his comrades' Shermans. 'Our turn next,' he said.

From the turret, however, there were no orders forthcoming. He looked up to Bill Shebbeare, expecting him to tell them what to do. But Shebbeare had fallen into a state of shock: 'transfixed, speechless, frozen in a horrified stare at the appalling scenes ahead'.

Moments later, Peiper's men scored a direct hit on C Squadron's leading tank, the shell smashing into the turret. Bill Shebbeare was killed instantly. The gunner, Sam English, the driver and one other managed to get out of the tank, but caught fire as they did so. Their flesh burning, they put the flames out as best they could by rolling furiously on the grass.

C Squadron was now leaderless, with most of its tanks on fire. Many men were dead, others had horrific burns on their hands and faces. Within minutes, almost all the remaining Shermans had been destroyed by the German onslaught. Those that were still operational offered a minimal fightback, taking out a German anti-tank gun and a Tiger tank, before heading back to the cover provided by the railway line.

In all, C Squadron lost twenty tanks in the few minutes of the battle and was effectively wiped out.

First the Fife and Forfar, now this: the LAH had had a very successful day.

Operation Goodwood continued for another couple of days, with more tank victories for Peiper and the other German forces, successfully defending the area south of the city of Caen. Finally, on 20 July, the offensive had to be called off. The British had lost around 3,500 men and hundreds of tanks. German losses, by comparison, were minimal.

It was clear that if Monkey Blacker had not been promoted to second-in-command on the eve of the battle he would probably have suffered the same fate as his friend Bill Shebbeare. In later years Blacker would sometimes wonder what might have become of Bill.

'Personally known to Attlee, almost certainly eventually a junior minister in the post-war Labour government, he had a brilliant mind and would have started on level terms with others of his age and with a Service background such as Denis Healey. Too nice, perhaps, for politics, but beneath the charm there was a tough streak. Anyway — it was not to be.'

32

Normandy, July–August 1944

Jochen Peiper had demonstrated the superior destructive force of his Panzer unit. Yet despite inflicting a heavy defeat on the British during Operation Goodwood, the LAH had suffered casualties of its own, and unlike the Allies — who seemed to have an endless supply of tanks to replace the ones lost on the battlefield — the Germans had to use what they had. Most Panthers or Tigers that were successfully 'brewed up' by the enemy constituted a complete loss for the Germans: there were practically none in reserve to take their place.

There was little time to rest or recover from battle. Allied troops could be relieved by multiple waves of reserves coming over the Channel. But for German soldiers in the front line this was a luxury they could not afford. Millions were involved in the fighting on the Eastern Front, while the whole 15th Army was still waiting in the Calais region for the Allied assault that must inevitably come from Dover and south-east England. The men fighting in Normandy were practically the only combatants that the Germans had available.

Then there were the incessant artillery bombardments and attacks from the air. Even hardened officers, like Peiper's former commander in the LAH, Sepp Dietrich, found the conditions worse than when fighting the Red Army.

'Normandy, in July and August '44,' Dietrich wrote, 'was the worst time I have spent in my fighting years . . . It used to take me six hours to move ten kilometres from my headquarters to the front.'

Peiper was also suffering. After the flush of victory at the Bourguébus ridge, he found himself under frequent bombardment. He had set up his regimental headquarters at the chateau of Garcelles-Secqueville, where the basement had been fortified and turned into a shelter. Radio silence had to be maintained at all times for fear of alerting the Allies to their position. Nonetheless, British ships in the Channel pinpointed him and fired shell after shell. The roof fell in, and two SS men were killed.

Peiper had two Panthers parked outside the chateau with ditches dug underneath as shelters in case his HQ came under bombardment. His men could dive out of the windows and take cover, the steel of the tanks offering more protection than the bricks and mortar of the building itself.

One day, during such an attack, a member of the motorcycle reconnaissance platoon found himself lying next to Peiper under one of the Panthers:

'I remember very clearly how one day I, too, found myself under this command tank of Peiper's. I had just arrived with a report from Kuhlmann when a formation of enemy bombers 'laid down a carpet'. A second and third wave followed, and bombs rained down. The bombs were bursting at such short intervals that Peiper — in spite of his famous calm and imperturbability — said, 'Now's it's time to get out and under the tanks!'

'We lay there close together — Peiper, Hans Gruhle, signals commander Helmut Jahn, and I — and waited. And then, in that depressing atmosphere, Peiper said, 'They're trying to finish us off here and now — (pause) — but I believe we will win this war, just like the First!'

'These words by Peiper did not have a shocking effect on me. I had also had serious doubts about our chances of winning the war since the previous winter's difficult battles . . . '

After years of heavy fighting, and now at the receiving end of a merciless Allied bombardment, Jochen Peiper was close to cracking up.

More fighting was to come, however. Caen was finally in the Allies' hands, but after Operation Goodwood, they once again launched an offensive designed to push south from the city towards the town of Falaise — Operation Spring.

Peiper's tanks, as before, were in their way, and as before, they put up fierce resistance. At the village of Tilly-la-Campagne it was the turn of the Canadian 3rd Infantry Division to receive the brunt of the LAH's force, and it suffered heavy casualties. A similar fate awaited armoured divisions that tried to attack the LAH near Rocquancourt.

As with Operation Goodwood, the Allies had made only small gains and at a high cost. But the bombardment and stress of command had finally taken its toll on Jochen Peiper. He was having a nervous breakdown. By 2 August he was relieved of his post as commander of the 1st SS Panzer Regiment and sent from the front to recover.

It was clearly embarrassing for a man of such high military repute to have a nervous condition: it did not fit with the SS ideas of a warrior-officer bravely and calmly leading his troops from the front. So the real reason why he had been relieved was covered up: when he reached the SS hospital he was officially diagnosed as suffering from 'jaundice caused by an inflammation of the gall bladder'.

Back at the front, however, things were developing quickly. While the LAH had been holding back the Canadians taking part in Operation Spring, further west the Americans had timed their own big push south to coincide. So while the British and Canadians had to fight against the best German forces in Normandy, including over six Panzer divisions, the US troops only faced one and a half German armoured divisions.

The result was that General Patton, now relieved from playing the head of FUSAG — the imaginary army group dreamed up by the deception planners in London — managed to push out of the Cotentin Peninsula into Brittany and further south.

His point of breakthrough, however, was narrow, and there was only a thin corridor of US-held territory linking the Cotentin and the newly liberated areas. It was here that Hitler decided to launch a counter-attack. Operation Lüttich was designed to be a master counterstroke, splitting the US army in two and halting its advance deeper into France.

Hitler's best forces, who until this point had mostly been fighting in the eastern sector against the British and Canadians, were now ordered west to fight the Americans. The tanks of the LAH, but without the respected and admired Jochen Peiper to lead them, moved out from their positions south of Caen and headed towards the US lines.

Operation Lüttich — what the Americans called the Mortain counter-attack — was a disaster for the Germans. Most of the divisions involved, including the LAH, were under strength, and many failed to reach their assembly areas in time for the attack owing to Allied air attacks whenever they tried to move across country. As a result the operation had to be delayed by a day. When finally things got going, during the early hours of 7 August, the Germans enjoyed some success, but once daylight broke, and the tanks could be spotted from the air, RAF Typhoons swarmed over them, causing havoc. In one day the LAH alone lost thirty-four Panthers and ten Mark IV tanks.

Operation Lüttich was called off. The German army in north-west France was in disarray and on the run.

Now that the LAH had been moved westwards to fight the Americans, the British and Canadians finally broke through and started heading from the area south of Caen towards Falaise. Meanwhile US forces were coming up from the west and south, encircling the German 7th Army, along with units from the LAH and other Panzer divisions, in a lethal pocket. Tens of thousands of German soldiers raced to get out to safety before the gap at the eastern end of the pocket was closed. Many did make it, but the majority — over 50,000 men — were trapped. The result was a bloodbath, and the biggest defeat for the Wehrmacht since Stalingrad a year and a half earlier.

The Battle of Normandy was lost: all they could do was fall back. The LAH as such now barely existed. It had lost some 5,000 men, along with all of its tanks and artillery.

Some wondered if everything would have gone so wrong during Operation Lüttich if Peiper had been with them.

'If Peiper had been there this would not have happened!' a staff commander remarked. Despite being pulled back from the front, and the near destruction of his regiment, Peiper's fame as a commander of genius lived on.

Peiper was luckier than many of his comrades and managed to flee the enemy advance, eventually recovering in an Upper Bavarian hospital, near his family home. Physically and mentally wrecked, he could only sit and watch as the Allies pushed deep into northern France.

33

London, Normandy and Paris, August 1944

In London, Garbo was drafting a letter to Kühlenthal insisting that FUSAG was still an imminent threat to the Pas-de-Calais, while explaining away the fact that General Patton was now obviously commanding forces in northern France. As ever, Kühlenthal accepted his agent's information at face value.

Meanwhile, on the night of 31 July to 1 August, Pujol's compatriots in the 2nd Armoured Division finally reached Normandy, disembarking in choppy waters at Utah beach: Spanish soldiers in a French unit wearing US Army uniforms and driving American tanks. For many in La Nueve, including Lieutenant Amado Granell, it was an emotional moment, and they cried as they bent down to pick up handfuls of sand from the beach. In their minds the conquest of France would be just the beginning. Once the Nazis had been pushed back over the Rhine, Franco's days in Madrid would be numbered. There would be another Allied landing soon, they were certain, this time on the Spanish coast.

Numbering some 150 men with Shermans, half-tracks and jeeps, these soldiers were here not only to liberate French soil; they had an ideological hatred of the enemy and scores to settle from their own Civil War. Some were anarchists, others Trotskyites; a handful were communists. Some, like Granell, were simply soldiers who had fought — and lost — on the Republican side.

Many in the French 2nd Armoured Division considered them unruly, a difficult bunch to handle. General Leclerc had put Captain Dronne, a Spanish speaker, in charge of them; he managed to keep them under control, more or less. But they were good fighters, among the best in Leclerc's force, so they were often at the vanguard of the action, sometimes as much as 15 kilometres ahead of the rest of the division.

They arrived in time for the collapse of the German 7th Army in the Falaise Gap. Here, in the small town of Écouché, they found themselves surrounded by fleeing remnants of the 1st SS Panzer Division LAH and the 2nd SS Panzer Division Das Reich. The Germans were broken and defeated, yet pockets were still resisting. Knowing that the enemy was made up of members of the SS only made the soldiers of La Nueve fight even harder. They suffered seventeen casualties on 16 August, but the enemy was now on the run, heading westwards towards Paris, chased by the Allies. What would happen in the City of Light itself, though? Would the Germans put up a fight? The city might be destroyed, yet it held the key to the whole country. Whoever was in control of the capital was effectively in control of France.

General de Gaulle wanted the Allies to march in and take Paris as quickly as possible. General

Eisenhower, the Supreme Allied Commander, however, was more cautious. He wanted to engage the Germans first to the north of the city and defeat them before entering the potential bloodbath that a battle for Paris might turn out to be. Besides, there was a race on for Berlin against the Soviets. A diversion to empty Paris of Germans could prove costly.

Nonetheless, the French decided to move in the direction of Paris anyway: on 19 August resistance fighters in the city had started an uprising. It was imperative to reach them and bring an end to Nazi rule. Further to the east, in Warsaw, an uprising by the Polish resistance was being mercilessly quashed by the Germans as the Red Army halted in its tracks and refused to move in on the city in support. The same thing could not be allowed to happen in Paris.

After the rapid collapse of the Germans in the wake of the Allied breakout from Normandy, it was time to take advantage of the situation.

Early in the morning of 23 August La Nueve started rolling eastwards. Eisenhower had finally given in to de Gaulle's pressure, and Leclerc's 2nd Armoured Division had permission to strike on Paris. The French forces were not alone, however: the US 4th Infantry Division were also marching towards the capital. There was a competition to be the first to arrive. By midday on 24 August Spanish soldiers reached the Parisian suburb of Antony. The road into Paris, where the resistance fighters were struggling to take the city with little more than handguns, appeared to be clear.

But now, just when the prize appeared to be in sight, La Nueve received orders to hold back and support other units on the outskirts of the city.

Reluctantly they turned around to head to La Croix de Berny, where a German 88mm artillery weapon was causing havoc. Before long, La Nueve dealt with it and the gun was put out of action.

At this point Leclerc himself arrived, and spoke to Granell and Dronne.

'What the hell are you doing here?' he demanded.

'*Mon général*, I'm following the order to pull back,' Dronne replied.

'No, Dronne. Head straight for Paris, enter Paris. Don't allow yourself to be held up. Take whichever route you want. Tell the Parisians and the Resistance not to lose hope, that tomorrow morning the whole division will be with them.'

Leclerc was adamant: they had to move in to support the resistance fighters. Hitler had given orders to destroy the city in the event of an Allied attack: they had to move before it was too late. And they had to reach central Paris before the Americans. La Nueve should leave at once.

And so the Spanish Republican troops, with Captain Dronne at their head, pushed into Paris itself. At first, Parisians hid in fear at the sound of their tanks, thinking that they might be Germans. Once they saw their uniforms, however, they emerged on to the streets again with the cry that 'the Americans' had come. Only on looking closer did they realise that these were men of the Free French forces come to liberate them. Few realised that they were actually Spanish.

By 2045 that evening, pushing through the cheering crowds, La Nueve reached the Porte d'Italie. Beyond lay central Paris itself. Yet the path through was not easy: Granell and Dronne had little idea how much German opposition there might be. And then there were barricades along most of the streets, thrown up by the French resistance to hamper any movement of German troops.

The armoured column of La Nueve started zigzagging its way through the streets. At one point they decided to split into two sections: one under Granell, the other under Dronne, each taking slightly different routes to the Hôtel de Ville.

Granell diverted away from the avenue d'Italie, striking west before reaching the rue Nationale and heading up once again towards the Seine. Dodging the German positions, he then reached the boulevard de l'Hôpital, at the end of which he crossed to the Right Bank by the pont d'Austerlitz. Here his column turned left and moved along the river bank before finally, without firing a shot, at 2122 he reached the Hôtel de Ville.

Granell, a Spaniard from the small Mediterranean town of Burriana, was the first Allied soldier to reach the heart of Paris. Soon his tanks and cars were surrounded by euphoric members of the resistance, who had taken the Hôtel de Ville from the Germans a few days earlier.

Granell's first act was to send a message to Dronne, saying that they had made it.

'Send reinforcements,' he called.

Word quickly spread of what had happened,

and soon the bells of Notre Dame were ringing over the city, followed by those of other churches. Hearing them, one of the German defenders still in the city wrote in his diary: 'I have just heard the bells of my own funeral.'

Granell himself described the scene:

'It was very moving and emotional to hear the bells of Notre-Dame. Fighting hadn't hardened us completely. There was shouting, cheering and songs — particularly *La Marseillaise* — accompanying the sound of the bells. We all had tears in our eyes and a lump in our throats. I tried to sing *La Marseillaise* with the others, but I couldn't . . . Explosions, people firing into the air . . . all that excitement was freedom itself, victory. I couldn't even blink for fear that I would really start crying. Our senses felt shorn of all impulse. The lines from the Rubén Darío poem had come alive: 'Even the most beautiful woman smiles at the most ferocious conqueror.' The ferociousness of the conquerors had been washed away by the emotion of the moment.'

In the jubilant scenes that followed, the president of the resistance committee, Georges Bidault, had his photo taken with a smiling, if tired-looking, Granell. On the next day it was on the front page of the newspaper *Libération*, with the headline: '*Ils sont arrivés!*'

On 25 August, when the rest of Leclerc's forces and the US 4th Infantry arrived, Paris was effectively cleared of the occupiers. In the afternoon, after a brief battle outside his headquarters at the Hôtel Meurice — again involving La Nueve — the German military governor,

General Dietrich von Choltitz, officially signed the German surrender in the billiard room of the Prefecture of Police.

Paris was delirious with joy, and the warm August evening soon turned spontaneously into one of the greatest celebration parties in history. Exhausted French, Spanish and American liberators who had fought their way to the capital through the bloody fields of Normandy were now embraced by the city's populace. Everywhere they went, men and women — but particularly women — threw themselves at them, wanting to kiss and touch the brave men who had ended the Nazi terror in their city.

As the evening wore on, the celebrations became more intense, more intimate, in what Simone de Beauvoir later called the *débauche de la fraternité*. Few soldiers slept alone that night. Either bivouacked in the Bois de Vincennes or in the gardens behind Notre-Dame, the Spaniards of La Nueve, the Frenchmen of the 2nd Armoured and the Americans of the 4th Infantry were mostly in the passionate embraces of Parisian girls and women keen to show their gratitude as warmly as they could.

In two and a half months the war had taken a decisive turn in favour of the Allies. Now it was only a question of time before Germany was defeated. In London, reading more complimentary reports from Kühlenthal congratulating the Arabal network for the quality of its intelligence, Pujol and Harris could be satisfied that their story-telling and lies had helped win the battle for France.

PART NINE

'Too much sanity may be madness. And
maddest of all to see life as it is and not
as it should be.'
Cervantes

34

London and Madrid,
August 1944–May 1945

While Spanish, French and American soldiers enjoyed the fruits of victory in Paris in late August, Juan Pujol continued his Garbo deception in London, although at a reduced pace. As far as the Germans were concerned, he was keeping a low profile after his arrest in Bethnal Green. In fact he was still working with Harris to perpetuate the threat to the Pas-de-Calais. Even as Paris was falling into Allied hands, the German 15th Army was still based firmly in the northern corner of France, waiting for the promised second wave of the invasion to come.

The Allies had swept out of Normandy and were hurriedly conquering much of the rest of the country; General Patton was now clearly in charge of the US 3rd Army, which was pushing deep into France and had nothing to do with the fictitious FUSAG supposedly based in Dover.

Yet still the Germans believed that FUSAG existed and was an imminent threat. MI5 concluded that Hitler now had 'an almost mystic confidence' in his Spanish spy.

On 31 August Garbo finally broke the news to them. Owing to the success of the Normandy campaign, the Allies had decided to dismantle

FUSAG and cancel the planned strike over the narrowest stretch of the Channel. The German 15th Army had been successfully tricked into sitting on its hands while much of France fell to the Allies.

The deception of Fortitude was complete, and was more successful than anyone could have imagined.

'Just keep the [German] Fifteenth Army out of my hair for the first two days,' General Eisenhower had asked the deception planners in London before the start of the invasion. 'That's all I ask.'

In the end, through deception and double-cross, the threat had been kept at bay for almost three months.

'Prior to D Day,' Harris wrote, 'the unofficial estimate of our probable success in holding the enemy from reinforcing the Cherbourg battle front [Normandy invasion beaches] was, that if it could afterwards be proved that we had been instrumental in causing <u>one</u> Division to hesitate <u>48 hours</u> before proceeding to oppose our landing in the Cherbourg peninsula, we would have been well repaid for the energies expended in organising this deception . . . Our success was infinitely greater than we had dared to hope . . . The climax was reached when, with the use of entirely notional forces we continued to maintain the threat to the Pas de Calais area until Allied Forces had by-passed it and annihilated the forces which we had been instrumental in persuading the Germans to retain there until after the Normandy battle had been won.'

The Allies were cock-a-hoop. Many in the late

summer of 1944, with the collapse of the German resistance in much of France, thought that the war itself might be over very shortly. In the end the enemy put up a fightback, and victory could not be celebrated until May of the following year, but for the deception teams of SHAEF, the London Controlling Section and MI5 it was a moment of triumph.

Pujol himself would receive an award for his efforts. After the Iron Cross granted by none other than Hitler himself, Harris worked behind the scenes to ensure that the British did not fail to decorate their Spanish hero in equal measure.

Before they did so, however, there was another final threat to Pujol's secret to deal with.

As Pujol was announcing to the Germans the end of FUSAG, in Madrid a Spanish spy with close ties to the German secret service was approaching the British Embassy offering to sell some highly valuable information. Roberto Buénaga was an associate of the Dirección General de Seguridad — Franco's equivalent of MI5 or the FBI — and he put himself in touch with Section V's man in the capital at the time, Jack Ivens.

For the right amount of money, Buénaga told Ivens, the British could have the name of the head of the Germans' best spy ring in London.

Ivens had been with Bristow and Philby back in early 1942, when news first reached Section V about Arabel. It was clear to him that Buénaga's information about the 'Nazi' spy was good, that he knew the name and even the address of Juan Pujol.

Something needed to be done. Pujol might have taken something of a back seat in the Garbo operation by this time — as far as Kühlenthal was concerned his deputy, Pedro, Agent 3, was doing more of the work, meaning that Harris himself, an MI5 officer, now had a direct line of communication with his German counterpart. Yet the whole network could still be blown, endangering lives and closing any chance of perpetrating any future deception plans.

The problem was that if the British did nothing with Buénaga's information and the Germans found out that he had betrayed them, it would be obvious that Garbo was a double agent. But if they agreed to do a deal with Buénaga, Kühlenthal would be forced to shut Garbo down as a German spy on the assumption that the British had now rumbled him.

After so many years of dealing with threats of this kind, it must have come almost as second nature to hand things over to Pujol to sort out. His solution, as elegant as ever, was to turn the problem into one for the Germans. He had, he told Kühlenthal, learned through his sub-agent J(1) — the courier working the civilian flight route out of Lisbon — that someone was moving in secret circles offering to sell information about the Germans' spy ring in Britain. And he named the person as Roberto Buénaga.

As a result, he — Garbo — was now going into hiding in Wales with Stanley, Agent 7, who could keep him safe for the time being.

Kühlenthal fell for it yet again. He congratulated Garbo on discovering the threat, and on his quick action in response. Pedro was now fully in charge of the Garbo network, having occasional contact with his chief — Garbo — from his Welsh hideout.

Pujol was, of course, still in London all this time. The Buénaga threat remained until the end of the war, yet he was successfully stalled, the British never accepting his offer to sell his information, the Germans believing that their spy network was safe and that its chief had managed to find a secure hiding place.

Towards Christmas of 1944 Pujol finally received official recognition of his services from the British. At midday on 21 December he was presented with the MBE. It was a private, secret moment. No mention of his name appeared in the *London Gazette*, yet the ceremony was presided over by the head of MI5 himself, Sir David Petrie, who made a speech in praise of the little Spaniard who had done so much to help the Allied cause. Among those present were Harris, Tar Robertson, John Masterman and Guy Liddell.

Afterwards the small group went for lunch at the Savoy. At one point, and perhaps bolstered by a few glasses of wine, Harris started beating the table with his hand, calling out Pujol's name. Within moments the others were doing the same, and Pujol stood up to make a speech of his own, thanking them for his medal.

'Garbo responded to the toast in halting but not too bad English,' Liddell wrote in his diary. 'I think he was extremely pleased.'

This was followed the next day by a second

celebration — one to which wives and ladies were invited. Liddell was present again at a dinner at the Dorchester along with Sarah Bishop, Harris, Harris's wife, Hilda, Pujol and perhaps more importantly, Araceli. For one night at least, it seems, the tensions of the past months and years were forgotten in the splendour of the moment. It was what Araceli had always dreamed of back when they were struggling in Madrid and Lisbon — mixing in high circles, the dream of a glamorous and more comfortable life. And in the magnificent surroundings of one of the best — and then relatively modern — hotels in London, she shined.

'Mrs Garbo was in tremendous form,' Liddell wrote, 'and related to me in animated and broken English the part she had played in the early days of her husband's double agent career.'

She told him of the events three years before, when Pujol had been at his lowest ebb in Lisbon, and she herself had taken the initiative to talk to the Americans, to persuade them to listen to her husband's story. It was the final move that had brought Pujol to the attention of the British and eventually to London as their top double agent.

Listen, Araceli was saying, none of this would have happened without me. I deserve this — you owe it to me.

Pujol himself was more subdued that evening, perhaps wisely allowing his wife to have her moment, to bask in the glory of his MBE. He had grown a beard — all part of his new role of 'spy in hiding'. Later he would try to get some photos of himself in this 'disguise' over to

346

Kühlenthal by post to show what measures he was taking against getting caught. Liddell thought the beard made him look rather like Lenin.

Yet despite the hidden tensions at the table — the hostility between Harris and Araceli never appeared to abate, while we can only speculate about the levels of intimacy between Pujol and Sarah Bishop — the evening was a success, at least as far as Liddell was concerned. Pujol and Araceli were, he concluded, 'very likeable characters'.

In truth the marriage was still in trouble. The war was close to an end and Araceli longed to be back in Spain, yet for Pujol his work remained unfinished.

Something of his feelings for Araceli, and the problems they had been through, can be sensed in a handful of letters he wrote in the early months of 1945, part of his ruse to convince Kühlenthal that he was hiding from the British. He wrote to his wife, date-lining the letters from various cities in Spain, to where he was pretending he had now successfully escaped. In fact he was sending them from Britain to Madrid, where Kühlenthal played his part and had the letters franked in Spain itself and sent back to Britain, thereby providing his agent with 'proof' for the British authorities that he was out of the country.

In the first letter Pujol talked about being back in Madrid, and how the city was a 'plague of memories' for him of his previous life there with Araceli, which only made the pain of their separation that much harder to bear.

I have no plans; I am like a little boat at the mercy of the waves of the Atlantic, waiting for a ray of light to show the way in my dark future. How different everything would be if you were here. I don't want to say too much about Madrid, because I know it will only make you as sad as I am as I walk the streets and realise that you aren't by my side. I don't plan to stay long in the capital; I'm hoping to leave next week because a journey is the best thing for me in my current state of health, which is in a terrible way with my nerves and the way I feel right now.

In a later letter, in which he talked about a supposed business venture that he was getting into, he again expressed his feelings for her:

Just remember, day after day, how much I love you and that everything I am doing is for both of us. That way the loneliness won't feel so bad, and you will be able to stand up strong against any adversity that comes your way.
I love you very much and send you millions of kisses.

If Pujol's wish was to rekindle the fondness of their early years together, to try to persuade Araceli to stay with him in London for a while longer, it failed. Her calls to be sent back to Spain continued, although at the last minute she wavered over whether to return when she heard that the naval officer she had been having an

348

affair with earlier in the war was being repatriated from his POW camp. By now, however, MI5 were tiring of her. Apart from the matter of marital infidelities, Harris commented that 'the domestic situation in the Garbo household had become extremely complicated'. Araceli struggled to find a servant and was having to look after the two small children and do the housework on her own — a situation that was becoming untenable owing to an unspecified illness.

On 1 May 1945, one day after a defeated Hitler committed suicide in the Berlin bunker, she and the children finally flew back to Madrid, at M15's insistence. The marriage was not over — not yet — but it was staggering towards an inevitable breakdown.

35

Britain, the Americas and Spain, May–September 1945

Just as he was saying goodbye to his wife, wondering how long his marriage could survive, Pujol was also busy with what would turn out to be the last Garbo messages sent between London and Madrid.

Harris and MI5 were keen to keep tabs on the German spy network in Spain after the war. The conflict was coming to an end, but there were fears that diehard Nazis might linger on and even stage a fight-back at a future date. As a result it was decided that Garbo should maintain contact with Madrid.

There was another reason, more personal for Pujol, to carry on, however. Until that point there had never been any suspicion that Kühlenthal had any inkling that his top London spy had been working for the British. Yet there was always the danger that one day Pujol's cover might be blown, in which case he and his family would potentially be under threat. He needed to be certain that no one on the German side knew anything about his true loyalties.

Through all this, Pujol had to keep up the pretence of being a 'German spy' on the run from the British authorities. As such he had to think of escape routes to relative safety overseas.

He put forward a number of possibilities to Kühlenthal, including sailing to Cuba with a tobacco smuggler, or getting to Canada using Fred's — Agent 4's — ID papers. In the end Kühlenthal suggested the Cuba plan was the best.

By this time the war in Europe was in its final days and Franco, keen to ingratiate himself with the winners and distance himself from his former friends, was rounding up German officials and placing them under house arrest. The British had learned that Friedrich Knappe, Pujol's first contact inside the defunct Abwehr, was detained in Catalonia, while Kühlenthal had been given permission to live in Ávila. Nonetheless, he was still able to respond to the Garbo messages.

On the evening of 1 May, just hours after Araceli and the children flew off for Spain, Garbo, ever the fanatical Nazi, offered to carry on fighting for the cause.

I am convinced that, providing we take the necessary steps in order to organise ourselves adequately and efficiently at the present time, we will be able to maintain contact with Three and Five after my departure, and thereby control a network, the benefits of which may be of incalculable value for the future.

For their part, the Germans thanked him for his continuing support in the face of 'the rapid course of events and the confusion reigning all over the world'. They would organise the

351

necessary documentation to get him out of Britain and make sure he received some funds to help him along. But it was time to close down the network. The situation was critical and he had to think of the safety of his collaborators.

Over the next few days more messages were sent back and forth detailing the particulars of shutting down the network, of getting funds across to Garbo, and about escape plans.

Then, at nineteen minutes past nine in the evening of 8 May — VE Day, just as the crowds were drinking and celebrating in the streets of London — Pujol and Harris sent their final message to Madrid. Garbo insisted on pressing the Germans for some sort of contact in Madrid, a way that would enable him to stay in touch with them. Now, four years after he first penned his fake reports on Britain from Lisbon, delighted at the outcome of the war and perhaps even under the influence of a glass of champagne or two from Harris's wine cellar, it was as important as ever to stay in character:

I understand the present situation and the lack of guidance due to the unexpected death of our dear Chief shocks our profound faith in the destiny which awaits our poor Europe, but his deeds and the story of his sacrifice to save the world from the danger of anarchy which threatens us will last for ever in the hearts of all men of goodwill. His memory, as you say, will guide us on our course and today more than ever I affirm my confidence in my beliefs and I am certain that the day will arrive in the not too distant future when the noble struggle will be revived which was started by him to save us from a period of chaotic barbarism which is now approaching.

The reply from Madrid was exactly what they were waiting for: details about how to keep in touch now that the war had ended:

To make contact with the person employed in Madrid we ask you to frequent the Cafe Bar la Moderna, 141 Calle Alcalá, every Monday between 20 hours and 2030 hours, starting June 4th. You should be seated at the end of the Cafe and be carrying the newspaper 'London News'. A person will meet you there one Monday who will say that he has come on behalf of Fernando Gómez . . .

It was the last message the Germans ever sent.

Pujol later remembered the celebrating crowds in Piccadilly on VE Day, drinking beer and dancing in the street. Victory had come, and there was an overwhelming sense of joy. Yet in that scene the story of how the war had ended was so different in the minds of each person there. The soldiers and servicemen and women had their own experiences to shade and give colour to a momentous occasion, yet they did not know what the little Spaniard and his friend from MI5 knew about how — or why — the Allies had prevailed.

Yet if we were to remove those two men from the picture, from history altogether, the scene would collapse. There would be no celebration, no party in Piccadilly. Normandy, the Second Front, would have failed, and things would have turned out very differently indeed.

Nonetheless they passed unobserved by the crowds, happy, yet still with work to complete. Doing their bit, as so many millions had done. Vital yet invisible. Storytellers who had helped shape an ending that was far from certain.

★ ★ ★

Pujol now had to get to Spain, but he did so in a roundabout fashion. By travelling to the USA and Latin America first he would be able to pick up a new passport from a Spanish consulate — pretending to have lost his old one — and thereby disguise any trails back to his time in London.

There was another reason to go, however. The head of the FBI, J. Edgar Hoover, had heard about the Garbo case, and he wanted to meet the men behind it.

In early June Pujol and Harris took off in a Sunderland flying boat from Southampton for a twenty-four-hour flight to Baltimore. From there they headed to Washington, where they had dinner with Hoover in an underground bunker that the ever paranoid FBI chief had beneath his official residence.

'Hoover showed great interest in my activities as a double agent,' Pujol remembered, 'and was most affable throughout, but he never asked me to work for him.'

Pujol had already turned down an offer from the British to take a comfortable, well-paid job at the Eagle Star insurance company. He was happy to continue working for them in secret, keeping an eye on any Nazi resurgence movements that he came across, but he was thinking about his own future, about his family, and a chance perhaps to repair things with Araceli. After so many years of difficulties — from his years in hiding during the Spanish Civil War, to his knife-edge existence in Madrid and Lisbon as a freelance double agent, to the long hours and strain of his work for MI5 — he owed it to his wife and children to start something new. Besides, he had the feeling that tyranny followed him wherever he went — first the lawlessness of Republican Barcelona, then Franco and finally Hitler: he wanted to settle somewhere tranquil, with no threat of revolution or dictatorship. A fresh beginning. Perhaps now at last he and Araceli might enjoy the kind of life that they had dreamed of all those years ago while working at the Majestic Hotel in Madrid.

There was one more task to perform, however: re-establishing contact with the Germans in Spain.

Pujol arrived in Barcelona by boat on 9 August 1945, the same day that the Americans dropped a second atomic bomb on Japan, over Nagasaki. After an emotional reunion with his mother and family, he travelled to Madrid, where Harris was waiting for him with their old friend from MI6, Desmond Bristow.

At first they tried to contact the Germans by radio, but no signal came back. Then Pujol went to the Café Bar la Moderna, as instructed in the last German message, but no one came to meet him. When he visited Knappe's Madrid flat, he found that his former contact was not at home, but Knappe's sister informed him that he was now living somewhere in Catalonia.

This was the information that the British already had — that he was living in Caldes de Malavella, near the French border. Now Pujol could satisfactorily explain to the German how he knew this.

It was late August by the time he made it there. Knappe became nervous when he saw his former agent standing at his door: the Spanish authorities did not allow him to have visitors. They agreed to walk around to a nearby forest where they could talk more freely.

Knappe was depressed. Germany had lost the war, and his own situation, now under house arrest, was uncertain. To Pujol he looked lost, saddened and worried about what might happen to him. It was clear that he had almost no contact with any of the others in the German secret services; he was on his own.

He did, however, have Kühlenthal's address in Ávila; he gave it to Pujol, suggesting that he go and see him.

Their conversation lasted some three hours, but by the end Knappe was becoming increasingly nervous and brought things to a conclusion. He was determined, he said, not to be sent back to Germany. He would rather live as a fugitive here in Spain.

Pujol never saw him again.

Back in Madrid, Pujol told Harris and Bristow what he had heard from Knappe, before heading to Ávila to meet his former German spymaster, Kühlenthal. As he drew into the city, he imagined that the great medieval walls somehow reflected the cool response his arrival would elicit. Instead, he was surprised to find Kühlenthal delighted to see him.

By this time Pujol was something of a superman in Kühlenthal's eyes. Not only had he run a highly successful Nazi spy ring from the heart of enemy territory, he had also managed to escape detection when the authorities had cottoned on to him, and now here he was, unscathed.

Or at least that was how Pujol later recounted his meeting with Kühlenthal to MI5. There are questions about Kühlenthal, however. Was he really duped as comprehensively as the records suggest? Did he never suspect that Pujol was acting as a double agent? The German historian Arne Molfenter has interviewed members of Kühlenthal's family. They insist that their relative *did* have his doubts. Perhaps, in the end, like so many in the Abwehr — even the organisation's head, Admiral Canaris himself — Kühlenthal was playing a double game of sorts, never fully loyal to the Nazi State, perhaps motivated more by self-preservation owing to his Jewish blood than anything else. Garbo, the Germans' greatest spy inside Britain, gave him a get-out-of-jail card, yet by passing on his agent's supposed intelligence as genuine he was also helping to undermine the regime that was murdering the Jews.

It is impossible to say. Perhaps Kühlenthal was cleverer than anyone realised, only acting the fool. Or perhaps his family want him to be perceived in that way, in an attempt to recover the good name of a man who has largely been ridiculed by history.

Whatever the truth of the situation, Pujol was relieved to see — in his eyes at least — that there was no hint of suspicion in Kühlenthal. Even now, after all that had happened, the German intelligence officer appeared none the wiser. Pujol suggested establishing contacts with other spies still active, and keeping his network alive. But Kühlenthal refused. It was not possible in the current situation. Nonetheless, he wanted Pujol to see him as 'a colleague and brother with whom he would always wish to share whatever good fortune might come his way in the future'.

There was nothing but praise for Pujol. Kühlenthal regretted that he was not able to give him his Iron Cross. There had been some bureaucratic complications which meant that it had never arrived in Madrid. Hitler himself had been involved in the matter, and had insisted that the medal be sent, but the end of the war had intervened in the meantime.

Kühlenthal was keen to know what Pujol planned to do now; perhaps his super-spy could help him get out of Spain. Like Knappe, he was anxious not to be sent back to Germany. Pujol

358

said he would talk to his sub-agents and see what they could do.

He, meanwhile, was going to leave Spain as quickly as possible. He told Kühlenthal that he thought that British spies were already on to him, and that he intended to cross into Portugal.

'How are you going to do that?' Kühlenthal asked him as Pujol was about to leave. 'How are you going to get over the border?'

Pujol gave him an enigmatic look, and simply said: 'Clandestinely.'

★　★　★

Pujol travelled back to Madrid, then on to Lisbon, where he met up once more with Harris. They flew to London, where Pujol was debriefed on what he had learned from both his meetings with his former German case officers.

His time as a double agent had come to an end; it was time to make his goodbyes to those who had been part of the Garbo operation. To Charlie Haines the radio operator; to Tar Robertson and John Masterman; to Hilda, Harris's wife; to Sarah Bishop, who had spent so many hours with him at the Jermyn Street office; and to Harris himself, the other half of Garbo: over the years the two men had become the best of friends.

MI5 were not ungenerous. Garbo had brought them some £31,000 in funding from the Germans, providing the final irony that the enemy had ended up paying several times over for the very service that had been used to fool them. Now a

359

portion of that money was given to Pujol to help him start his new life.

It was September 1945. Just as, four years previously, he had popped up magically out of nowhere, now Pujol — like his namesake Greta Garbo — simply vanished.

PART TEN

'A tale, fictitious or otherwise, illuminates truth.'
Rumi

36
Britain, Spain and Venezuela, 1945–84

For the majority of people after the war the name 'Garbo' referred to one person: the actress whose films thrilled audiences with scenes of rumba dancing and skiing while German bombs were falling on London. Only a very select number — members of the intelligence community — had any inkling of another, secret 'Garbo', a Spaniard who had played a crucial role in defeating the Nazis. And of these, a mere handful knew his real name.

There were rumours — stories of a double agent who had done incredible things. It was too good a tale to suppress completely. But who was this Garbo? As the years passed, no one could say for certain that he was even alive any more. Something about him succumbing to malaria in Angola. Or was it a snake bite? Others insisted he had died in the jungles of Mozambique.

Then in 1972 the general public was alerted to the existence of this other Garbo when John Masterman, former head of the Twenty Committee, published a book on the Allies' deception work during the war. *The Double-Cross System* was a bombshell, outlining as it did for the first time how the wool had been pulled over the Germans' eyes, how the entire German spy network in Britain had been either neutralised or turned and controlled by the British themselves, and how the Allies had then used this to great military advantage for D-Day and the Normandy campaign.

It was something of a sop to help bolster the image of the British intelligence services, whose reputation by this point lay in tatters after the scandals of the Profumo Affair and Kim Philby's defection to Moscow. We are good at spy work, Masterman wanted to say. The Soviets may be getting the better of us now, but look at this great success we enjoyed during the war.

Many players were mentioned in Masterman's book — the double agents, all referred to by their code names. There had been almost forty double agents at one time or another. It was a team effort, and ever the sport lover, Masterman revelled in drawing comparisons between his task in charge of the Twenty Committee and running a cricket eleven. But even the most integrated teams have their stars. For Masterman and the entire deception operation, it was clear who that star player had been: Garbo, the Spaniard, a man who, in Masterman's words, 'turned out to be something of a genius'.

Masterman's book came out at around the same time that the journalist Sefton Delmer published *The Counterfeit Spy*, an account of the Garbo case. Delmer had worked as a propagandist against the Germans, a role which had allowed him to meet some of the intelligence officers who could tell him the story of the great deception that had helped win the war.

Delmer changed all the names in his book, even that of Garbo, which became 'Cato'. Neither did he give away the double agent's real name: Pujol was referred to throughout as 'Jorge Antonio', while Harris became 'Carlos Reid'.

The story was now becoming popularly known, but the mystery remained. Who was Garbo? Was he still alive? If so, where was he?

Could anyone find him?

One man was determined to seek Garbo out. Inspired by Masterman and Delmer's accounts of the story, the writer and historian Nigel West began a search in the early 1980s to discover his true identity. The tales of snake bites and malaria did not ring true, he thought. Somewhere, Garbo was out there, and he was determined to find him. All he knew was that he was Spanish.

The problem was that many of those who might have helped in his quest were now dead. West knew that Harris had been Garbo's case officer during the war, yet Harris was killed in a car crash in Mallorca in 1964. Hilda, his wife, had been with him at the time, and although she was unharmed in the accident, she died not long after without revealing the secret of Garbo's identity.

Whenever he had the chance, West asked former officers about the Spanish double agent. They had all heard of Garbo, but none knew his real name. It seemed as though the man might never be found after all.

But then, in 1981, West was given the opportunity to interview Anthony Blunt. Two years earlier Blunt had been publicly exposed as the fourth member of the Cambridge spy ring. A former member of MI5, he had been Guy Liddell's assistant for much of the war, as well as a close friend of Harris.

There was much to talk about — his spying for the Soviets, his relationship with the other Cambridge spies, Burgess, Maclean and Philby — but during the interviews, the subject of Garbo came up. West was surprised when Blunt told him that he had met the Spaniard on one occasion.

It was 1944, and Harris and Garbo had met Blunt for lunch at their usual haunt close to the office on Jermyn Street, the restaurant Garibaldi's. Almost forty years had passed since that day, and now in his mid-seventies Blunt had only a couple more years to live. And yet his memory was still good, and he told West that Garbo's name had been something like Juan or José García.

It was a start, if not a promising one: in Spanish it was about as unusual as 'John Smith'. Yet at least West had something to go on.

Then some time later West met Desmond Bristow, the Section V officer who had been one of the first to deal with Garbo on his arrival in London.

'Tell me about Garbo,' West said. And before Bristow could clam up, West added: 'It's all right, I know his name. It was Juan or José García.'

Bristow took the bait and corrected West.

'Juan PUJOL García,' he said.

West finally had Garbo's name.

Bristow went on to tell him that Garbo had dropped his first surname during his period in

366

London to protect his identity. The former MI6 officer had no idea whether Pujol was still alive, but he suggested trying in the Barcelona area: Pujol was a Catalan surname and that was the city where he had been born.

West hired an assistant to call up all the Pujol García households in the Barcelona phone book, asking them whether there was a member of the family called Juan, and if so whether he was about seventy years old and had spent time in England during the war.

The answers were all negative. Only one family stood out — the man who answered the phone had been defensive, wondering what the questions were about. After further calls, however, he opened up, finally admitting that his uncle Juan had spent a lot of time in London during the war. He had gone to live in South America, however, and his nephew had not heard from him for over twenty years. The last time they had had news from him he was living in Venezuela.

West was now convinced that he was on Garbo's trail, and the focus of his search moved to the other side of the Atlantic. A researcher was hired in Caracas, and after ten days searching the country for a 'Juan Pujol García' he called West telling him to ring a certain number at a certain time.

When he rang, a man answered at the other end. West had prepared a number of questions: whether the person answered them correctly or not would tell him if he had found Garbo. It was a nervous moment.

The Juan Pujol García at the other end of the line answered West's questions without hesitation, confirming that he had spent a good deal of time in London during the war, and adding that he had been in Hendon. He had also known Tommy Harris, and still kept a medal that was awarded to him by the British government in 1944.

This was the proof that West needed. Far from having died in Angola of malaria, Garbo, he now knew, was alive and well, and living in Venezuela. What was more, the former double agent agreed to meet West the following week in New Orleans.

West dropped everything and caught a plane. The venue was the Hilton Hotel. West was told to show up at a certain time. It was 20 May 1984 and the celebrations for the fortieth anniversary of the Normandy landings were only days away.

When he arrived, West realised with some horror that the lobby of the hotel was vast. Not only that, it was full of people. He had no photo to help him identify Pujol, and for an hour he walked around, looking in vain for the man he had spent so many years trying to track down. Giving up, he went back to his own hotel, having concluded that Pujol had decided not to show up. Pujol had, after all, escaped detection almost his entire life, turning evasion into something of an art form. Perhaps he had had second thoughts and did not want to be discovered after all.

West's then wife, however, had travelled to New Orleans with him, and now she — Araceli-like — saved the day. Go back, she told West. We haven't come all this way for nothing. Go back and find Garbo.

So off to the Hilton went West for a second time. On this occasion, a short bald man accompanied by his wife crossed the lobby and introduced himself.

The prey had found the searcher.

37

Venezuela and Spain, 1945–84

The forty years since leaving Britain had been eventful for Pujol. After an intense career as a double agent he might have been seeking a quieter life, but such was not to be his fate. His life in Venezuela had brought much pain and many failures. Like Oskar Schindler, his luck appeared to be concentrated in one specific moment in his life — the war — with the result that, in hindsight, few of his ventures either before or after enjoyed great success.

Things appeared to start well in Venezuela. Flush with his pay-off from MI5, Pujol took a grand house on Avenida de Bolivia in Caracas. There he housed not only Araceli and his two sons, but also his brother-in-law and his family, as well as his own mother Mercedes for a while. Pujol, it seemed, had great plans.

A visitor to the Caracas home in these early days was Tomás Harris. Harris, it will be recalled, as well as being an artist, had directed the Spanish Art Gallery in London, where works by the great Spanish masters were exhibited and sold. Now that the war was over, he gave that up to return to his career as an artist as well as starting a collection of prints, but he was still looking out for his friend Pujol.

News about a big art exhibition in Venezuela,

including paintings by El Greco, Velázquez and Goya, appeared in the local papers in December 1945. The artworks, the reports said, were being shipped from London, had a value of around £200,000 and were the property of a Spaniard resident in Venezuela by the name of Juan Pujol García. The idea was to try to sell the paintings to the Venezuelan government, thereby creating at a stroke the greatest art collection in the whole of Latin America.

The news did not go unnoticed by the Spanish Embassy in Caracas, and soon a secret investigation was launched. Who was this Juan Pujol, and where had these paintings come from? Were they artworks that had been looted during the Spanish Civil War?

For the following months, the Foreign Ministry in Madrid looked into every document in the possession of the Spanish State referring to Pujol, trying to find out about him. They discovered a lot — about his time as an officer in Franco's army during the Civil War, his time at the Majestic Hotel, his move to Lisbon in 1941. Even that he had lived in London for much of the war. But they never found anything to make them suspect that he had been an MI5 double agent.

Nonetheless, questions about the art collection remained. Araceli, Pujol's wife, was also investigated. She was reported by the Francoist authorities as being back in Spain in 1946, travelling with her brother in an expensive car and attending the most select 'society' parties. Was this part of the art dealing that her husband

371

now appeared to be engaged in? No one could say for certain.

In the end, however, the deal never went ahead. Still keeping their eye on him, by 1947 the Spanish authorities reached the conclusion that Pujol himself was not the owner of the paintings, rather that they belonged to persons unknown in Britain. Pujol was merely acting as an intermediary, and the Spanish State had no legitimate claim over the collection. The Venezuelan government did not buy the paintings in the end; the investigation was dropped.

It was the first of the series of failures that now characterised Pujol's life. But what was really going on?

Given the close relationship that he had built up with Harris in London, Harris's visits to Venezuela at the time (at least twice, according to someone who was there), and the art angle to the story, it seems more than likely that Harris had a part to play in Pujol's brief reinvention as a member of the art world.

'No other source in London could have provided a 'collection' of major Spanish works' at the time, says art historian Juliet Wilson-Bareau.

Was it a cover story concocted by Harris to give Pujol a new persona for his life in Venezuela? It is a possible explanation, and Harris's trips to Caracas may simply have been part of the narrative that was being built up around Pujol at the time. Wilson-Bareau also suggests a link with Harris closing down his Spanish Art Gallery at the end of the war.

'It was at that time that he began what must have been a major operation to close the London gallery and dispose of the stock.'

So a cover story with a large element of truth in it, perhaps, with Pujol acting as a middleman in Venezuela for a potential art deal involving Harris's merchandise.

Nonetheless, allegations have been made that something more sinister was afoot. In the 1980s, back in Spain and long divorced from Pujol, Araceli became friendly with Desmond Bristow and his wife. She told them that Pujol and Harris had been involved in faking paintings of the old masters. They had even, she claimed, managed to sell some of them in Caracas before a local art expert spotted them and blew the whistle. Bristow believed the story and concluded that Harris's friend Anthony Blunt would have acted as authenticator of the 'forgeries'.

Questions raised in the Canadian parliament in 1980 showed that Harris and Blunt had indeed been involved in the art business together after the war: the National Gallery of Canada had bought Poussin's *Augustus and Cleopatra* from Harris in the 1950s, with Blunt certifying its originality (as he did for many other museums around the world). Doubts have been raised in recent years about this attribution, however, and art historians now believe it was done by an unknown Italian artist. An article in the London *Daily Telegraph* in 2001 also pointed out that two other paintings bought by the Canadians from Harris around the same time on Blunt's recommendation — *St John the Baptist* by

Jusepe Leonardo and *The Three Angels* by Bartolomé Esteban Murillo — were later found to have been looted during the Spanish Civil War.

Araceli's accusations against her ex-husband and his former case officer — a man she did not get on with — have never been proven. They were made to Bristow in 1986, two years after the Garbo story became publicly known. Pujol, by this point, was a hero, but her ex-husband had airbrushed her — and the considerable role that she played in his success — out of his autobiography. Was she bitter? Her recollection of what had been going on between Harris and Pujol in Venezuela forty years before would have been uncertain at the least. Perhaps she wanted to pay Pujol and Harris back for the misery of her London life, even after so much time had passed. In Bristow she found a willing audience. Having been made head of station for Spain and Portugal after the war, Bristow had left MI6 in 1954 after becoming suspicious of many of his former colleagues in the secret service following the defection of Burgess and Maclean. Conspiracy theories about his former friend Harris were grist to his mill, and through him Araceli found a mouthpiece for her attempts to tarnish the Garbo name.

Neither does the Canadian angle to the story do any more than confirm that Harris and Blunt were working together in the art business. Blunt's attribution has been questioned in recent years but there is nothing to suggest that he did not believe it to be a work by Poussin at the time. Similarly, that two of the artworks sold to the Canadians were later proven to have been looted does not incriminate Harris. The positive identification of looted art began late and is still ongoing.

Whatever Pujol's role in the matter — as a bona-fide front man for a real art deal by Harris, or simply pretending to be a collector as part of a new cover story — his first venture in Venezuela fizzled out.

His next step was to take the money remaining to him and buy a large farm near the city of Valencia, three hours from Caracas. It was 1947 and Pujol brought in new, modern machinery, some of which had never been seen in the country before; elaborate irrigation systems were set up and the farm workers were given much better wages and work conditions than on any of the other farms in the area.

But again Pujol's luck had deserted him. In 1948 there was a revolution in Venezuela, and in the ensuing chaos Pujol's farm was attacked and destroyed. Financially ruined, he returned to Caracas, but this turned out to be the final straw for the marriage. Whether Araceli left him or he told her to leave is not clear, but she now travelled back to Spain for good, taking their three children (a daughter had been born to them in Venezuela) with her.

It was 1948; Pujol was alone and broke. But news came from an unexpected source: MI5 wanted him to work for them again. Bristow, still in MI6, came up with a plan for Pujol to infiltrate a group of Czech expatriates in

Venezuela in the hope of eventually getting inside Soviet spying operations then active inside France. Pujol was keen on the idea, as was Harris, and a meeting was arranged between the three of them in Spain.

Before the Madrid reunion, however, Pujol visited Harris alone at his home in Mallorca. In the meantime, it seems, Harris had mentioned Bristow's plan to Philby back in London. Philby was now the head of MI6's anti-Soviet espionage group — irony of ironies — and he, not unnaturally, poured cold water on the scheme. As a result, Harris had become doubtful about the plan, and subsequently so did Pujol. At the Madrid meeting with Bristow they told him that they thought it would not work.

Bristow's scheme was shelved. Pujol went back to Caracas, but soon he had cause to get in touch with the British again. A letter from his brother-in-law in Spain mentioned that a German called Knappe had been looking for him. At their final meeting in the woods near the Spanish-French border at the end of the war, Pujol had told Knappe that he would try to help him escape Spain. Now, it appeared, Knappe was calling in that favour. Pujol immediately got in touch with MI5, who told him to carry on and make contact with Knappe. But soon afterwards the trail went cold, and the former German spy disappeared. Pujol never heard from him again.

The two events — first with Bristow and then with Knappe — made him decide, however, that he needed to cut his links with the British. His wife and family had gone; he had lost all his money: this was a perfect opportunity to start life anew.

'Garbo' had to die.

It was the last contact there would ever be between Pujol and Harris, the two men who had created the characters and network of imaginary Nazi spies. As a final favour to his double agent and close friend, Harris now spread the rumour that Garbo had passed away in southern Africa. Perhaps through a case of Chinese whispers, different versions of what had actually happened began to emerge. Even the British Ambassador to Spain helped confuse things by telling Araceli that her husband had died in a Mozambique jungle. Struggling financially in Madrid, Araceli did not believe a word of it.

But for Pujol it must have been a relief. He was still only thirty-six and he could begin again.

By now he had started a relationship with a Venezuelan woman, Carmen Cilia Alvarez. They opened a newsagent in Maracaibo, but the wealth they had expected to earn from the expanding oil industry in the area failed to materialise, and so Pujol found work as a language teacher for Shell — giving Spanish lessons to the new arrivals, and English to the locals. Putting some money aside from his new job, he and Carmen got rid of the newsagent and opened a gift shop in the luxury Lagunillas Hotel instead.

Their first children were born in the early 1950s — a daughter and a son. And for a while Pujol was happy with his life, forging new friendships, stamp collecting, reading.

In the late 1950s Araceli got in touch: she

wanted a divorce. She had met an American — an art dealer — called Edward Kreisler, and they wanted to get married. Pujol signed the necessary papers and Araceli got her final wish — living the high life that she had dreamed of for so long. Kreisler moved in top circles, and their friends included the US Ambassador as well as celebrities such as Charlton Heston and Sofia Loren. Francoist Spain did not allow divorce, so Araceli and Kreisler were married in Gibraltar in 1958.

In the early 1960s Pujol ventured back to Spain for the first time since his meeting with Bristow and Harris in 1948, taking his new family with him for a holiday. He wanted to fulfil a promise he had made back in 1938, when he had jumped out of his trench on the front lines in the Spanish Civil War, and crossed over to the Francoists. The Republican search party had almost found him hiding at the bottom of a valley, but a cloud had covered the light of the moon just at the right moment and he had managed to escape. He had attributed his luck at the time to the aid of the Virgen del Pilar — the patron of the city of Zaragoza. Now, at last, he wanted to visit the city's cathedral and thank her.

The trip to Spain gave Pujol a new idea, though. He saw the beginnings of the mass tourism boom in the country and thought he should try something similar in Venezuela.

Soon after they returned, he packed in his teaching job with Shell and invested their savings in a hotel in Choroní, his wife's beautiful home town on the coast. The Hotel Marisel was created with grand ideas: Pujol offered tourists package deals, driving people in from Caracas, giving them full board, entertaining them with films shown from a projector at weekends, and generally providing them with everything they could want.

The location was perfect, and today it is a prime resort. But Pujol was ahead of his time. The roads to Caracas were mud tracks and were often flooded in the rainy season: a one-way journey could take anything up to three hours. Like his previous plans, the hotel was destined to fail, and within a few years he had to sell up and return to the only thing he had left — the gift shop. His wife and their three children went to live with relatives while, for the next two years, Pujol worked, ate and slept surrounded by nick-nacks. The family were not reunited until 1968, when they could finally afford to rent a small flat.

Outside Venezuela, however, people were beginning to talk about Garbo, speculating about whether this mysterious double agent was still alive, and if so what his true identity was. Some of the stories were repeated by local journalists, and Pujol started to feel insecure. When the British got in touch with him again in 1973, he could not be sure if it was a set-up, and took his son, Carlos, along with him for the meeting in Caracas, telling him to wait outside and call the police if he had not come out within half an hour. Carlos was nervous — all his father told him was that it had something to do with his wartime activities, and he borrowed a gun from a friend to take with him in case he needed it.

In the end the British approach turned out to be legitimate. The embassy officials merely wanted to tell Pujol that certain papers relating to his work for MI5 were now going to be declassified. There was nothing to worry about, however, because the story that he had died had been circulating for some time. It may not be accidental that the meeting coincided with the publication of both Masterman's and Delmer's books.

With the threat of discovery hanging over him, Pujol now passed through some of his unhappiest years. In 1975 his daughter with Carmen Cilia, María Elena, died in childbirth at the age of only twenty-two. The news shocked Pujol so much that he lost his Catholic faith and became agnostic.

A couple of years later he himself came close to death due to heart problems. His family raised some money, and he was flown to Houston where a quadruple heart bypass was performed.

In time he recovered and was well enough in 1979 for the family to take another holiday to Europe, this time visiting Germany and Italy as well as Spain. It was the one and only time that Pujol visited the country he had done so much to defeat in the war. Hiring a car in Luxembourg, they crossed the border and drove towards Bonn. After only a few kilometres, however, he was pulled over by a police patrol, who immediately asked him for his identity papers. Pujol nervously obliged, and then through sign language the German policeman indicated that he was giving him a ticket for speeding. Pujol simply smiled to himself and handed over the money.

By the early 1980s, Pujol had sold the gift shop and he and Carmen Cilia were living in Caracas with their son. Then, in May 1984, there was a phone call from London: a man named Nigel West wanted to ask some questions about the war . . .

38

Spain, Germany, France, Canada and Britain, 1945–Present

Tomás Harris's death in a car crash in Mallorca on 27 January 1964 came just a year after his close friend Kim Philby disappeared from Beirut and defected to the Soviet Union. Months later, another friend, Anthony Blunt, admitted to the British authorities that he too was a Soviet spy.

Given his connection with the Cambridge Five and the timing of his death, some have speculated whether Harris might not also have been working in some way for the Soviet Union. In the paranoid years of the Cold War, with the growing recognition that respected and leading members of the British intelligence community were secretly working for Moscow, accusations were made against many people. Some of the claims were substantiated, others were not. In Harris's case, nothing has ever been proven.

Harris's detractors included the journalist Malcolm Muggeridge, who had worked in MI6 during the war. Muggeridge appears to have been the one who began a rumour that Harris acted as a paymaster for the Cambridge Five, although he did not know Harris very well and no evidence was forthcoming to back the claim.

For some historians, however, Harris's art dealings with Blunt after the war help to cast

doubt on his true loyalties. Nigel West has speculated about the 'paymaster' theory. One possibility,
he says, is that the Soviets passed on paintings
looted during the Spanish Civil War from Republican-
held territory to Harris. He would then have sold
them and the money would have been used to
pay the Cambridge spies.

Juliet Wilson-Bareau, who worked closely with
Harris for the last ten years of his life, rejects the
idea that he might willingly have been involved
in any art scam, although, she says, 'he was
persistent and adept at following trails, and took
risks as a collector.'

After the war, Harris was awarded an OBE
and wrote up a report on the Garbo case for
MI5, which he finished in November 1945. He
left the Security Service, sold the art gallery (his
father Lionel had died in 1943) and moved to
Spain with his wife Hilda, staying initially in
Malaga before, in 1947, moving to a large house
in Camp de Mar, Mallorca, where he concentrated on his art — including sculpture, ceramics
and designs for stained glass and tapestries, as
well as paintings, prints and drawings. He kept
his print collections in London and travelled
back regularly to the studio building that he
retained at his Earl's Court address[1] (with the
large house let to Sotheby's director Peter
Wilson). But Spain was now his home.

Nigel West points to a further 'coincidence'
between Harris in this latter period of his life

---

[1] Logan Place was later home to Queen singer
Freddie Mercury.

and the story of the Cambridge Five, however. In 1951 Burgess and Maclean defected to Moscow and the story of the Soviet moles began to emerge. On fleeing to the USSR, Maclean had been forced to leave his American wife, Melinda, who was then pregnant with their third child. Sometime later Melinda moved to Geneva to get away from the public eye. Then in 1953, supposedly under surveillance by the British, she too vanished and showed up some time later in the Soviet Union. Her escape route had been complicated, involving a number of trains and pick-ups by people helping her and her children get to the East. How had the details of what to do been passed on to her?

According to West, a possible clue was spotted in the fact that only days before leaving Geneva she had been on holiday in Mallorca. The place where she stayed was at the other side of the island from Harris's home, but he speculates about whether instructions for her escape been given to her while she was there. And if so, whether Harris had anything to do with it.

To this day no one can say, but at the time the coincidence further fuelled suspicions against Harris — suspicions that were compounded by Philby's defection in 1963. Was Harris's death in a car crash a year later also just a coincidence? Or had he been assassinated by the Russians to silence him, as some later suggested?

Desmond Bristow was one of the first to hear about Harris's death. The phone rang at his home and Hilda, Harris's wife, told him about the car crash. Bristow immediately flew out to be with her.

Hilda told Bristow that she and Harris had both gone to Palma on the day of the accident so that Harris could visit an antique dealer. Hilda had gone shopping, and after the meeting Harris had met up with her at the port for lunch. They had a few drinks, and an argument began.

'Don't ask me what about,' she told Bristow. 'I haven't a clue: most probably I was angry with him for being late.'

After lunch they set off to visit a pottery, where Harris wanted some of his recent ceramics to be fired. But angry and slightly drunk, he drove his new Citroën DS too fast. Heading down the Lluchmayor road, they went over a humpbacked bridge, Harris lost control of the car, and they hit an almond tree. Hilda was thrown clear by the impact, but Harris died instantly.

'When I came to, he was still in the car, not moving or breathing or anything.'

Bristow checked the police report on the accident and everything tallied with Hilda's account. Inevitably, though, questions have been asked about it, particularly given its timing. Had someone tampered with Harris's car? Why else should he crash on a straight road that he had driven down so many times before?

Given the circumstances it seems reasonable to accept the official version of what happened. The combination of alcohol and a row with his wife might have been enough for him to lose control of the car in the first place. Add to this the fact that they had just gone over a humpbacked bridge at speed, thereby losing traction on the road, and one might almost be surprised had they *not* crashed.

Wilson-Bareau recalls comments that owing to the bouncy suspension of the Citroën, Harris had hit his head on the roof — perhaps going over the bridge — and had been knocked out, thus causing the crash. He was under enormous strain at the time, she remembers. He had curated a major exhibition of Goya's prints and drawings at the British Museum, which opened just a few weeks before on 12 December 1963. He was also involved in a parallel Winter Exhibition at the Royal Academy devoted to Goya, as well as rushing to finish the publication of his catalogue *raisonné* of Goya's prints, which was planned to coincide with the two events. He had returned to Mallorca, intending to go back to London for the end of the exhibitions in February and continue work on the final catalogue proofs (dummy volumes had been provided for display at the British Museum). It finally appeared, posthumously, that autumn — a major work in two volumes. It is still considered the 'bible' for the study of Goya prints.[1]

At the time of his death Harris was only fifty-five. His wife Hilda returned to England shortly afterwards, where she died in December 1972.

Since the collapse of the Soviet Union, not all

---

[1] In 1962 Harris had offered to place his Goya collection on permanent loan to the British Museum, and in 1979 the bulk of it was accepted in lieu of tax on his estate.

the KGB files have been opened. Some have, however, and those that mention Harris refer to him simply as an MI5 officer. There is nothing in the documents that have been seen in the West so far to suggest that he was ever working for the Soviets.

In her last interview before she died, Harris's sister Enriqueta, who had collaborated in a minor capacity on the Garbo case and had worked for MI5, insisted that her brother had never betrayed his country.

Wilson-Bareau was introduced to Harris in 1954 when Blunt, her director of studies at the Courtauld, responded to Harris's request for help editing his Goya catalogue. She worked as Harris's assistant and carried the catalogue through to its publication after Harris's death. Today she remains uncertain, although unconvinced, about a possible Soviet connection.

'It's still an open question,' she says. 'I remember that Harris was aghast when Philby defected, and I thought it was impossible that Harris could have been involved as well. But following the shock and disbelief when Blunt was later exposed I felt that you could never be sure.'

Blunt never forgot his friend. He wrote an entry on him for the *Dictionary of National Biography*, and in 1975 an introduction for an exhibition of Harris's work, drawn from his three sisters' collections, at the Courtauld Insitute.

★ ★ ★

Just six months after his withdrawal from the Battle of Normandy, suffering from a nervous breakdown, Jochen Peiper was once more on the front lines with the 1st SS Panzer Division LAH fighting the Allies. The Battle of the Bulge was an audacious fightback by the Germans to defeat the Allies on the Western Front by pushing through the US lines in the Ardennes area and splitting their armies in two. Peiper's role in the battle would seal his reputation as one of the most effective and ferocious commanders in the Waffen-SS.

Driving a spearhead of new 'King Tiger' tanks — more powerful and dangerous than their already feared predecessors, the Panthers and Tigers used in Normandy — Peiper pushed deep into Allied territory using techniques similar to the Blitzkrieg tactics that had won the Germans so many victories at the start of the war. It was mid-December 1944, there was heavy snow on the ground, and his move caught the Allies by surprise.

Bold though the attack was, however, it failed, not least because the King Tigers needed a large amount of fuel and the Third Reich was already running out of supplies to keep them moving. By Christmas Eve, Peiper had to give up, and was forced to trudge on foot through the snow with 800 of his men back to the German lines.

When he was finally captured, Peiper was put on trial by the Allies for what became his single most infamous act of the war — the massacre of over eighty American soldiers during the Battle of the Bulge at Malmedy. The 'Malmedy massacre trial', as it became known, was held in

1946 at Dachau, where Peiper had first trained to become an SS officer. He was found guilty along with several others, and sentenced to death by hanging.

The death sentence, however, was controversial. Already by 1946 there was a growing sense that the wounds of the war should be healed, a call for no more executions or retribution. In addition, doubts were raised about some of the prosecutor's methods during his interrogation of Peiper and the other defendants, with suggestions of torture and mock trials to get them to confess to their crimes.

The case was brought to the US senate, and a committee was set up to investigate — interestingly, one of the members was Senator Joseph McCarthy, then a relatively unknown politician. Eventually it concluded that improper procedures had been used by the prosecution — although not torture — and that this had affected the trial process. There was no doubt about Peiper's guilt, but the result was that after several postponements of his hanging, his sentence was commuted to life imprisonment.

Eventually, towards the end of 1956, he was released on parole after serving eleven and a half years.

Through an organisation that helped former SS members, Peiper got a job with Porsche and quickly moved up the company hierarchy. He was forced to leave, however, when union members objected to his being given a senior management role. He later went on to become a car sales trainer.

During the 1960s he was called to trial in a number of cases involving his activities in the war, including one in which Simon Wiesenthal backed claims that he had deported Jews from Italy, but he was never convicted.

In 1972, now in semi-retirement, he bought a home in the town of Traves, in the Haute-Saône department of France, just east of Dijon. He still used his given name, and within a couple of years was identified by a former French resistance member in the area. Reports on Peiper were circulated among French Communists, and in 1976 the Communist newspaper *l'Humanité* published an article on Peiper's whereabouts.

Death threats soon followed, and Peiper sent his family back to Germany while he stayed in the house.

There, on the night of 13–14 July there was a shoot-out and the property was set on fire. Peiper's burned body was later found inside, with a bullet wound in his chest. No one was ever brought to trial for his murder.

★ ★ ★

Karl-Erich Kühlenthal continued to live in hiding in Spain until 1950, when he returned to his native Koblenz. His wife Ellen was the heiress of a clothes and fashion business in the city, called Dienz, and husband and wife took over the running of the company.

Kühlenthal made a better businessman than he did a spymaster. Dienz flourished, and the Kühlenthals became respectable members of the community. He died in October 1975.

Did he ever know the true story of 'Alaric', his top spy in London, who was really 'Garbo', a British double agent?

Harris, his British opponent in MI5, was damning in his conclusion: 'His characteristic German lack of sense of humour . . . blinded him to the absurdities of the story we were unfolding.'

The records suggest that he was fooled; his family insist that he was not.

Today the Dienz company is owned by his son, Edgar Kühlenthal.

★　★　★

Cecil 'Monkey' Blacker won the Military Cross following Operation Goodwood and continued to fight with the 23rd Hussars across northern France and Germany, being made regimental commander in 1945.

He stayed in the army, rising through the ranks and serving in Northern Ireland and Yemen. Throughout this time he continued his horse racing activities, riding Sir John in the 1948 Grand National. They fell at a fence before the Chair, and Blacker had to stand at the side and watch as the race was won by Sheila's Cottage.

After becoming Vice Chief of the Imperial General Staff in 1970, his final position was that of Adjutant General to the Forces, one of the highest officers in the Army.

He retired in 1976 and died in 2002. His son is the writer and journalist Terence Blacker.

On the day after the liberation of Paris, Amado Granell and other members of La Nueve escorted Charles de Gaulle in the victory parade down the Champs-Elysées. It was a great moment of pride for the Spanish lieutenant. Soon all France would be free and the eyes of the world could turn to deposing another fascist dictator. Franco.

But while the French gave him honours such as the Croix de Guerre and the Légion d'honneur, no one was in the mood to start waging war in Spain by 1944. In Europe, Germany and Hitler were the target, nowhere and no one else.

The political battles within liberated France now enveloped Leclerc's 2nd Armoured Division, and towards the end of 1944 Granell decided that he had had enough. He went with the conquering Allied armies as far as the Rhine, where he washed his hands and face in a symbolic gesture, and then retired from military service.

He was a great loss to La Nueve. His commanding officer, Captain Dronne, wrote that with Granell's departure his company had lost 'part of its soul'.

Granell's dream of re-establishing democracy in Spain did not end there, however, and he became friendly with a number of Republican politicians, including Francisco Largo Caballero, the former Republican prime minister. For a while, in the late 1940s, he provided a line of communication between exiled Republicans and Don Juan, son of former King Alfonso XIII and heir to the Spanish throne, in an attempt at reconciliation. Don Juan, like the Republicans, was also in exile, living in Portugal, forbidden by Franco to return to Spain.

Franco's own contacts with Don Juan in 1948, in which he promised to pass power to Don Juan's son, Juan Carlos, on his death, brought the discussions with Granell to an end.

In 1950 Granell opened a small restaurant in Paris, Los Amigos, where known Spanish Republicans often gathered. But within two years he returned clandestinely to his beloved Spain. At this stage death sentences were still being carried out against those who had fought against Franco during the Civil War, and Granell was forced to live secretly in Santander, Barcelona and Madrid.

In 1971 he opened a white-goods shop in the town of Orihuela, to the south of Alicante. On 12 May 1972, while driving to Valencia to talk to the French consul about his war pension, he was involved in a car crash and died. He never learned of the critical role that another Spaniard — Juan Pujol — had played in the Allies' victory in France.

In his diary, Dronne suggested that anyone checking Granell's car, turned upside down in the rice paddies around the town of Sueca, would have found bulletholes. Just as with the crash that killed Harris eight years earlier, there was a suspicion of foul play. No evidence to support this has ever been found.

* * *

At the end of the war, Private Jack Poolton of the Royal Regiment of Canada was liberated by US soldiers moving into central Germany in April 1945. His captors gave up the fight, refusing, at the end, to carry out an order by Himmler to shoot all prisoners.

Poolton had been in POW camps for almost three years after the disaster at Dieppe, and his health was suffering. A troopship took him back to Britain, where, on arriving at Waterloo station, he telegraphed his parents back in Canada to tell them that he was safe. Thin, dirty and louse-ridden, he spent much of his time eating to get his strength back, but struggled to keep his food down. He lost so much weight that friends and relatives did not recognise him.

In July 1945 he sailed back to Canada, slowly recuperating. The return to civilian life was painful; he suffered from depression and considered committing suicide, unable to cope with the sense of guilt that he had survived while so many of his comrades had been killed.

With time, he built a new life for himself, working as a mechanic until his retirement. He married and had three children.

In 1992 he returned to Dieppe for the fiftieth anniversary of the raid. Despite his shaking the hands of German servicemen who also attended, a certain bitterness over what happened that day in August remained.

'I am convinced', he wrote in his memoirs, 'that the Germans *did* know of the Dieppe Raid in advance, and those who planned it were aware of this.'

★ ★ ★

Johnny Jebsen was held in German concentration camps until the last days of the war. He never told his captors what he knew about the British double-cross system, and the secret was kept safe.

No one knows what happened to him. Was he one of the last victims of the Nazis, who killed as many of their prisoners as they were able to before the enemy could liberate them? Or did he manage to escape and begin a new life under a different name?

In February 1950 a court in Berlin pronounced him officially dead, but the question has never been satisfactorily answered.

★ ★ ★

Mavis Batey continued working at Bletchley Park until the end of the war, but left shortly afterwards. She became an academic, teaching at Oxford University's extra-mural courses, and wrote extensively on the role of the Enigma code-breakers in the defeat of Nazism. She and her husband Keith Batey had three children. They continued to share a love of crossword puzzles but never spoke to each other about their respective work within the secret world.

Mavis was made an MBE in 1987 and in 2009, Mavis's biography of Dillwyn Knox, *Dilly:*

The Man who Broke Enigmas, was published.

She spent her last years in Sussex and often spoke about the code-breaking work at Bletchley during the war and the important achievements of Dilly Knox's team. She died in November 2013 at the age of 92.

39

London and Normandy, June 1984

Juan Pujol might never have allowed himself to be revealed as Garbo had Nigel West not got in touch with him when he did. His second son with Carmen Cilia, Juan Carlos, was studying in New Orleans at the time, and had suffered racial abuse on account of the dark complexion that he inherited from his mother. The revelation that his father was the famous Second World War double agent Garbo, Pujol reasoned, would prove that he had no reason to feel inferior to anyone.

Unaware of this, Nigel West had a hook of his own to get Pujol over to London for the fortieth anniversary celebrations of the Normandy landings. By agreeing to appear now, he said, he could get a publishing deal to tell his story, and would also have an opportunity to meet Prince Philip at Buckingham Palace.

The latter was not strictly true — West had not yet had any contacts with the Palace over Pujol. But he felt certain that Prince Philip, an amateur spy-buff, would jump at the chance to meet the famous Garbo in person.

In effect, West 'did a Garbo' on Garbo. Pujol accepted the invitation, and West hurriedly arranged things. In the end, the Palace reacted as he had expected them to.

Before his audience, however, West arranged a meeting with the surviving members of the deception group who worked on the Garbo operation all those years before. Present at the Special Forces Club were Tar Robertson, Roger Hesketh, Cyril Mills and Desmond Bristow. None of the intelligence veterans believed West's claim that he had found the real Garbo.

When Pujol walked into the room, however, everyone fell silent. Here he was, the man they had worked with during the war, someone who had been reported dead at least once over the past decades.

Cyril Mills was the first to say anything.

'I don't believe it,' he said. 'It *can't* be you. You're dead.'

Tar Robertson was so moved that he burst into tears and rushed over to embrace Pujol.

Other reunions were held: a gathering with Sarah Bishop, Charlie Haines and Harris's sisters, who had also been engaged on the Garbo operation at various stages. Later there was a private lunch between Sarah Bishop and Pujol to which West was not invited.

The audience with Prince Philip followed on 31 May, at which Pujol was publicly awarded with the MBE that had secretly been given to him back in 1944. Prince Philip thanked him for his help during the war, asking Pujol why he had decided to assist Britain.

Pujol looked at him. Prince Philip was Greek, yet had served with the Royal Navy during the conflict.

'Why did *you* help the British?' Pujol asked.

398

Prince Philip smiled.

Photos were taken of the newly discovered war hero, and Pujol's face appeared the next day on the front cover of the *Daily Mail*. From forced obscurity he was famous overnight.

The Spanish press soon caught on to the story, and Pujol agreed to lengthy interviews with a magazine and on Catalan television. The fact that he was now known about in Spain opened up old wounds: he had not been in touch with Araceli or the three children he had with her since they left Venezuela to return to Spain in the 1940s. To this day Nigel West feels there is still some rancour on their part for his having uncovered a past that they preferred to leave buried.

Months later Pujol returned to his home in Caracas, where he wrote an account of his life. Nigel West wrote chapters dealing with the inside workings of double-cross, which Pujol was never fully aware of, and the jointly written book was published in 1985.

Pujol glossed over many aspects of the story, however. Araceli's role, his exact relationship with some of the other members of the Garbo team, the art dealing after the war — all this and much more was left out.

The truth behind the gaps in his own account died with him. Three years later, on 10 October 1988, Pujol suffered a stroke and died. His son called the British Consulate to inform them, but the official on duty forgot to pass the word on to London. Neither did word reach Spain.

Pujol's death was only marked by a short

announcement in the local newspaper. He was buried in the cemetery at Choroní, by the waters of the Caribbean.

Months later, once the news had finally spread, his family received letters of condolence from all over the world.

It was only after he had appeared publicly that Pujol got a true sense of the scale of his own achievement, of the importance that Garbo had had during the war. The double-cross system and the vast apparatus of deception that the Allies had built and which they used to bolster, back up and complement his work was kept largely secret from him while he was in London. His work was important — that much he was told. But not quite how much depended on it.

After the reunions with the Garbo team members in London, Pujol was taken by plane on 6 June 1984 to the Normandy beaches for the commemoration ceremonies taking place that day marking the fortieth anniversary of the landings. Prime Minister Margaret Thatcher, President Reagan and President Mitterrand were all in attendance, as were thousands of veterans who had taken part. A camera crew followed Pujol around as he visited several sites along the coastline, and news quickly spread that 'Garbo', the double agent who had done so much to ensure the campaign's success, was present. Elderly medal-wearing men, some in uniform, pressed around to shake Pujol's hand and hear his story.

The most emotional moment, however, came when Pujol went to the American military cemetery at Omaha beach. Thousands of pearl-white crosses and Stars of David stand in arrow-straight rows across the perfectly kept lawns, with views over the cliffs to where so many men were killed on the morning of the invasion. Even today, so long after the events, it remains the single most moving site along the Normandy coastline.

Pujol wandered off on his own at one point, pacing gently among the gravestones, with their simple inscriptions to each person buried there. One in particular seemed to draw his attention — the white cross of a Sergeant. Arthur B. Buschlen of the 16th Infantry Regiment, who was killed on D-Day at Omaha beach. Pujol was clearly affected by what he saw, and soon began to weep. He knelt down and made the sign of the cross, before walking back to Nigel West and the television crew.

West asked him if he was all right. They had come here, after all, to celebrate his amazing achievement.

'They told me,' Pujol said, wiping away his tears, 'that the work I did saved thousands of lives.'

He looked back at the endless lines of the dead.

'Only now, coming here, I see I didn't do enough.'

Epilogue

What If?

To understand the importance of what Juan Pujol and Tomás Harris achieved with Garbo and the stories they told the Germans, it is essential to ask the question: 'What if?'

Today, historians hail Garbo as 'the greatest double agent in the Second World War'. But what if Garbo had been a failure, or had not existed at all? Serendipity played a crucial role in his tale, the meeting of specific people at the right time in the right place. What if none of these factors had turned out as they did, and he had not become a British-run double agent?

Roger Hesketh, who worked in Eisenhower's deception unit, Ops B, and who was a key figure in the double-cross operation, wrote a book on the Fortitude plan after the war. In it he asked a pertinent question: Of all the elements employed in deception for the Normandy campaign, from the fake runways and aircraft, to the dummy airborne troops, and the double agents feeding lies to the enemy, which one had the greatest effect? Which part of Fortitude had actually fooled the Germans?

There were many different and important parts to the overall puzzle, but on examining the German records after the war, and interviewing their commanders, one key piece stood out over all the others: Garbo's message of 9 June 1944 in which he clearly elaborated the theory that the Normandy landings were a trap meant to divert the best German troops away from the Pas-de-Calais. Other factors had helped — the other double agents feeding the Germans the story of FUSAG and the fictional build-up of Allied troops around Dover. But it was Garbo's D+3 message that made Hitler himself give the counter-order that stopped the German reserves — and importantly the 1st SS Panzer Division LAH — from attacking the Allied soldiers struggling to get a toehold on the Normandy coastline in the first few days of the invasion.

Keitel himself, Hitler's Chief of Staff, said as much. When shown the text of Garbo's message he agreed that it had been the reason why the Führer ordered his crack reserves to stay close to the narrowest part of the Channel.

'There you have your answer,' he told his interrogator. 'If I were writing a history I would say, with ninety-nine per cent certainty, that that message provided the reason for the change of plan.'

No other double agent or factor within the deception set-up had such a dramatic and powerful effect. Garbo was the single most important part of the success of Fortitude.

'Taking the evidence as a whole,' Hesketh concluded, 'the reader will probably agree that GARBO's report decided the issue.'

And would Operation Overlord, the invasion of Normandy, have succeeded without the deception plan? Could all those thousands of soldiers have managed to fight their way off the beaches and deep into France had Fortitude not been set up to protect them from the best German troops then available in Western Europe?

Some historians prefer to downplay the importance of Fortitude, yet Allied commanders at the time were convinced that it was pivotal. It was the reason why the deception was carried out in the first place.

Considering the numbers of German troops available in France and Belgium, and the speed with which the Allies could get men and equipment ashore, the success of Fortitude was not a mere bonus that would help keep casualty rates down, it was crucial to the success of the invasion itself. Deception planners in London had already envisaged a scenario where no deception was carried out, estimating a timetable showing how quickly the Germans would pour men into the invasion area once the assault started. If the enemy correctly assumed that Normandy was it — that there was no second invasion coming in the Pas-de-Calais — and as a result sent the bulk of its forces in to repel the invaders, then by D+25 they would have some thirty-one divisions in Normandy, including nine Panzer divisions. That scale of build-up, Eisenhower and the other Allied commanders knew, was impossible to match. They had the floating Mulberry harbours, which they could use to ship supplies and men into France at a rapid rate. But even with these it would not be sufficient to bring in enough soldiers and armour to combat such imposing numbers.

'In short, if Fortitude did not work, if the Germans pulled their Fifteenth Army away from the Pas-de-Calais and hurled it against Normandy, Overlord would fail.'

In a conflict involving so many millions of people, in which so many died, it seems frivolous, perhaps, to boil it all down to one or two men, a mere handful whose words and decisions changed the course of history. Other factors could also have had a decisive effect on the success of D-Day — the weather in the Channel over those crucial few days in early June, for example. And others also played their part — not least the soldiers who landed on the beaches, risking their lives to begin the slow process of liberating Europe from the Nazis. And yet the importance not only of the deception operation, but of Garbo's role in it, seems incontrovertible, as Eisenhower himself acknowledged to Harris.

'You know,' he told Harris after the war, 'your work with Mr Pujol most probably amounts to the equivalent of a whole army division. You have saved a lot of lives.'

So we turn to the even greater question: What if, in the absence of Garbo, Overlord had failed? What if the Allies had been pushed back into the sea, as so many commanders and politicians — including Churchill himself in his darker moods — predicted? What would the history of the Second World War read like today? What kind of world, even, would we be living in?

We are moving into the realms of extreme speculation here, but it is useful in order to understand the significance of Garbo, and more importantly, it is fun, an intellectual game — because we know what really happened.

The first thing to point out is that even in a scenario where the Allies failed successfully to invade France, Germany would still have been defeated in the Second World War. It was already too late for the Nazi State to survive unless Hitler could have found some way to arrange peace or an armistice of sorts with Stalin. The two dictators had managed to find common cause with the Nazi-Soviet Pact of August 1939, so there was a precedent. But by this stage, and with so much blood spilled on the Eastern Front, it is hard to imagine Stalin agreeing to anything short of the annihilation of his ideological nemesis. Hitler had duped him once before, breaking their pact by invading the Soviet Union in June 1941. Pragmatic though Stalin could be, he was unlikely to let that one go unavenged.

So the Red Army keeps pushing towards Berlin. In the west the Allies have failed to establish a bridgehead on the beaches of Normandy, and it will take them a long time to prepare another assault, so now Hitler can focus the vast majority of his forces to fight the Soviets. This would have slowed them down, but would not have stopped them. The fall of Berlin, Hitler's suicide in the bunker — these events are still likely in a Garbo-less world, but perhaps at a later date.

And then what? It seems probable that Stalin does not stop in Germany, but pushes on into France. The whole of Europe might well fall into Soviet hands.

'It should not be forgotten that D-Day began the liberation of the western half of the European continent; a liberation without which the Red Army would surely have appeared on the banks of the Rhine — if not the Atlantic Coast — with profound consequences for the post-war world,' Roger Moorhouse argues.

And what are the Allies doing while all this is happening? With a disaster in Normandy, the US might well shift its focus to the Pacific, where its war really started. Yet would it really stand by, and watch as Europe falls to Communism?

'A climax would have come late in the summer of 1945,' Stephen Ambrose suggests, 'with atomic bombs exploding over German cities. What a finish *that* would have been.'

The Red Army marching over the entire continent, whole areas devastated by terrifying new weapons, perhaps a new war involving Britain and America against the Soviets. Today we look at the footage from the end of the war of crumbling towns and cities, of piles of corpses and of a world emerging from a conflict of mythical proportions and unimaginable brutality. And we shudder at the unspeakable grimness of it all, thankful that we have not had to live through such horror.

Yet it could have been much, much worse.

Nobody changes the world by sticking to the rules. Through Garbo, Pujol performed a great service by drawing on a sense of playfulness and mischief and by seeing beyond everyday ideas about 'good' and 'bad'. In this he drew on a long tradition in Spanish culture of the lovable rogue, the *pícaro* who deftly weaves his way through the world, smart, wily and slippery like mercury.

In common with the leading character in *Lazarillo de Tormes*, the classic picaresque novel of the sixteenth century, Pujol was a trickster and an adventurer. In other circumstances he might well have ended up in jail. Certainly the Germans would have killed him without hesitation had they had any inkling of what he was really up to.

Yet by taking advantage of the bizarre opportunity provided by the war, and by joining with Harris to create Garbo, he also became a magician, a Prospero-like character, returning a happy order to the world through the power of words and thought. Somehow, thanks to his wit and skill, he managed to slip through the nets that might otherwise have caught him, and survived.

Untruths told in the service of a greater truth. We owe the world that we live in today in large part to Garbo's ingenuity, imagination and sense of fun.

And that's the truth.

Appendix I
The Flow of Deception Material from the Allies to the Germans through Garbo (June 1944)

Most of the communications on the German side are being decrypted by Bletchley Park and fed back into the Allied intelligence system, creating a loop.

Eisenhower and Allied Chiefs of Staff
|
Deception planners — SHAEF Ops B,
London Controlling Section
|
Masterman and Tar Robertson,
XX Committee and MI5
|
Harris
|
GARBO (Harris and Pujol)
|
....
|
Kühlenthal and the Madrid station
|
Schellenberg, German secret service

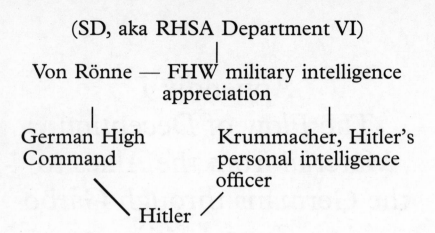

(SD, aka RHSA Department VI)
|
Von Rönne — FHW military intelligence appreciation
|
German High Command

Krummacher, Hitler's personal intelligence officer

Hitler

Appendix II
The 29 Names

Below, in CAPS, are listed the 29 names that made up Pujol's network of agents, along with their code names and numbers as used by MI5, and Pujol's personal group of informants (known as J's network).

Juan Pujol, known as:
1. GARBO by the British
2. ALARIC by the Germans (head of the Arabal/Arabel spy network)

J's network:
3. J(1) — THE COURIER: official on the regular Lisbon — UK flight during the war, carrying Garbo's letters to Lisbon, thereby avoiding the British censors. German codename: Smith.
4. J(2) — THE AVIATOR: RAF officer who provided Garbo with his first piece of 'genuine' intelligence passed on to the Germans from London.
5. J(3) — THE WORK COLLEAGUE: Garbo's boss at the Spanish Department of the Ministry of Information. In time the Germans were led to believe that THE WORK COLLEAGUE was W.B. McCann, the real head of the department. German

411

codename: Ameros.

6. J(4) — THE CENSOR: employee at the Ministry of Information who passed on 'Stop' and 'Release' press notices to Garbo.

7. J(5) — THE MISTRESS: secretary in the Secretariat of the Ministry of War with whom Garbo started an affair in September 1943. Pujol described her as the most important member of the Garbo network. German codename: Amy.

8. Agent 1 — Senhor CARVALHO, the Portuguese: Pujol's first invented spy, based in Newport. A 'commercial traveller', he mostly reported on south-west England.

9. Agent 2 — William Maximilian GERBERS: German-Swiss living in Bootle, Liverpool; reported on shipping movements in the Mersey.

10. 2(1) — Mrs Gerbers THE WIDOW: after her husband's death, Mrs Gerbers moved to London and became Garbo's assistant, firstly as a housekeeper and later as an encriptor.

11. Agent 3 — PEDRO the Venezuelan: last of the spies invented before Pujol left Portugal for England. An independently wealthy man who had studied at the University of Glasgow. He became Garbo's deputy and effectively ran the spy ring towards the end of the war, when his role was played by Tomás Harris.

12. 3(1) — THE RAF NCO: drunkard and gambler based in Glasgow who passed on information to PEDRO.

412

13.   3(2) — THE LIEUTENANT in the 49th Infantry Division: talkative officer whom PEDRO met on a train; passed on information about troop movements in Scotland.

14.   3(3) — THE GREEK SEAMAN: communist deserter from the Merchant Navy who gave information to PEDRO because he believed he was working for the Soviets. German codename: Ben.

15. Agent 4 — FRED the Gibraltarian: waiter who had been evacuated from the Rock and resettled in England. He was sent to work in the Chislehurst Caves for a while before ending up in the NAAFI on the south coast. German codename: Camillus.

16.   4(1) — THE OPERATOR: left-wing wireless technician who sent Garbo's radio messages to the Germans believing that he was communicating with Spanish Republicans. He was played by MI5 radio operator Charlie Haines.

17.   4(2) — THE GUARD: working at the Chislehurst Caves, this man passed information on to FRED about who was allowed in and out.

18.   4(3) — THE AMERICAN NCO: Franco-sympathiser who befriended FRED in Soho in order to practise his Spanish. Usefully for Garbo, he was happy to show off how much he knew about US formations and their battle plans. German codename: Castor.

19. Agent 5 — THE BROTHER: PEDRO's sibling, also of independent means. Initially based in Glasgow, he moved to Toronto, where his role was played by Ciril Mills. German codename: Ahorn or Moonbeam.

20. 5(1) — CON: Agent 5's cousin, a commercial traveller based in Buffalo who collected intelligence on the US. German codename: Prescot.

21. Agent 6 — DICK: anti-communist South African of independent means who introduced Garbo to J(3) at the Ministry of Information.

22. Agent 7 — STANLEY: Welsh nationalist in the Merchant Navy, first introduced to Garbo by FRED. German codename: Dagobert.

23. 7(1) — THE SOLDIER: member of the 9th Armoured Division.

24. 7(2) — DAVID: former merchant seaman and founder of the pro-Nazi Welsh nationalist group 'The Brothers in the Aryan World Order'. German codename: Donny.

25. 7(3) — THERESA JARDINE: English secretary of 'The Brothers in the Aryan World Order' and the mistress of RAGS. Her role was eventually played by Peter Fleming in Ceylon. German codename: Javelin.

26. 7(4) — RAGS: Indian poet and lover of THERESA JARDINE, with a fanatical belief in the superiority of the Aryan

race. German codename: Dick.

27. 7(5) — THE RELATIVE: member of DAVID's family and also of 'The Brothers in the Aryan World Order'. German code-name: Drake.

28. 7(6) — THE LOW GRADE SPY: office worker in South Wales, also a member of 'The Brothers in the Aryan World Order', who only worked half-heartedly as a spy. German codename: Drommond.

29. 7(7) — THE TREASURER: leading member of 'The Brothers in the Aryan World Order', later stationed in the Harwich-Ipswich area to report on troop movements.

Select Bibliography

Primary sources

Arxiu Municipal de Barcelona (Barcelona city archive)

Harris, Tomás, *Garbo, the Spy who Saved D-Day*, with an introduction by Mark Seaman, 2000

Interviú (Spanish news magazine) Nos 435–440: interviews with Juan Pujol, 1984

The Guy Liddell Diaries (ed. Nigel West), two Volumes, 2005

The National Archives, Kew, files KV 2/39 to KV 2/42, and KV 2/63 to KV 2/71; KV 2/101 and KV 2/102

Pujol García, Juan and West, Nigel, *Operation Garbo*, 1985 (republished 2011)

TV3 (Catalan TV station): *Encontres* interview with Juan Pujol 1984

Other sources

Ambrose, Stephen E., *Ike's Spies: Eisenhower and the Espionage Establishment*, 1981 (2012 edn)
Citizen Soldiers: From the Normandy Beaches to the Surrender of Germany, 1997 (2002 edn)

Andrew, Christopher, *The Defence of the Realm: the authorised history of MI5*, 2009

Bailey, Roderick, *Forgotten Voices of D-Day*, 2009

Batey, Mavis, *Dilly*, 2009

Beevor, Anthony, *D-Day: the battle for Normandy*, 2009

Paris after the Liberation (with Artemis Cooper), 1994 (2007 edn) Bennet, Ralph, *Ultra in the West*, 1979 (2009 edn)

Blacker, Cecil, *Monkey Business*, 1993

Blunt, Anthony, introduction to Tomás Harris catalogue for art exhibition held at Courtauld Institute, 1975

Brenan, Gerald, *The Literature of the Spanish People*, 1951 (1976 edn)

Bristow, Desmond, *A Game of Moles: deceptions of an MI6 officer*, 1993

Burns, Jimmy, *Papa Spy*, 2009

Carter, Miranda, *Anthony Blunt*, 2001

Cave Brown, Anthony, *Bodyguard of Lies: the extraordinary true story behind D-Day*, 1975 (2002 edn)

Collins, Larry and Lapierre, Dominique, *Is Paris Burning?*, 1965 (1991 edn)

Cowley, Robert (ed.), *What If?*, 1999

Crowdy, Terry, *Deceiving Hitler*, 2008

Daglish, Ian, *Goodwood*, 2005

Delmer, Sefton, *The Counterfeit* Spy, 1973

d'Este, Carlo, *Decision in Normandy*, 1983 (2004 edn)

Elliott, Geoffrey, *Gentleman Spymaster*, 2011

Ford, Ken, *Dieppe 1942: prelude to D-Day*, 2003

Fraguas, Rafael, *Espías en la transición*, 2003

Giangreco and Moore (eds), *Eyewitness D-Day*, 2005

Gilbert, Martin (ed.), *Churchill: the power of words*, 2012

Handel, Michael (ed.), *Strategic and Operational Deception in the Second World War*, 1987 (2004 edn)

Hastings, Max, *Overlord: D-Day and the battle for Normandy 1944*, 1984 *All Hell Let Loose*, 2011

Haufler, Hervie, *The Spies Who Never Were*, 2006

Hesketh, Roger, *Fortitude: the D-Day deception campaign*, 1999

Holt, Thaddeus, *The Deceivers: allied military deception in the Second World War*, 2004

Howard, Michael, *British Intelligence in the Second World War, Vol. 5 (Strategic Deception)*, 1990

Irving, David, *Hitler's War* (online edn)

Jeffrey, Keith, *MI6: the history of the Secret Intelligence Service 1909–1949*, 2010

Jones, R.V., *Most Secret War*, 1978

Juárez, Javier, *Juan Pujol, el espía que derrotó a Hitler*, 2004

Kahn, David, *Hitler's Spies: German military intelligence in World War II*, 1978 (2000 edn)

Keegan, John, *Six Armies in Normandy*, 1982 (1992 edn)

Knightley, Phillip, *Philby: K.G.B. masterspy*, 1988 (2003 edn)

418

Levine, Joshua, *Operation Fortitude: the story of the spy operation that saved D-Day*, 2011

Lewin, Ronald, *Ultra Goes to War*, 1978

Lochery, Neill, *Lisbon: war in the shadows of the City of Light 1939–1945*, 2011

Macintyre, Ben, *Operation Mincemeat*, 2010 *Double Cross*, 2012

Masterman, J.C. *The Double-Cross System*, 1972 (1995 edn) *On the Chariot Wheel: an autobiography*, 1975

Mesquida, Evelyn, *La Nueve*, 2008

Miller, Russell, *Codename Tricycle*, 2004

Montagu, Ewen, *Beyond Top Secret U*, 1977

Philby, Kim, *My Silent War*, 1968 (2002 edn)

Pincher, Chapman, *Too Secret Too Long*, 1984

Poolton, Jack A., *Destined to Survive*, 1998

Prados, John, *Normandy Crucible: the decisive battle that shaped World War II in Europe*, 2011

Rankin, Nicholas, *Churchill's Wizards: the British genius for deception 1914–1945*, 2008

Reynolds, Michael, *Steel Inferno: I Panzer Corps in Normandy*, 1997 (2009 edn) *The Devil's Adjutant: Jochen Peiper, Panzer leader*, 1995 (2009 edn)

Ripley, Tim, *Steel Rain*, 2001

RNE (Radio Nacional de España) documentary on Juan Pujol, December 2012

Ros Agudo, Manuel, *La guerra secreta de Franco 1939–1945* (2002)

Sebag-Montefiore, Hugh, *Enigma: the battle for the code*, 2000

Smyth, Denis, *Deathly Deception: the real story of Operation Mincemeat* (2010)

Talty, Stephen, *Agent Garbo: the brilliant, eccentric secret agent who tricked Hitler and saved D-Day*, 2012

Trevor-Roper, Hugh, 'Penetrating the Enemy Secret Service', unpublished lecture delivered at Christ Church Oxford, 2002

van der Vat, Dan, *D-Day, the Greatest Invasion: a people's history*, 2003

von Luck, Hans, *Panzer Commander*, 1989 (2002 edn)

West, Nigel and Tsarev, Oleg, *The Crown Jewels: the British secrets at the heart of the KGB's archives*, 1998

Westemeier, Jens, *Joachim Peiper: a biography of Himmler's commander*, 2007

Wheatley, Dennis, *The Deception Planners: my secret war*, 1980

Wingate, Ronald, *Not in the Limelight*, 1959

Zaloga, Steven J., *Campaign 194: liberation of Paris 1944*, 2008

Acknowledgements

Many thanks to Mavis Batey, Nigel West, Arne Molfenter and Juliet Wilson-Bareau for sharing their insights into this wonderful story with me.

Ana Domínguez Rama proved to be an excellent researcher and assistant when delving into the labyrinths of the Barcelona city archives. My thanks to the ever resourceful Enrique Murillo for facilitating things.

Nigel Jones and Roger Moorhouse gave useful background information and advice on Second World War matters, for which I am very grateful.

My father, John, leaped gleefully out of retirement to become my reasearch assistant for much of the writing of the book. My thanks for his input and advice.

Thanks also to Lisa Abend, Sabine Kern, Francisco Centofanti, William Ryan, D.E. Meredith, Mike Ivey and Gijs van Hensbergen.

This book would probably not have been written without the support of Peter Ettedgui, who has shared my fascination with the Garbo story from the start. Many years have passed since our first conversation about it at a terrace café in the Plaça de Catalunya, and now, finally, here we are. *Gràcies.*

Everyone at Random House has been very helpful — and patient. Thanks to all there. Mary Chamberlain remains the best copy-editor one could wish for. And Jenny Uglow, as ever, gracefully helped guide things along.

My thanks to Peter Robinson, for his unwavering support and good advice.

And finally to Salud, *por todo.*

422

We do hope that you have enjoyed reading this large print book.

Did you know that all of our titles are available for purchase?

We publish a wide range of high quality large print books including:
Romances, Mysteries, Classics
General Fiction
Non Fiction and Westerns

Special interest titles available in large print are:
The Little Oxford Dictionary
Music Book
Song Book
Hymn Book
Service Book

Also available from us courtesy of Oxford University Press:
Young Readers' Dictionary
(large print edition)
Young Readers' Thesaurus
(large print edition)

For further information or a free brochure, please contact us at:
Ulverscroft Large Print Books Ltd.,
The Green, Bradgate Road, Anstey,
Leicester, LE7 7FU, England.
Tel: (00 44) 0116 236 4325
Fax: (00 44) 0116 234 0205

BLOOD MED

Jason Webster

Spain is corrupt and on the brink of collapse. The king is ill, banks are closing, hospitals are in chaos, homes are lost, demonstrators riot and right-wing thugs patrol the streets. The tunnels below are at once a refuge and a source of anger. And as the blood flows, Cámara roars in on his motorbike. He is back in Valencia, with his partner Alicia and his anarchist, marijuana-growing grandfather Hilario. In the old police headquarters, the mood is tense as the chief hunts for cuts — who will go, Cámara or his friend Torres? The two men are flung into action investigating the suicide of an ex-bank clerk and the brutal murder of a young American woman. And as the city erupts around them, their case takes them into the heart of the trouble . . .